BOOKS THROUGH BARS

BOOKS THROUGH BARS

STORIES FROM THE PRISON BOOKS MOVEMENT

EDITED BY MOIRA MARQUIS AND DAVE "MAC" MARQUIS

THE UNIVERSITY OF GEORGIA PRESS   ATHENS

© 2024 by the University of Georgia Press
Athens, Georgia 30602
www.ugapress.org
All rights reserved
Designed by Erin Kirk
Set in Warnock Pro
Printed and bound by Friesens
The paper in this book meets the guidelines for
permanence and durability of the Committee on
Production Guidelines for Book Longevity of the
Council on Library Resources.

Title page art and part numbers by John Vasquez Mejias

Most University of Georgia Press titles are
available from popular e-book vendors.

Printed in Canada
28 27 26 25 24 P 5 4 3 2 1

Library of Congress Cataloging-in-Publication Data

Names: Marquis, Moira, editor. | Marquis, Dave "Mac", editor.
Title: Books through bars : stories from the prison books movement / edited
    by Moira Marquis and Dave "Mac" Marquis.
Description: Athens : University of Georgia Press, 2024. | Includes
    bibliographical references.
Identifiers: LCCN 2023035285 | ISBN 9780820365879 (paperback)
Subjects: LCSH: Book donations—United States. | Prisoners—Books
    and reading—United States.
Classification: LCC HV7428 .B66 2024 | DDC 365/.66-dc23/eng/20231012
LC record available at https://lccn.loc.gov/2023035285

A Sarah Mills Hodge Fund Publication

This publication is made possible, in part, through a grant
from the Hodge Foundation in memory of its founder, Sarah Mills Hodge,
who devoted her life to the relief and education of African Americans
in Savannah, Georgia.

All proceeds from the sale of this book will fund
prison books programs.

CONTENTS

Community

How to Start a Prison Books Program

The Future Of Prison Books

Your Honor, years ago I recognized my kinship with all living beings, and I made up my mind that I was not one bit better than the meanest on earth. I said then, and I say now, that while there is a lower class, I am in it, and while there is a criminal element, I am of it, and while there is a soul in prison, I am not free.

Eugene Debs, after being convicted of sedition for resistance to the World War I draft

This book is dedicated to all the people
who work against humanly created violence.
May we recognize each other in our common
purpose and uplift each other for a better future.

BOOKS THROUGH BARS

RETURN TO SENDER

UNAUTHORIZED ITEM:

_____ COLOR PAPER/COLOR ENVELOPE

_____ POST CARD/CARD STOCK

_____ LABELS/STICKERS

_____ MARKERS/CRAYON

_____ SCENTED/LIPSTICK

11-3-20

11-12

PRISON BOOKS: A LOVE STORY Moira Marquis and David "Mac" Marquis

In this book, you'll find stories that show how regular people, without a lot of money and with no powerful allies, work together for mutual aid as we laugh, dance, and organize. The folks who have come together to write this book organize prison books programs across the United States. We are a diffuse, autonomous, and nonhierarchical movement who gather books others discard, and mail them to folks inside prison walls who write to us, asking for books. Each week, we collectively send thousands of books, legal resources, and letters to imprisoned people throughout the country, all free of charge. These packages of books cross the lines our culture constructs to divide us. These small acts reach out to our fellows on the inside, rejecting the judgment that aims to take life and joy from people through incarceration. Mailing books is mailing care—oftentimes care that has been systematically denied to people. This book is a book of joyful caring that we hope empowers you to reach out to our fellows inside.

Prison books programs (PBPS) operate on shoestring budgets, with all-volunteer workforces and largely donated libraries. We partner with local, independent bookstores and hold creative events to fundraise for mailing costs. Although we face many challenges from books being banned or rejected by prisons, to finding stable spaces to house the libraries, sending books through bars gives us hope and joy. We have so much fun selecting the perfect books to send someone inside or organizing a benefit show. Being involved in undermining the isolation and judgment of the carceral state for others helps us undermine the isolation and judgment in our own lives. We all exist in a culture that sees us as disposable. We have found that acting

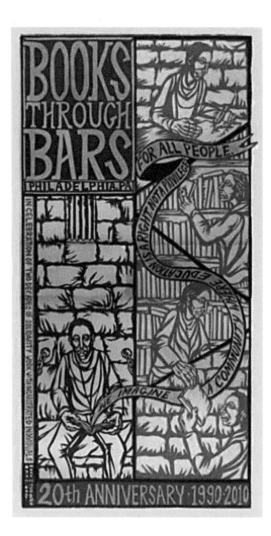

Books through Bars
Philadelphia.

together for another kind of culture really does bring it into being. This work continues to uplift us and remind us of our common purpose.

As Lorenzo Kom'boa Ervin discusses, prior to pioneering lawsuits brought by jailhouse lawyer Martin Sostre in the 1960s and 1970s, no books were allowed in jails and prisons except for Bibles. Thanks to lawsuits by others, including Kom'boa Ervin, imprisoned people successfully challenged bans on books and radical literature. All current PBPs are indebted to these actions taken by incarcerated people. After these lawsuits, prisons could not legally refuse books, and PBPs began forming throughout the country. The first organized PBP in the United States was either in San Francisco or Boston—what most folks think are the longest-running programs. They probably began as mutual aid to people's friends who were jailed for civil rights, anti-war, antinuclear, and other protests. It is also possible that these programs grew out of other mutual aid organizations such as the Anarchist Black Cross. Over time, PBPs have evolved into organizations that send books to anyone locked up in the most populated prison system the world has ever known. Although staggering enough to seem hyperbolic, single U.S. states incarcerate more people than all other nations in the world combined.[1] Many people spend their entire lives in prison. For people inside, there is intense boredom and isolation even though there is no privacy. Books are one of the few escapes available from incarceration's monotony and loneliness. Most people inside hear about PBPs from other people. In some prisons and jails, PBP addresses are scratched onto cell walls. Some PBPs stamp their addresses on the insides of books that get passed around—despite sharing being against

Tranzmission
Prison Project

prison rules. Other times, someone gets a package from a PBP that is announced during mail call, and this spreads the word.

One of the few things people can have in prison—albeit in limited quantity—are stamps. Incarcerated people use those precious stamps to write letters to PBPs and ask for books. Many times, people will write letters on paper from prison bureaucracy—their commissary request form, medical request form, and so on—which is folded and taped together to create a makeshift envelope. Other times, people will have real stationery and spend hours drawing elaborate pictures on the envelopes as thanks for books they've received. Many of these envelopes adorn PBP spaces—taped to bookshelves or covering the rare wall space not taken up with stacks of books. If someone hasn't written a PBP to ask for books before, they might assume they have to prove they're worthy, writing about how they're indigent, they have no friends or family, or they're in lockdown and aren't allowed to go to the library. But PBPs don't have criteria people need to meet. If you're inside, we'll send you books.

PBPs run on volunteer labor. Usually there's a weekly meeting time, and people will gather and read letters, select books, and tape packages. It's quiet or loud depending on people's moods. Sometimes there's music. Some people bring their dogs or kids. Sometimes there's laughter. Sometimes cookies. After the weekly pack, one person usually takes the packages to the post office and mails them. At the post office, PBPs usually have to pay return fees—from prisons that reject and return packages. Sometimes there are reasons for returns, a person got released or the content is banned (see Michelle Dillon's chapter on banned books), and sometimes there's no reason. PBPs have to pay for the postage there and back, and the person inside doesn't get their books. If we can remedy the reason the package got returned, then we will mail the books again, essentially paying the postage three times for the same books.

This is largely what PBPs do, but there are bigger issues that have been building over years that threaten to disrupt this quiet solidarity and largely joyful mutual aid. While prisons have always tried to limit incarcerated people's access to books, new technology threatens to eliminate paper books from entering prisons at all. Quietly, states and the federal government are trying to limit people's reading to electronic tablets, supplied by the prison. While there are advantages to tablets, as Valerie Surrett points out in her chapter, these are owned by the state, and the content on tablets is therefore controlled. As Rebecca Ginsburg, Victoria Law, Michelle Dillon, Kwaneta Harris, and other contributors in this book note, prisons have a long history of limiting information. Books that are banned or rejected include books on the history of racism in America, sex education and how bodies work, and prisons as a profit-making industry. It is surely the case that tablets will enable even greater information control. The introduction of tablets is being justified by arguments that PBPs, and other people that mail packages to loved ones inside, contain contraband. Despite studies showing that guards are the actual conduit for drugs and other kinds of contraband in prisons (such as cell phones), policy targets books.[2]

PBPs are not surprised by this move. Ever since PBPs began sending books inside, there have been attempts to limit what we do. Prior approval is needed in many states. This is where a letter is written by the PBP to the imprisoned person that indicates what exact titles will be sent. The person inside has to get this approved—which can be impossible depending on the relationship between themselves and the guards or warden. That approval letter then needs to be returned to the PBP, which can then send the books. There are also restrictions that differ by facility. Some allow up to five books to be mailed at once, some only two. Some demand the books are new. Federal facilities have recently started requiring packages to be wrapped in white paper, rather than brown. Most jails do not allow free books. PBPs send invoices indicating that the books have been paid for even though incarcerated people do not pay. The books have been paid for by someone, after all. There are also states' banned books lists that include everything from books with tattoo illustrations to biology texts with illustrations to Toni Morrison. Sometimes these lists are published. Sometimes they're not, and we only find out content is banned when packages are returned with "Prohibited" stamped on the outside.[3] Oftentimes banning is enforced by mailroom staff at prisons and differs based on the personalities and knowledge levels of those people.

Those of us working in PBPs know that all our freedoms are mutually dependent. We push back against prison policies that limit people's access to reading because we want to keep sending books to people inside until there is no more incarceration. By giving direct aid to people locked up, we demonstrate the kind of society we want: one where no one is disposable. With the rise of abolitionism in mainstream discourse we're heartened by the thought that more people will begin to demand the cessation of this system. Until it

When you reach the quarantine facility in the Michigan Department of Corrections (MDOC), you lose even the small access to a county jail library. Instead, the only books available are those circulated among the inmates around you in whichever unit of traditional levels of cells you're assigned a single or double bunk in. The paperbacks typically have several pages missing: almost always the covers and any hot scenes a reader may have found. Sometimes you may not realize what's missing until you reach the end . . . All this while you're cooped up in your cell all day save for three calls out to chow, one hour on the yard, the occasional opportunity to use the in-unit phones or JPay and any call-out you may have as part of your processing to the MDOC. Good luck reading when everyone is yelling to talk to each other. Better wait till most people are napping end even then you might doze off while trying to read yourself as depression and a lack of nutrients and activity consume you.

At most facilities you gain access to the library. Fill out a form to request half an hour during the time the General or Law Library is open to peruse the books and check out up to three books for two weeks, with the option to renew once. Your people on the outside can only purchase books for you that are shipped directly from the publisher or a recognized retailer. They must come with a receipt, or else they'll be held hostage until your people mail a copy of the receipt to you. I just had my first book rejected for apparently mentioning the MDOC—it was written for us inmates to aid in our rehabilitation while incarcerated.

Prison does provide time to catch up on reading you've neglected in the world so long as you can find quiet time in your cell or cube or unit. And reading a book provides your mind with the stimulation that there is much more to life than all this.

Drake Misek

ends, however, our friends on the inside need books. They need to know they aren't forgotten. They need to know we want them free. Until prisons are no more, we need to help people escape—even for an hour—one book at a time.

Moira's Prison Books Story

I first heard about prison books programs at a party. It was 2006, and I had been working (as much as I could since my son, Liam, was only four) with the *Asheville Global Report* (AGR): a free weekly newspaper put together by a group of folks who thought it was important to report news stories the mainstream media marginalized. But the AGR was closing, for reasons largely related to costs, and I was looking for another activist avenue. At this house party, I asked a lady I knew through the AGR what else was going on. She said, "Well, there's prison books." I was a little skeptical. I asked her if they were for real—like if people were honestly working on something. She got very serious and said, "Absolutely."

I went to my first prison books packing night a short time later. I was surprised to find it in the former dining room of a stately house near a public park in a very nice part of town, complete with chandelier. I thought I might be in the wrong place when I first drove up. But inside this dining room were wall-to-wall bookshelves, crammed with books of all kinds, and in the middle of the room was a large pallet table with scissors, tape, brown paper bags, and a shoebox tightly packed with letters. That night I instantly fell in love. I got to select books! I got to read letters from folks who wanted books, look through hundreds, and select the ones I thought they would enjoy the most! I didn't have to charge them any money, and I could share the wealth of human thought of which we are all inheritors. I was filled with joy. We finished early that night—amazingly since most prison books programs struggle to keep up with the demand. I was disappointed when there weren't any more letters, but I knew I would be back. I wound up working with Asheville Prison Books for the next seven years.

I went to the stately house every week and read letters and filled requests for books. I also did all the other things you need to do for a PBP: fundraised, gathered books, tried to get people to volunteer, built a website, and applied for 501c3 status. I've heard it said that in order to really commit to service of any kind, it needs to give back to you. It must be that prison books gives back to me because I constantly go back to it.

During the time I worked for Asheville Prison Books, I started teaching English in public school in Asheville. I had started my teaching career as a world history teacher, but those jobs were few and far between. I took this job teaching English and, for the first time, became responsible for teaching students how to read. Some of my students were so bright and could remember anything but couldn't understand a thing they read, and I struggled to understand how that could happen. It was an enormous challenge. Many of my students had never passed a reading test—given since third grade.[4] These teenagers were well past the age of easy readers and were self-conscious about their reading level. I struggled to learn literacy pedagogy—I asked my neighbors, started a master's degree, and read all I could, but there

Photo of Moira and students.

just wasn't a lot out there about how to teach teenagers reading. It seemed that once kids got out of elementary school, most people assumed they were a lost cause if they couldn't read. I had to agitate to get glasses for one of my fourteen-year-old students who had this need documented since third grade but hadn't gotten them. I saw a pervasive attitude that some people just weren't worth the effort reflected in teachers and administrators: all the people who were supposed to be working to help. I was even told things such as, "Well, the world needs toilet bowl cleaners." This comment wasn't from a uniquely bigoted person, either. The idea that we live in a meritocracy is undone by exposure to people who've been locked up. The sidebars you'll find throughout this book titled "Dear Prison Books" are written by people inside. They have typos and misspellings, which we've kept to illustrate how most people imprisoned in this country have not had access to quality education, opportunity, and cultures of care. Dictionaries are the single most requested book, as many people teach themselves to read in prison having been failed by public education. James King's chapter talks about the Black radical tradition of self-education behind bars, which exists because of the systemic, racist underserving of Black boys and girls in our schools. Over

60 percent of adults in prison are functionally illiterate—meaning they can't understand most of what they can pronounce as they read.[5] They don't understand contracts for cell phones or rentals, let alone the legal documents they are coerced into signing in the process of their prosecution and incarceration. The rate is even higher in youth detention—85 percent of children in prisons cannot read at a fourth-grade level.[6] You might be surprised that children get sent to prison, but it's true. In public schools, "resource officers" are armed police officers who can charge children with real criminal charges and take them to jail. I've had students arrested for things such as throwing a firecracker "in the direction" of a police officer. And as a result, kids as young as fourteen have served time. This seems consistent within the punitive culture of public schools, where kids get sent to detention or suspension for dress code violations (flip flops, hats, shirts "too low," etc.). I even witnessed a serious discussion about expelling kids for starting a harmless and fun-loving food fight during lunch one day.

I tried as hard as I could, and I had small victories, but I felt then, as I feel now, that I failed more than I succeeded. It was so hard to try to save someone from a culture that sees them as unworthy from the time they are still so small. When I select books for people inside, it gives me a second chance to help. I knew those people at the other end of the letter: they are like my students. They were kind and funny and silly and sweet. They were badly treated and neglected and denied help. I knew they were told they weren't smart, weren't worthy, and I got to reach out to them and tell them, "I hope you like these books. Please write back and let me know and I'll send you some more. <3 Moira." It's not perfect, but we live in a cruel culture. Sending books to folks inside helps me to feel less defeated by the senselessness of it all.

When I moved to Chapel Hill, I briefly worked with a prison books program there before finding out about a literacy nonprofit that had tutoring privileges with a local prison. I signed up. I tutored imprisoned folks to help them pass a reading test that was required by the state to take classes offered by the local community colleges. Working inside the prison, I learned that most people in prison don't see themselves as victims of a system that wasn't designed for them to succeed. Instead, most people talked about what bad choices they made, how they're "never gonna do that again," and how they've learned their lesson. If prisons are designed to "rehabilitate" people to act in less criminal ways, my own anecdotal experience indicates the vast majority are already repentant—but most have many, many more years inside to face.

My first student, I'll call him Spenser, was a middle-aged and genial guy. We went through the workbooks for the test, and I targeted the kinds of questions the test asked: tables of contents and cardinal directions. As in public school, I found that literacy tests do not test your reading level but your cultural competency. Why are there questions about a table of contents, which test not whether you can read words but whether you have read the kinds of books that have tables of contents? It's because standardized testing is not designed as a meritocratic measure of achievement but as a cultural benchmark whose goal is assimilation. Once I told Spenser what these things are, along with the other elements he didn't understand, he passed the test with flying colors. The folks at the nonprofit were delighted (if a bit surprised), and Spenser was allowed to continue tutoring without having to worry about tests. I suggested we start reading some real books together.

When I first gave him the option of choosing a book to read, he selected *The Girl with the Dragon Tattoo*. It's not a great book, but folks might be able to read it and enjoy it if you're quick about it—like in a night. But Spenser needed more time to read this long (and not great) book, and it felt pretty tedious for a couple of weeks. When we were done, I asked if he minded if I chose the next book. He said that was fine, and I gave him *Kindred* by Octavia Butler. It was a hit, and I enjoyed it much more. I didn't realize that this book is on North Carolina's banned books list for prisons. Yes, prisons ban books. Spenser loved the afterlife of slavery in the contemporary world narrative of *Kindred*. I suspect that in all his years in school, Spenser might never have been given a novel by an African American author. Many, many important novels by African American authors are on the banned books list including *The Bluest Eye* by Toni Morrison and *I am Not Your Negro* by James Baldwin.[7] After reading *Kindred*, Spenser's love of reading skyrocketed, and you have to wonder why books that encourage such a positive pastime would be banned. As Rebecca Ginsburg notes in her essay, books by African American authors and books about the history of racial violence in the United States are targeted by prison authorities. Spenser started reading books by himself and summarizing them for me. He particularly loved Mildred Taylor's books, which he consumed as fast as I could get them for him. She writes for young adults, so Spenser could read them independently, but the themes of racism in Jim Crow South and the everyday struggles of Black folks to keep their families together through this violence resonated deeply with Spenser.

THE IMPORTANCE OF BOOKS

The Saginaw Correctional facility library is very limited in a variety of books, especially on the topic of Afrikan History. All prison facilities here in the state of Michigan censor books coming in and have a list of banned books. Sadly, here at the facility there are not a lot of prisoners reading books and the books they read are fiction without substance. I've got my own, private library of books consisting mostly of Afrikan history, Islam, etc. An Afrkian proverb says: Each one, teach one. So, I do share the books from my own private library here in the prison community.

Books to me open an individual mind to new worlds. The late Malcom X said it best: "My alma mater was books, a good library. . . . I could spend the rest of my life reading, just satisfying my curiosity." I personally go the distance with books by exercising my mind as I read. Strong mind, strong body.

AhJamu Khalifah Baruti

Because of the legacies of enslavement and settler colonialism in the United States, African Americans and Native Americans are overwhelmingly, disproportionately incarcerated. African American men are almost six times more likely to be imprisoned during their life than white men.[8] Native people are the single largest group per capita in U.S. prisons, experiencing incarceration at a rate almost 40 percent higher than the average across other races.[9] It made me very sad that Spenser didn't recognize his imprisonment as connected to this system but saw it as the result of his own personal failings. It is very challenging to accept and continue to live in a culture that is almost unilaterally stacked against you. I remember having a literature circle discussion on *Malcom X Talks to Young People* with a group of young men in my time teaching public school. Malcom X taught himself to read in prison. His critique of the structural racism of American society is profound, and I got carried away with my thoughts. I made some comments about the pervasiveness of institutionalized racism that were too emphatic. One of my students said, "Easy there, teach. We got to have some hope." That

Stanley Tookie Williams wrote *Blue Rage, Black Redemption* (2004) while on death row. The book is largely memoir, detailing Williams's childhood and his attempt to protect himself from violence through the formation of a gang. While in the book Williams demonstrably shows his rejection of violence, he was executed by lethal injection in 2005.

snapped me back: we can all only take so much. Working in both public schools and in prisons, I encountered the same tension between individual accountability and systemic violence. While people do, as individuals, commit crimes, the law is not some impartial code, implemented by disembodied and objective reason or an all-knowing and omnipotent god. Laws are created by people. This is critical race theory's significant insight: laws reflect the society that creates them. We live in a culture that uses a legal system to sanction some kinds of violence but blames individuals—who are often the first victims of culturally created violence—as if people have total power to determine our own lives. Recognizing we live in such a system can be a disempowering realization, however. It needs to be balanced with the firm belief that we can construct a different kind of society—just as we are maintaining a violent one today. But for many incarcerated people, this is almost a heavier burden to bear than individual culpability. Living every day with the knowledge that we live in humanly created and maintained oppression can be debilitating—especially when you're inside. Often it's easier for people to assume responsibility for their actions so they can be empowered to at least try to live.

For other people, the systemic racism of contemporary America motivates them into taking action against violence. In that prison I also met the librarian—an incarcerated person I'll call T.J. He took his job seriously, telling me that he hid the "urban" fiction because "it isn't good for them [the other people inside]." Urban fiction is a genre like blaxploitation films and traffics in violence, gangs, heteronormative gender norms, and capitalist desires. T.J. wanted his fellows to read books that helped them understand these systems as constructs that largely prevent people from self-determination. One day he asked me to take books from the prison library. I was surprised. "Why?" I said. "They're bad books, and I don't want them in here," he said. I trusted that T.J. knew more than I did about what he needed as the librarian, and I agreed. I offered to bring in other books if he wanted. I was soon bombarded with requests for languages: Chinese, French, Spanish. Did I have language CDs? How about dictionaries? "There's a guy here who can teach people Mandarin," T.J. said, "but we need a book or two." I didn't realize at the time that prisons ban non-English language books in the paranoid assertion that people will master another language in order to communicate without carceral authorities understanding and effect an uprising or escape. I started to accumulate donations, and everything was fine until one day I brought a large donation: about eight boxes of books. I was held up at the gate by a woman officer who said that I couldn't bring them in unless I had a specific form filled out and signed by the warden. Every other guard had let me bring books in. It's this kind of haphazard enforcement that makes prison regulations meaningless. The books were taken by the guards but were eventually given to the chaplain. Fortunately, at that facility, the chaplain had been formerly incarcerated, and he passed most of the books along to T.J. This moment illustrates how our small, everyday actions can either contribute to another's well-being or reinforce injustice. It's not that hard to intervene in systems of oppression through small, everyday actions that can make a very real difference in other people's lives. It's also possible to enforce violent systems and thereby perpetuate them. There are several other stories in this book that affirm this simple truth. Rod Coronado and the Asheville Prison Books origin story both note how something as simple as making free photocopies can really mean all the difference to another person or the success of a group.

While prisons have libraries, most are poorly stocked and contain really bad books: romance novels, westerns, urban fiction, *National Geographic* magazines from the 1980s. . . . For institutions that claim to want people to be reformed, they have a startling number of books that reinforce violence, competition, and domination. T.J. is not alone in wanting to get better books, but institutions put many obstacles in the way of imprisoned people receiving books. In addition to creating capricious restrictions (such as demanding books are mailed in white paper only—not brown), institutions seem genuinely suspicious of providing reading materials to incarcerated people. I tried to start a reading group at a women's prison in Western North Carolina (WNC). I was shuffled around to different bureaucrats for permission for months and asked for many justifications about why I wanted to read books and talk about them with other women. After eight months of trying, I moved out of the area and never got to organize the group. I also volunteered to run a reading group at a nonprofit that houses women transitioning out of prison in Piedmont, North Carolina. This nonprofit does a lot of great work. However, when I offered to run a reading group, I was told, "We'll call you later," and I never was. This program prioritizes "practical skills" for women that include making lip gloss and body scrub. It seems strange that the foundational skill of reading is so suspect and marginalized by people working at all levels of imprisonment and even prison aid—especially given the high correlation between poverty, literacy, and imprisonment. This is especially frustrating since religious groups of any Christian denomination are given ready access in prisons. There are weekly Bible studies, religious services, and pastors. Bibles and other Christian religious materials are some of the most readily available books in prisons—way more so than dictionaries. I finally made some headway in starting the reading group at the women's facility in WNC when I sent a flyer for the reading group that featured an angelic image. I got a fast reply to that email and directions about next steps. It seems that most people understand "rehabilitation" in a moral sense—that people who are in prison have sinned (whereas the rest of us have not?) and therefore need redemption from God, not care from other people.

There's also reluctance on the part of imprisoned folks to ask for books. Many letters to PBPs document that people often feel unworthy of asking for something without paying. Many folks who write to prison books programs feel the need to talk about their poverty as justification for requesting free books. We know that education and poverty are connected—half of U.S. adults who are functionally illiterate live at or below the poverty line.[10] People are imprisoned because, through no fault of their own, they have been deemed not worthy of care. The only attention most of these people get is when they become identified as criminals. But many people inside feel they are personally flawed and feel shame for their inability to read, their poverty, and their incarceration.

Higher education programs in prisons are one of the few opportunities incarcerated people have to get support, but like PBPs they are heavily regulated and often have to deal with undue burdens, especially when compared to religious programming. Although incarcerated people were denied the ability to get financial aid for college for many years, that ban has recently been lifted.[11] Mac and I started Saxapahaw Prison Books (SPB) in 2020, and I transitioned it to a student-run program at Claflin University, a historically Black university in South Carolina. I offered SPB assistance in sending additional books to the people enrolled in the university's Pathways from

Prison Program, which offers classes for incarcerated people at several prisons in South Carolina. The director spoke on the phone with a person at the South Carolina Department of Corrections about sending books to people in this program. He told her that if we mailed books to students, they "would be guaranteed not to receive them." There's no rationale for this censorship. It isn't even state policy. It's just one person preventing lots of other people from accessing reading material. Unfortunately, this is all too common. However, there are few people within the prison complex who will contest these kinds of decisions, especially if the person making it is "in charge." While housing PBPs at universities is a great idea, as Julia Chin's chapter addresses, partnering with higher education institutions or programs doesn't necessarily guarantee any better outcomes. It's still a struggle. Unfortunately, after I left Claflin, there was no faculty member who agreed to assume oversight of Saxapahaw Prison Books, and we were forced to stop the program.

A recent letter to Saxapahaw Prison Books.

Claflin University students with packages of books ready to mail

Prison books programs strive to create bonds of care to those who have been denied them. I am so lucky to have learned about PBPs and to have been able to work with some of the amazing people in this book throughout the years. While we recognize the need to fundamentally alter our culture's belief that punishment and isolation are justice, it helps me maintain my own well-being to care for others. Sending books inside helps reinforce, in me, the knowledge that I do not agree with a culture that deems some people disposable. Being part of prison books communities that collectively work to let incarcerated people know that we see and care about them helps me maintain hope that one day, we can all be free.

Mac's Prison Books Story

I grew up in a working-class factory town in New Jersey just a short train ride from New York City. I was a bit of a juvenile delinquent and barely missed becoming part of the school-to-prison pipeline. Of course, I was unaware that there was a name for such a thing. By the time I was in grade school I was already labeled a discipline problem. One teacher recognized that this was, in part, because I was bored. She gave me a wide variety of books to read and let me sit on the back stoop and read unsupervised. I was never a problem in her class. I was able to develop a similar rapport with a few other teachers. Nonetheless, I had several brushes with the law before I arrived at high school that led to the police coming to my home to bring me in for questioning. It's a funny thing answering the door at twelve years old, seeing the police, and realizing they are looking for you. Most of my problems in school were disciplinary. I spent quite a bit of time in the suspension room and was routinely threatened with expulsion—for violating the dress code with ripped jeans or for refusal to stand for the Pledge of Allegiance.

My refusal to stand for the pledge resulted in suspension, but it also taught me an important lesson, though not the one the administration was trying to teach me. I argued my case from teacher to vice principal to principal and finally was brought before the superintendent. I had been bluffing and suggested that we were all aware of a court case that had been in the news recently in which the court decided it was unconstitutional to compel students to stand for the Pledge of Allegiance. The superintendent agreed that this may be the case but informed me that we both also knew that my family did not possess the means to take the school district to court. In short, he was arguing that I did not have the money to rely on the protection of the law. Afterwards, I stood for the pledge but never forgot that lesson. My disciplinary issues continued, and I quickly became one of the usual suspects. When a fire alarm was pulled, fireworks were set off in the hallway, or a stink or smoke bomb was deployed, whenever anything bad happened, you could bank on it that within ten minutes you would hear, "David Marquis to the principal's office. David Marquis to the principal's office, please." Sometimes I was informed that it did not matter if I had done that specific thing or not: "Well, we know you did something," so you are going to be punished anyway. This is how people get sorted.

This type of sorting meant that teachers with whom I never had any previous interaction were already convinced I was "bad." Someone defaced a bust in the library when I was in there one day, and the teacher covering the study hall pulled me aside to blame it on me. I declared my innocence (I actually didn't do it). He responded with "I don't care you little shit, get the fuck out of here. I don't ever want to see you in here again. Don't make me beat your ass." This was a new one, even for me. I was banned from the library, not officially, but under threat of violence. I did not return to the library for the rest of my high school career. That teacher had a reputation, and friends informed me that he did indeed hit students. I don't know if that was true or not, but I do know that children were physically assaulted by teachers at that school.

I don't want to give the impression that none of the teachers were positive influences. There were some good ones, but public education is not a panacea. There is no doubt that the public education system has failed many people, but there is also no doubt that we ask too much of public education and conversely do not give it the financial support it needs. Sure, we had a free lunch program in our school for those who qualified. But friends who did not eat breakfast and had a subpar dinner might not be able to concentrate during the first half of the day while they looked forward to your free lunch. In grade school, receiving the free lunch did not seem like a big deal, but high school was in the neighboring town, and there the class lines were more rigid. Schools by themselves cannot end poverty or racism, and the rightful place for the shame of a free lunch should be on the system that enforces poverty.

The shining city on a hill, American Dream, pull yourself up by your bootstraps narrative did not seem to square with the world I saw around me. Pedophile priests, mafia payoffs, and corrupt police were all seemingly ignored or accepted. I witnessed so much hypocrisy that it made it difficult to buy in. There were teachers in my school who cursed at and assaulted children; there was even a teacher who had sex with and impregnated a student. His big punishment was to be banned from extracurricular activities. Extracurricular activities indeed.

After graduation I moved to the closest big town, New Brunswick, New Jersey. There I started reading the books I found interesting. I began with the young anarchist starter kit of Howard Zinn and Noam Chomsky. I became active in a number of causes, but it was during this time that I first engaged in support for incarcerated people. There was an Anarchist Black Cross chapter in a neighboring city, and I began to help them get the word out about "political prisoners," mostly former Black Panthers if I recall correctly. I ultimately found this work a little too provincial and questioned the usefulness of the term "political prisoner" in the face of the largest prison complex in the world. It is important to support people who have sacrificed their freedom to create a more just society, and I think these organizations do important work. Nonetheless, it was not where my heart was at the time, so I moved on.

Although I continued to support people incarcerated for their polit-ical beliefs and actions, I shifted my focus to make it a part of a larger effort to fight those same systems of oppression that landed so many people in jail. I spent years raising awareness of the injustice of the imprisonment of Mumia Abu Jamal while also engaged with a num-ber of other social movements, such as Earth First! I enjoyed spend-ing time with people who wanted to help create a more just, healthier world. I continued to move through social justice and environmental activist circles while occasionally taking college classes and working construction and restaurant jobs. Eventually I ended up in Asheville, North Carolina. While in Asheville, I worked with the Asheville Global Report (AGR) and helped get Asheville Prison Books up and running.

One of the wonderful things about volunteering in social justice and environmental movements is the sense of community. Oftentimes there is cross-pollination between groups and among similar orga-nizations in other locations. I moved from activist hotspot to activ-ist hotspot throughout the 1990s, sometimes making my way to new towns by catching a ride on a freight train. For instance, when I spent a few weeks in Austin, Texas, I volunteered at Inside Books, a local PBP. I was impressed with the way Inside Books was run. They kept track of who ordered packages and what books they sent folks; this kept them from sending duplicates.

Most of the activism in which I have been involved is a form of mu-tual aid, and all prison books programs are mutual aid organizations. Mutual aid is the idea that regular folks can help each other, in big and small ways, through the sharing of resources and acts of care. The con-cept of mutual aid challenges the narrative that glorifies competition in our society. The competition narrative suggests that success is a zero-sum game. That we can only achieve financial and emotional security at another's expense. Underlying this narrative is a projection of scar-city—with limited resources only some can receive what they need to survive and thrive. In our own way, prison books programs demon-strate that there is enough for all, if we make the effort to share our resources more equitably. It's amazing how many books are discarded in the United States. It's also amazing how free books will be readily snatched up by so many people. This gap, between availability and ac-cess, is but one example of the fundamental failure of our social system,

YOU DID NOT SEND ME A SINGLE BOOK THAT I HAD ASKED FOR AND IT MADE ME MAD. I GOT OVER IT AND READ WHAT YOU SENT ME AND ALL THREE OF THEM WERE REALLY GOOD, SO THANKS.

Mac commuting to an activist gathering.

but it also is an opportunity for intervention. Mutual aid actions can take what is plenty and share it equitably with all.

For me, the love story is working with others to change the system that creates inequality and injustice. It is inspiring to be around other people who are committed to a different, more caring world. I have made many good friends while working to change the world, some of them are even represented in these pages: Moira Marquis, Annie Masaoka, and Sarah West. Although I helped run the Asheville Prison Books Program during some of its early years, I eventually experienced some burnout, in part because we kept losing our space and had to repeatedly move the project—which, with tons of books, was no small task. Predictably, Patrick Kukucka—who wrote two of the chapters in this book—and some other folks, including Moira, stepped in to keep prison books afloat. Indeed, they took it to the next level by finding a semi-permanent home for the project and acquiring official nonprofit status. I eventually moved to a little town just outside of Chapel Hill, North Carolina, called Saxapahaw. Having realized that so much of the activist work was actually a form of public education, I returned to school to finish my

Photo of *Asheville Global Report* staff.

undergraduate degree. It was not long before I was once again seduced by the siren song of prison books and ended up volunteering at the PBP that was in Carrboro, North Carolina (now located in Durham). Many good things have happened to me through my volunteer activities, and my experience with Carrboro prison books was no different. There was a new volunteer who identified herself as a historian. Having recently returned to school to finish my B.A. in history, I was intrigued. Once we got to talking, I realized she was a labor historian, Cindy Hahamovitch. I almost fell off my chair since I was in the process of finishing my senior thesis on a southern labor union. Long story short, she eventually became my dissertation adviser. I finished my Ph.D. in the spring of 2022.

In spring 2020, Moira and I started our own program in the small village of Saxapahaw. We decided to focus on Georgia because at the time there were no other PBPs focusing on Georgia. Asheville Prison Books Program served incarcerated people in Georgia for many years. However, after getting completely overwhelmed with mail, Asheville Prison Books decided to scale back and serve only people incarcerated in North and South Carolina. Shortly after Saxapahaw Prison Books formed, X Books formed in the Atlanta area and also served Georgia. While many prison books programs serve several states—some even serve as many as forty-seven!—the volume of letters these programs receive make their work challenging. When local PBPS serve their state or neighboring states, mailing costs are lower, and wait times decrease for folks inside. When Moira told Julie Schneyer from Asheville Prison Books that Saxapahaw Prison Books would be serving Georgia and asked that letters be passed along from Asheville, Julie was relieved that Georgia would be receiving some attention.

Shortly after starting we were contacted by some folks at UGA Press who were interested in helping us serve incarcerated folks in Georgia. Our conversations quickly led to proposing this book to promote all the wonderful PBPS across the country that operate in relative obscurity. We knew all these volunteers and incarcerated people had a story to tell. We also knew that it was a story people needed and wanted to hear. It is our hope that you, reader, will find your way to your local prison books program, or perhaps start one of your own. We know that you will fall in love with the project once you open a letter and hear the voices so often silenced by the walls that surround them. You won't be able to ignore the siren song of prison books.

Chapters

The authors in this book have extensive experience with prisons and PBPS. Some authors were or are incarcerated; some have been working with PBPS for decades. Their contributions are divided into broadly thematic sections that we hope will guide readers through this collection. Interspersed between and within these chapters are several sidebars. "One time at prison books . . ." are largely funny stories about working with PBPS. "Dear Prison Books" are taken from letters sent to PBPS from folks inside that illustrate what books mean to people inside. "Written on the Inside" details some of the amazing pieces notable people have written while incarcerated. Throughout the book we've featured lots of art created for and by PBPS. We are grateful to all the amazing artists who have devoted their time to supporting PBPS throughout the years. From fundraising flyers to logos, PBPS would not be visible without you. Unfortunately, artists are not valued in our culture, but please keep on. We need you!

Part One: Why We Need Prison Books Programs addresses the need for PBPS. From censorship to access to books and the need for education, to the myriad and deleterious issues prisons create, the writers in this section offer short essays that explain why we need books inside and describe some of the obstacles PBPS face. Victoria Law starts off our book with a chapter, "Prison Books: A Lifeline," that outlines why prison book programs are needed. Michelle Dillon's chapter, "We Need You, Dear Reader: On Banned Books Lists," addresses censorship that includes banned book lists and attempts by states to limit the kinds of books incarcerated people can receive. Melissa Charenko's chapter, "Until There Is a World without Prisons: Books for LGBTQ People," details the struggles LGBTQ people face in obtaining literature about sex and gender identities and highlights the vulnerability of LGBTQ people, in particular, inside. "Knowing Students Inside," by Lauren Braun-Strumfels, addresses the challenges students and professors face in trying to pursue higher education while incarcerated. Rebecca Ginsburg's chapter, "An Ongoing Case of Prison Library Censorship," continues this theme by detailing the raiding of a prison library established as part of a higher education initiative where nearly all the books confiscated were about

We had so many books. . . . And we had BAD books. I mean, we had a book where Confederate soldiers traveled in time, got machines guns, and went back and won the Civil War. We had conversion therapy books. We had books about taking colloidal silver for wellness. And the walls were closing in on us. We also, as usual, had no money. What can you do with all those awful books? You don't want anyone to read them. Can't bring them to Goodwill. It could damage someone for life. We could be cultivating the next Ted Bundy. These books should just be removed from the world—and from our prison books library. Always on the lookout for a good benefit and a little healthy cultural agitation, we decided to have a book burning. Yup. Get rid of those books that would corrupt our minds and souls and, in the process, burn the bad juju they gave off. For five bucks, people could show up and help stoke the flames.

We did not realize just how much old books burn . . . It was like the fires of hell. With a lot of ash. Like, a LOT. Not the most lucrative benefit either. But I'd like to think it did the world some good.

ONE TIME at PRISON BOOKS

Black history and culture. "*Big House Books v. Hall*" is written by two attorneys at the Mississippi Center for Justice, Beth Orlansky and Robert McDuff. This chapter explains the lawsuit the PBP, Big House Books, brought against the state of Mississippi for attempting to limit the kind of books incarcerated people can receive to only religious books. The Mississippi Center for Justice successfully fought off this attempt. James King's chapter, "The Case for Contraband Education and Radical Pedagogy in Prison," addresses how many imprisoned people have been failed by education that often obscures or reinforces racism. This chapter explains the necessity of self-education for many Black people and the role books play in that journey.

Part Two: Origin Stories begins with an interview of Lorenzo Kom'boa Ervin, a former Black Panther who talks about how the early movement to get books inside was organized by incarcerated people. Kom'boa Ervin discusses how jailhouse lawyer extraordinaire, Martin Sostre, brought lawsuits against the New York State Prison System beginning in 1969. Up until Sostre's successful lawsuits, all books were contraband except for the Bible. This interview addresses the necessity of books for people inside as well as how learning during his incarceration enabled Kom'boa Ervin's significant contribution to radical political thought, *Anarchism and the Black Revolution*. While this book does not detail the oldest programs, Asheville Prison Books Program and Appalachian Prison Books Project could not be more different, and we hope these origin stories will inspire you to start your own program—as well as laugh. The Asheville Prison Books origin is explained through the discussion of three longtime APBP organizers, Annie Masaoka, Mac Marquis, and Sarah West. They recollect how the program began as a way for friends to get together and demonstrate that making a difference in the world did not have to come at the expense of having fun. "Appalachian Prison Books Project Origins" by Ellen Skirvin details how this college-affiliated program got off the ground, continues to recruit students, and has aligned courses. It's a very different model from Asheville, but it has also stood the test of time and continues to educate new people through its affiliation with a university. This is a great chapter for folks with links to higher education as a guide for thinking through establishing a PBP at your school.

Part Three: Community tackles some of the challenges of decentralized organizing. While many, many prison books programs exist in the United

States, we aren't an organization like the Red Cross. All our programs operate independently. Most are collectives, where members and volunteers come together to discuss what the group will do, sometimes once a month-ish. For a long time, PBPs would communicate with other folks we knew through activism or community only. Now, prison books programs are connected through a listserv. "The Genesis of Communications in the National Prison Books Program Movement" by Andy Chan talks about how the email listserv came about and how it helps our decentralized network tackle large-scale challenges and support each other. Jodi Lincoln's chapter, "The National Conference," recollects the PBP conference in 2019 and how it created a space to share knowledge and make connections for PBPs. "Independent Bookstores and Prison Books Programs" by Patrick Kukucka explains how independent used bookstores are vital for PBPs. Most states require that books be sent from "authorized distributors," that is, brick-and-mortar businesses. Partnership with bookstores enables PBPs to mail books under their aegis. Without independent bookstores, PBPs would not be able to send books. As a lifelong environmental activist and the subject of the recent documentary "Operation Wolf Patrol," Rod Coronado gives an interview in this section where he addresses the need for books inside, especially for Native people. Coronado notes now incarcerated Native people lack reading materials on Native history and culture, reflecting and exacerbating settler culture's erasure and marginalization of Native people. Coronado testifies to the emotional and psychological support PBPs give by sending decolonial and Native-authored books to incarcerated Native people.

While spaces, time, and books are donated, prison books programs always need money for mailing costs. Mailing books is frequently the only cost most programs have. Many prison books programs come up with creative fundraising strategies, including art shows, where artists donate their work and proceeds go to the prison books program, and concerts, where bands play for free. These events coalesce communities around prison reform in addition to generating money for mailing. Patrick Kukucka's chapter "Fun(draising): The Halloween Cover Band Show" talks about the Asheville Prison Books Program's annual Halloween cover band show fundraiser. While it's always work and sometimes drama, the show continues to be an example of successful grassroots fundraising that also serves as a means to advertise and raise awareness of PBPs and the need for them.

Benefit flyer for Books Through Bars.

Fundraising takes lots of time and generosity from those who contribute—especially artists who are not valued enough in our culture. But these activities are so much fun and contribute to our ability to create the kind of world we want to live in—one where we have fun while helping each other—and not the one that we have inherited, where we all feel alone and unsupported. This section concludes with an interview with Daniel McGowan, a prison booker with NYC's Books Through Bars. McGowan talks about his time inside and how important books were for him as well as how he continues to devote his time to prison books and abolition.

We hope these chapters illustrate how you can also support prison books programs in so many ways: donating books, creating a space in your house for a prison books library (amazing and fun!), attending benefits, making and distributing fliers, or becoming a regular donor. There is a place for everyone.

Part IV: How to Start a Prison Books Program details how to start and maintain your own PBP through your community or college. "Creating a PBP" is a graphic instruction manual, written by Moira Marquis and illustrated by

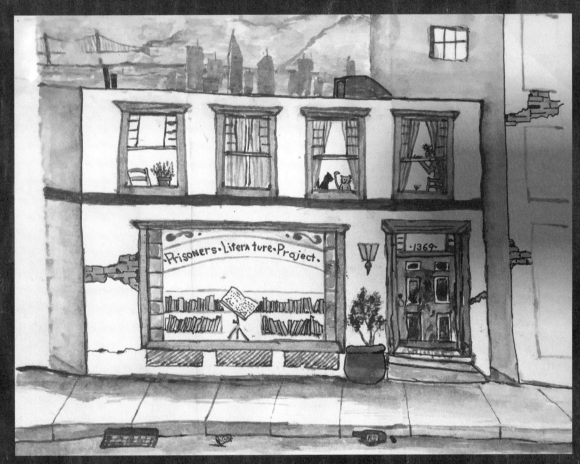

Prisoners Literature Project storefront

Nic Cassette. This graphic shows how it's easy to get set up now because we're all connected and there are so many resources for everyone, including an online list of restrictions for every prison, by state. We hope this chapter motivates you to start your own PBP. "Keepin' the Dream Alive: Maintaining Your Prison Books Program" by Julie Schneyer addresses the challenges nonhierarchical organizing faces and makes suggestions for how to resolve issues from the pragmatic—like money—to the interpersonal. Specifically for college students, "Starting a University-Based Prison Books Program: Pages for Individual in Prison" by Julia Chin speaks from a student perspective of how to establish a PBP at your college or university, with practical tips as well as obstacles to anticipate.

Part V: The Future of Prison Books addresses the innumerable barriers the prison industry puts up against the creation of community and the sharing of books. While our final section details some of the ongoing and impending challenges PBPs face, we hope that this short introduction will show people how prisons, rather than being the institutions for reform and rehabilitation, are censorship.[12]

Our purpose in the final section on the future challenges PBPs face is to show how small and largely unnoticed policy decisions have a profound impact on peoples' lives and create cascading effects that compound the already destructive consequences of incarceration. Kwaneta Harris's chapter, "Forbidden Knowledge," is written from her solitary confinement cell in Texas, where she is routinely denied books from the prison library that are not religious. This chapter is an invaluable and eloquent insight into the life of a person isolated with no end in sight and the respite and resources reading provides. Valerie Surrett's chapter, "The High Costs of Free Prison Tablet Programs," addresses the move by many states, the federal government, and private prisons to prevent paper books from entering prisons and jails, instead forcing people to use prison-sanctioned tablets. This chapter is an even-handed analysis of this complex issue that we hope will motivate people to voice their opposition to this strategy of information control. Zoe Lawrence's interview addresses how and why people in the general population need books. As a trans woman, Zoe also offers a perspective on how books on LGBTQ issues are needed and often denied. Paul Tardie's chapter, "Going Postal: Censorship, Policy and Correspondence Rejection with Texas Prisons," explains the bureaucratic roadblocks prisons put up to stop people from receiving books. These policies are often said to be necessary for ensuring safety, but as this chapter shows, this is far from the case. We hope that these chapters will motivate readers to realize that prison policies matter to us all and that the system itself should be dismantled.

In the afterword, Megan Sweeney, author of *Reading Is My Window: Books and the Art of Reading in Women's Prisons*, presents a mediation on the significance of the PBP movement from a person who has spent years researching, teaching, and writing about imprisonment. We hope you will find it, and this work as a whole, inspiration for working toward a society without prisons.

There is a list at the end of this book of all the PBPs in the United States. Reach out and join us!

NOTES

1. Wendy Sawyer and Peter Wagner, "Mass Incarceration: The Whole Pie 2020," Prison Policy Initiative, March 24, 2020, https://www.prisonpolicy.org/reports/pie2020.html; and Emily Widra and Tiana Herring, "States of Incarceration: The Global Context 2021," Prison Policy Initiative, September 2021, https://www.prisonpolicy.org/global/2021.html.

2. Jorge Renaud, "Who's Really Bringing Contraband into Jails? Our 2018 Survey Confirms It's Staff, Not Visitors," Prison Policy Initiative, December 6, 2018, https://www.prisonpolicy.org/blog/2018/12/06/jail-contraband/; and "Video Visitation: How Private Companies Push for Visits by Video and Families Pay the Price," Texas Criminal Justice Coalition, October 2014, https://www.texascjc.org/system/files/publications/TCJC GL Video Visitation Report (Oct 2014).pdf.

3. For an examination of censorship of books inside prisons as a form of targeted oppression, see Jeannie Austin, Melissa Charenko, Michelle Dillon, and Jodi Lincoln, "Systemic Oppression and the Contested Ground of Information Access for Incarcerated People," *Open Information Science* 4 (2020): 169–85, https://doi.org/10.1515/opis-2020-0013.

4. No Child Left Behind states that children in grades 3–8 must be tested in reading and math once a year. See Alyson Klein, "No Child Left Behind: An Overview," *Education Week* 11 (April 10, 2015), https://www.edweek.org/policy-politics/no-child-left-behind-an-overview/2015/04.

5. Elizabeth Greenberg, Eric Dunleavy, and Mark Kutner, "Literacy behind Bars: Results from the 2003 National Assessment of Adult Literacy Prison Survey," U.S. Department of Education, Washington, D.C., National Center for Education Statistics, May 2007, 13.

6. Ibid.

7. North Carolina Department of Public Safety, "Disapproved Publications Report," September 18, 2019.

8. Thomas P. Bonzcar, "Prevalence of Imprisonment in the U.S. Population, 1974–2001," Bureau of Statistics Special Report, U.S. Department of Justice, August 2003, 1.

9. Lawrence A. Greenfeld and Steven K. Smith, "American Indians and Crime," Bureau of Justice Statistics, U.S. Department of Justice, February 1999.

10. *Adult Literacy in America: A First Look at the Findings of the National Adult Literacy Survey*, National Center for Education Statistics, April 2002, 60, https://nces.ed.gov/pubs93/93275.pdf.

11. "U.S. Department of Education Announces It Will Expand the Second Chance Pell Experiment for the 2022–2023 Award Year," U.S. Department of Education, July 30, 2021, https://www.ed.gov/news/press-releases/us-department-education-announces-it-will-expand-second-chance-pell-experiment-2022-2023-award-year.

12. For an extensive list, see "Prison Abolition Syllabus 2.0," Black Perspectives: African American Intellectual History Society, September 8, 2018, https://www.aaihs.org/prison-abolition-syllabus-2-0/, with contributions by Dan Berger, Garrett Felber, Kali Gross, Elizabeth Hinton, and Anyabwile Love.

WHY WE NEED PRISON BOOKS PROGRAMS

PRISON BOOKS: A LIFELINE
Victoria Law

> I wouldn't have made it this far without books. In prison, reading is not so much a means of escape as a survival mechanism. Books become tools of diverse purpose within the penitentiary; not only do they combat loneliness, but they are also barriers against isolation. Books will build you up more effectively than any time spent in the yard's weight pit, and the information they impart will protect you far better than a sharpened shiv.—LEE DOANE

Lee Doane is serving a life sentence. Like many who are imprisoned for such long periods, his ties to the outside world—family and friends—have eroded. He relies on Books Through Bars (New York City) and other prison book programs for reading materials that get him through his day and, as he noted, combat the loneliness and isolation of imprisonment.

With over two million people in its patchwork of jails and prisons, the United States has the world's highest incarceration rate—698 of every 100,000 U.S. residents are behind bars.[1] Contrary to the myth that prisons are places of potential rehabilitation, there is no national mandate requiring jails and prisons to have a library or provide meaningful access to books. In fact, there is no mandate requiring them to provide access to any reading materials at all.

If a prison or jail does have a library, prison practices and policies frequently act as barriers to access. Movement is strictly controlled and can only happen at certain intervals. To visit the library, a person typically must request a pass to walk from their cell or dormitory to the library. Those who are enrolled in the prison's education or work programs may find that program hours clash with those of the library, and thus they can never go to the library. In many prisons, the library is frequently closed or has limited hours, thus preventing many people from visiting.

Then there are the eighty thousand to one hundred thousand people across the U.S. prison system who are held in solitary confinement.[2] In solitary confinement, also known as segregation, a person is locked into a small cell for twenty-two to twenty-four hours each day. Some are isolated as punishment for breaking a prison rule—anything from a fight or assault to having too many sheets, towels, or books in their cell. Others are there for administrative purposes; they have broken no rules, but prison administrators see them as a potential threat or disruption. Still others, like Kwaneta Harris in Texas, are isolated while awaiting the outcome of an investigation. "If people want to know how dire it is, they should go sit in their closets—no books, no TV, no phone, no human contact—and they are still in a better place than us," explained Harris, who is entering her fifth year in solitary. Although she cannot see or touch other women, she can't block out the constant screaming, including women threatening suicide, and can't avoid inhaling the tear gas unleashed by prison guards whenever someone attempts to follow through on their threat. "In an environment that exacerbates trauma, a book, magazine or paper is your only refuge."[3]

People locked in their cells under these torturous conditions are perhaps most in need of the mental and emotional escape that reading provides, but they are prohibited from visiting the library. Doane spent six years in solitary. His only human contact was with prison guards, who pushed meal trays and mail through the slot in his metal door and, three times a week, handcuffed and frog marched him down the corridor to the prison shower. New York prison rules dictate that people in solitary have access to the library, usually in the form of a book cart filled with a ragtag assortment of paperbacks and weeks-old periodicals and periodically trundled through the corridor, but the prison where Doane was held did not bother with that requirement. If it weren't for Books Through Bars (New York City), Doane would have had no reading material to get through those long days.

Books Through Bars (New York City) is one of fifty-three programs across the United States that sends free books and other reading material to people behind bars. While restrictions vary depending on the system, nearly all jails and prisons require that books be sent directly from bookstores or publishers. Family members and friends are unable to buy a used book and mail it

Volunteers reading letters and fulfilling book requests at NYC Books Through Bars

directly to their imprisoned loved one, and given that the vast majority of people behind bars come from low-income families and communities, the cost of new books is often financially out of reach. For thousands imprisoned across the country, prison book programs have been one of their few—if only—source of books.

Even for those not stifled by solitary, books are a lifeline. "Every day here reminds me of my limitations: the fences, razor wire, bells, count times, uniforms—everything," wrote Elena, who is in her third year of a twenty-to-forty-year prison sentence. "Focusing on those limits can be lethal; I must seek a safe way out so I do not suffocate. Books are that outlet. When I read, I am reminded of freedom, of love, of choice, of beauty. Books make me a part of the human experience again, a need as crucial to survival as any physical satiation. I fear that if I do not have books, my mind will become as bland, limited, and broken as this dysfunctional institution."

The need for books behind bars is great, as evidenced by the hundreds, and sometimes thousands, of requests received by each prison book program each month. Program volunteers read these letters and then match,

Former Black Panther and award-winning journalist Mumia Abu Jamal penned *Live from Death Row* (1995) from Pennsylvania's death row. "You will find a blacker world than anywhere else. African-Americans, a mere 11% of the national population, compose about 40% of the death row population." His book *All Things Censored* (2000) was written in response to the revocation by NPR of an offer to contribute to their radio show, *All Things Considered*. In it, Abu Jamal explains with incisive clarity many complex issues.

as best they can, the subject of the request from the selection of donated books. Often the letter writers explain their reasons for their specific requests. Some, like Elena, say that they want books that allow them to temporarily escape the confines of their cells or the chaos of their crowded dorms.

For many, books are a way to continue their education. A 2003 Department of Justice study found that over 41 percent of people in jails and prisons, compared to 18 percent of the country's general population, had not completed high school or obtained their GED.[4] Still, even basic education classes are hard to access within prisons—in 2020, the Bureau of Prisons, which is responsible for all federal prisons, announced that 16,400 people were on the waiting list for prison literacy programs.[5] This figure only encompasses the 226,000 people in federal prisons; it does not include the nearly 1.3 million people in state prisons or the 631,000 in county jails.[6]

Higher education programs are even more scarce. The 1994 Crime Bill prohibited using Pell grants for students behind bars. At the time, Pell grants to imprisoned students constituted only one-tenth of 1 percent of the Pell Grant budget. But politicians' race to be toughest on crime dominated the discussion and decimated nearly all of the 350 college-in-prison programs.[7] For nearly all prison book programs, the most commonly requested book is a dictionary. Some people explain that they want a better vocabulary or that they want to teach themselves English. Others have stated that they have a cellmate whom they are teaching to read and write and want a dictionary to aid their efforts.

Race and racism play a central role in who is targeted by police, pursued by prosecutors, and sentenced to prison. The imprisonment rate of Black adults is more than five times that of their white counterparts.[8] Black people make up 33 percent of the nation's prison population though they comprise approximately 13 percent of the nation's population.[9] For Latinx adults, who make up 23 percent of U.S. prisoners, the imprisonment rate is nearly three times that of their white counterparts.[10]

Reflecting the skewed racial dynamics in prison are frequent requests for books about the history and culture of marginalized peoples that are too often missing from school textbooks, classrooms, and prison libraries. "At this facility, the kaptives are predominantly people of color," said U'Bay Lumumba, who has been imprisoned in New Jersey since the 1990s. "However, there are no Afrikan centric books conductive to a person's history and culture." Books about chattel slavery, the civil rights movement, and the Black Power movement often fly off the shelves to meet requests faster than most books-to-prisoner programs can replace them. The same is true for books about the Aztecs and the Incas.

For U'Bay Lumumba, reading about the lives of Malcolm X and George Jackson changed his ways of thinking and seeing the world. "It was their respective transformation from the kriminal mentality to a revolutionary mentality that influenced my own transformation," he recalled. He began reflecting on how his own actions, including those that led to his imprisonment, affected the lives of his family and friends, and he wrote letters apologizing for the "senseless decisions that left them alone to deal with that overt and systemic racism" of both the prison system and the world outside.

Still others ask for books to answer healthcare questions that prison medical staff fail to explain; alarmingly, this includes requests for pregnancy information by incarcerated women. In one Oklahoma women's prison, an imprisoned peer educator asked for information about HIV and AIDS to counter the disinformation that HIV could be contracted from a washing machine or a plate in the prison mess hall.

In 2020, in an effort to stop the spread of the novel coronavirus, prison administrators across the country stopped even the limited access to prison libraries. In nearly all prisons, prevention efforts also included keeping people confined to their cells for nearly twenty-three hours a day, essentially locking everyone into solitary confinement. Meanwhile, guards and other prison staff entered and left the prison on a daily basis; every shift change harbored the potential of bringing COVID-19 into the prison.

As people were locked away with little to no information about this deadly new disease, books took on new importance both for educational purposes and to fill the yawning void of perpetual lockdown. "During the pandemic, it became painfully clear how many hours I had to fill and that I could not fill all of them with unmitigated productivity. Down time was a looming problem, one that could leave me anxious, depressed, or irritable," recalled

Elena. "I became intensely grateful for the peaceful absorption books provided. My mind could imagine courageous and daring exploits or delve into a new world of information. The destructive cycling [of depression] could not reach me in there; I was safe. The price of peace was as low as a tattered paperback, something even I could afford."

Sharing possessions—whether a towel, a cup of noodles, or a book—is prohibited in prison, but many incarcerated people buck this rule; one book can make its way to a dozen or more other readers in that prison. Elena not only shares her reading material but uses it to challenge the women around her about their racist or xenophobic beliefs. After reading an article or book, she leaves it in the prison's common area for others to read. This allows her to open conversations without seeming confrontational. She often uses fantasy novels, such as N. K. Jemisin's *Broken Earth* trilogy and S. A. Chakraborty's Middle Eastern-inspired *Daevabad* trilogy, to encourage discussions about differences in race, ethnicity, culture, and faith and to challenge those around her to rethink their bigotry. "I find that sharing books has encouraged the exploration of new cultures and had made a difference in what people are willing to consider," she reflected.

In New Jersey, some of the men on Lumumba's housing unit began turning to books to fill the long and lonely months of lockdown and quarantine. With no access to the prison's library, which Lumumba described as filled with Westernized fiction, adventure, crime thrillers, and science fiction novels with no connection to readers of color, many turned to Lumumba and his personal collection of books for reading material. "In addition to providing my books, I also provided katpives with the addresses of programs that send free books," he recalled.

Books can not only change ingrained beliefs, but they can also spark a movement. By 2008, Todd Ashker had been imprisoned in California's notorious Security Housing Unit (or SHU) at Pelican Bay State Prison for nearly twenty years. Like Doane, Harris, and the tens of thousands of others in solitary, he had virtually no human contact. He spent nearly twenty-four hours alone in his cell each day; his one hour of recreation took place alone inside another cage. Unlike Doane and Harris, however, he had no release date from isolation. In California, until a 2015 legal settlement, prisoners could be placed in the SHU for an indeterminate period of time—or indefinitely—based on allegations of gang affiliation. Twenty years into his indefinite

Books Through Bars logo

isolation, Ashker was sent a copy of a biography of Bobby Sands, an Irish political prisoner who died in 1981 after embarking upon a sixty-six-day hunger strike protesting British rule.

Reading about Sands inspired Ashker, who was soon shouting down the cement corridor to men in neighboring cells about organizing their own strike. "They soon agreed, something had to be done," Ashker wrote. They agreed on a mass hunger strike, hoping that their actions would bring widespread media and public attention to their conditions and force meaningful change.[11] They launched three hunger strikes—two in 2011 and another in 2013. Each strike spread to more than a dozen state prisons and included thousands of participants. The last strike began with more than thirty thousand state prisoners refusing meals and lasted for sixty days (though the number of participants dwindled over those two months). Ashker also filed a class-action lawsuit, which, combined with the increased attention that their strikes garnered, resulted in a groundbreaking settlement. Prison officials agreed to a number of changes, including limiting placement in the Pelican Bay isolation unit to five years.[12] Ashker was released from the SHU into a unit with fewer restrictions shortly after the 2015 settlement was finalized.[13]

Occasionally prison books programs provide a literal lifeline in the last days of a person's life. People on death row are generally isolated from the rest of the prison and, like those in punitive solitary, locked in their cells for nearly twenty-four hours each day. Books provide a mental reprieve from the execution hanging over their heads. "The time I spend reading is my only escape," a man on Florida's death row wrote to Books to Prisoners Seattle. "I become totally engrossed and vicariously experience whatever the characters are doing. Fiction, ironically, is the only real world I get."[14]

In 2002, while on Texas's death row, Stanley Baker requested—and received—books from Books Through Bars (New York City). Twenty-eight days before his execution, he wrote a brief note, which was not opened and read until weeks after he had been put to death.[15] "I would like to thank you for the books you sent me. I'm going to be executed May 30th but I'd like you to know that those books will give me much pleasure in the days remaining to me," he wrote in what would become a thank-you note beyond the grave.[16]

"Organizations such as Books Through Bars do much more than just provide reading material; in actuality, they furnish the incarcerated person with an individual survival kit, a way of getting from one day to the next, a little bit of hope bound up between the covers of books," Doane told me.

NOTES

1. Peter Wagner and Wanda Bertram, "What Percent of the U.S. Is Incarcerated? And Other Ways to Measure Mass Incarceration," *Prison Policy Initiative*, January 16, 2020, https://www .prisonpolicy.org/blog/2020/01/16/percent-incarcerated/.

2. Andrea Fenster, "New Data: Solitary Confinement Increases Risk of Premature Death after Release," *Prison Policy Initiative*, October 13, 2020, https://www.prisonpolicy.org /blog/2020/10/13/solitary_mortality_risk/.

3. Kwaneta Harris to Victoria Law, August 25, 2021, letter in author's possession.

4. Caroline Wolf Harlow, *Education and Correctional Populations: Bureau of Justice Statistics Special Report*, U.S. Department of Justice, January 2003, https://bjs.ojp.gov /content/pub/pdf/ecp.pdf.

5. *Federal Prison System: FY 2021 Performance Budget Congressional Submission*, U.S. Department of Justice, 32, https://justice.gov/doj/page/file/1246231/download.

6. Wendy Sawyer and Peter Wagner, "Mass Incarceration: The Whole Pie 2020," Prison Policy Initiative, March 24, 2020, https://www.prisonpolicy.org/reports/pie2020.html.

7. In December 2020, Congress lifted the ban on Pell grants to people in prison, but with the pandemic raging through the world, including U.S. prisons, it remains to be seen when and how college-in-prison programs will resume.

8. E. Ann Carson, *Prisoners in 2019*, U.S. Department of Justice, Office of Justice Programs, Bureau of Justice Statistics, Bulletin, October 2020, 10, https://bjs.ojp.gov/content/pub/pdf/p19.pdf.

9. Carson, *Prisoners in 2019*, 6.

10. Carson, *Prisoners in 2019*, 10.

11. Victoria Law, "What Does a Book Have to Do with a Movement?" *Waging NonViolence*, September 15, 2015.

12. Under the *Ashker v. Brown* settlement, the California Department of Corrections and Rehabilitation also agreed to place prisoners who have spent ten or more years in the Security Housing Unit in either general population or a new restrictive custody general population facility, which, while restrictive, allowed for in-person interaction, group programming, and contact visits with loved ones.

13. Eleven months after his release from the SHU, Ashker was placed in the administrative segregation unit, another form of solitary confinement, after prison officials received confidential information that he would be attacked, if not killed, if he remained in general population. Victoria Law, "'As Long as Solitary Exists, They Will Find a Way to Use It,'" *The Nation*, July 13, 2018.

14. Quoted in Michelle Dillon and Bo-Won Keum, eds., *Dear Books to Prisoners: Letters from the Incarcerated* (Seattle: Left Bank Books, 2019), 151.

15. Author's recollection of opening the letter months after Baker's execution date, then looking him up online.

16. Stanley Baker to Books Through Bars, "Letters," https://booksthroughbarsnyc.org/letters/.

WE NEED YOU, DEAR READER: ON BANNED BOOK LISTS
Michelle Dillon

One of the most pernicious issues in the provision of books to people who are held in carceral facilities is the censorship of reading materials. In a country that incarcerates nearly 1 percent of its adult population, jail and prison censorship is the predominant form of state censorship in the United States today. Unlike censorship in most other settings in this country, carceral censorship is total and insurmountable. If a school bans a book, a curious student may be able to borrow a copy of that book outside the school or find the text online. Not so in a jail or prison. The internet does not exist in most carceral facilities. Families and friends cannot mail books to or leave books with their loved ones when they come visit. In a carceral facility, the mailroom and the library (if one even exists at the facility) are the only channels for obtaining printed information. The state maintains total control over the bodies of incarcerated individuals, and that is precisely what makes the largely unregulated status of contemporary carceral censorship so dangerous; if we want to empower people who are incarcerated, we must fight for their right to read. To do so, we must first learn the extent of censorship and uncover the depth of what we still do not know about it. Banned book lists, as you will discover, epitomize censorship; these lists are fertile ground to fight for access to books in jails and prisons.

As a volunteer with Books to Prisoners Seattle, a prison book program in the state of Washington that sends free books into state and federal prisons across the country, I saw censorship repeatedly. Through this exposure, addressing and reversing carceral censorship has become my mission. Censorship is so ubiquitous in carceral facilities that scholars have created classification systems to better describe the scope of it. In 2019, PEN America differentiated between two primary routes to censor incoming materials: content-neutral bans and content-based bans.[1] A content-neutral ban limits which publishers, bookstores, and other distributors are allowed to provide materials. A content-based ban decides that a specific title will be censored.

Content-neutral bans often mean that reading materials can only be received from a few expensive outlets. Some content-neutral bans cases have explicitly banned free book distributors such as Books to Prisoners Seattle and other books to prisons programs. These bans restrict peoples' access to only new books obtained from commercial bookstores. Other content-neutral bans force incarcerated people to purchase books through their inmate accounts, which are accounts that are controlled by private companies that charge money for depositing into the account. For example, one company, JPay, charges $3.50 to deposit $5 into an inmate account.[2] Most egregiously, in 2019 the West Virginia Division of Corrections and Rehabilitation partnered with Global Tel*Link and began charging $.03–$.05 per minute to read books on digital tablets. To restrict books in this way creates a tax on reading in an environment where alternatives and money are extremely limited.

Recent content-neutral bans have included an attempt by the Pennsylvania Department of Corrections in 2018 to limit book access exclusively to a tiny (and expensive) set of digital books, as well as an attempt by the Washington Department of Corrections in 2019 to limit access to new books only—which would have stopped access from free prison book programs and made books unobtainable for many people given the costs of new books. In January 2021, the Benton County Jail in Arkansas attempted to remove all physical books except Bibles from its premises; the new policy was met with swift condemnation from the ACLU of Arkansas.[3] With the limited oversight on jail and prison policymaking that currently exists in this country, these bans can take effect

Playwright and novelist Oscar Wilde was sentenced to prison on "indecency" charges for being gay. While incarcerated, he wrote a letter titled "De Profundis," Latin for "From the Depths." This letter, written to Lord Alfred Douglas, is considered one of the greatest love letters of all time.

virtually overnight. They are always fluctuating between—and even within—carceral agencies and are often only uncovered by prison books programs after multiple packages of books have been rejected.

However, as difficult to track and navigate as content-neutral bans can be, content-based bans are magnitudes worse in terms of erratic and unjust implementation. Bans based on content are often made by individual mailroom staff with minimal outside guidance or standardized reporting procedures. Hundreds of books and letters (or even compact discs, in some prisons) arrive daily in a jail or prison's mailroom to be processed.[4] Whoever is assigned to the mailroom will sort through the incoming mail and judge, based on extremely nebulous definitions, whether a material constitutes a "threat to safety and security" for the facility. If a determination about "threatening" content is made, the materials will be denied to their intended recipients. If staff declare the material to be unsafe, that determination may be maintained permanently, and the material will be banned within that facility or prison system from that point forward.

Some facilities maintain review processes for denied materials that involve third parties or appeal processes wherein the sender or incarcerated individual can contest the ban, but many facilities simply allow the mailroom staff to act as the final word. The incarcerated person and sender may not even be aware that the material has been censored, as facilities are currently under no obligation to notify an inmate their books have been banned. Unsurprisingly, given the history, composition, and intent of carceral agencies, deep racial biases in the assessments of alleged threats have been found by the few published studies of content-based bans.[5] Thus, carceral agencies have established a system in which biases are freely imposed upon reading materials, the information allowed inside facilities has been extremely curtailed, and few mechanisms exist to even assess current bans, let alone overhaul the system.

I understood the extent of the dearth of knowledge about content-based bans only when I undertook a project in 2019 to gather comprehensive information about the scope of prison censorship. By that time, I had experienced firsthand the chronic frustrations of prison censorship through seven years of volunteer work with Books to Prisoners Seattle and two years of employment with the Human Rights Defense Center (the publisher of the monthly magazine *Prison Legal News* and frequent undertaker of litigation against jails and prisons when censorship of that magazine occurred). I knew that some prison systems codified their censorship as banned book lists: any

Michelle Dillon in 2019

censored material would be added to a centralized list to which every official in every prison would adhere—in theory.

The entries on many of these known banned book lists were erratic and nonsensical. For example, volumes 3 and 5 of a book series might be explicitly banned, but volumes 1, 2, and 4 from that series would not appear on the list and thus presumably would still be allowed. Under the pretense of "sexual explicitness," women's health books and self-help books about sexual trauma were frequently banned. Innocuous books such as dog breed encyclopedias and coloring books showed up on banned book lists.[6] Texas was notoriously restrictive—the Texas Civil Rights Project had obtained the state's banned book list in 2011 and found that it contained 11,581 titles. Even though Texas technically had an appeal process for censored materials, the report determined that more than 86 percent of appeals were ultimately denied.[7] The same lack of oversight that allowed single staff to throw out books also made these lists inscrutable; seldom were coherent rationales for censorship included in these lists. Even worse, the lists were rarely made public to prison books programs such as Books to Prisoners Seattle, which meant that we often had to reverse engineer lists and guess at which books could

A returned package received by Saxapahaw Prison Books
because it was wrapped in brown, not white paper.

be received. The inconsistency from state to state also made regulations difficult to understand, as a book might be censored on two states' lists but nowhere else, and it was impossible to accurately guess whether that book might be allowed for any of the states for which we did not currently have access to a banned book list.

Banned book lists stymied prison books programs and incarcerated people with equal frustration. In one Supreme Court amicus brief written on behalf of a lawsuit by the Human Rights Defense Center against censorship in Florida prisons, the legal representative wrote:

> Books are also regularly added or removed from banned-books lists, sometimes even daily, and prisons do not always share these lists with book clubs, who are left flying blind. Because they are usually small and often staffed entirely by volunteers, and because it is costly to send books that do not reach prisoners, book clubs inevitably self-censor. And when prison book clubs are chilled, prisoners forgo books that might interest them and spark a lifelong habit of reading.[8]

By 2019, Books to Prisoners Seattle had collected approximately two dozen lists from state prison systems across the country and created a resource page for those lists on the organization's website. These lists had been dredged from every known source: a few regularly updated lists made public by the Pennsylvania Department of Corrections and the Washington Department of Corrections; a handful of lists that had been received over the years from supporters; and occasional media coverage of the issue. The resulting collection, although valuable, was full of gaps and often woefully outdated. The most recent list for some states was nearly a decade old; other states had no lists uploaded at all. After an exhaustive search and consultations with other prison books programs, it was clear that the information to fill the gaps on the resource page was simply not publicly available at that time.

As the public records manager at the Human Rights Defense Center at that time, I knew that public records requests could be the most effective method to obtain the missing lists, but I also understood how time- and resource-intensive public records requests could be. Public records requests are any requests for information made by an individual to a government agency. Each state has implemented its own policies for responding to such requests. Some states take public records requests more seriously and have imposed time limits on government agencies to respond to the public as well as limitations on the amount of money that the agency can require that a requester pay before providing records. Other states take advantage of the lack of regulations to shield their public records. In 2015, for example, the Portland Police Department tried to charge a local newspaper $1,042,450.20 to provide records about the department's operations.[9] Tennessee still requires requesters to reside within the boundaries of the state, a truly ludicrous restriction in the era of the internet.[10] Without legal backing, a requester such as Books to Prisoners Seattle faced an uphill battle in many states where the prison system could drag its feet or similarly leverage high fees.

With the expectation of these barriers, the Human Rights Defense Center generously offered to act as a partner in the project, having already litigated against

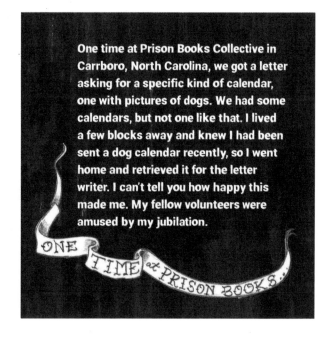

One time at Prison Books Collective in Carrboro, North Carolina, we got a letter asking for a specific kind of calendar, one with pictures of dogs. We had some calendars, but not one like that. I lived a few blocks away and knew I had been sent a dog calendar recently, so I went home and retrieved it for the letter writer. I can't tell you how happy this made me. My fellow volunteers were amused by my jubilation.

ONE TIME at PRISON BOOKS...

correctional agencies in several states both to reverse carceral censorship and to obtain public records about departmental operations. Enlisting a nonprofit with a such a track record could be the key to unlocking these records. Books to Prisoners Seattle was also fortunate to have been contacted by a group of graduate students in the Master of Library and Information Science program at the University of Washington who expressed an interest in working on this project. I worked with this group of students to draft and submit public records requests on letterhead for the Human Rights Defense Center asking for current banned book lists as implemented in every state prison system in the country. For months, we tracked the progress of each request, followed up with agency representatives, and (inevitably) waited as delays and excuses mounted.

We expected to find long lists filled with ridiculous and oppressive inclusions, but what we discovered was somehow worse. It turned out that the reason we had significant gaps in our resource page for banned book lists was that some states would not deign to collect that information altogether. Some states, such as Alaska, simply had not bothered to create a central list.

CDCR   **Disapproved Publications** June 2019   1

Note: publications on this list were disapproved at the time of compilation, but may have been subsequently approved upon appeal

*Each publication on this list was determined to meet the criteria of CCR Section 3134.1 on a case by case basis

Publications	Author
100 DEADLY SKILLS	Clint Emerson
100 EUROPEAN GRAFFITI ARTISTS	Frank Malt
100 JAPANESE TATTOO DESIGNS BY HORIMOUJA; PART II	Horimouja
100 NO EQUIPMENT WORKOUTS	Neila Rey
100 UK GRAFFITI ARTISTS	Frank Malt
1000 TATTOOS	Carlton Books
1000 TATTOOS	Henk Schiffmacher
1001 MOVIES YOU MUST SEE BEFORE YOU DIE	Jason Solomons and Steven Jay Schelder
101 THINGS NOT EVERYONE SHOULD KNOW HOW TO DO, FORBIDDEN KNOWLEDGE	Michael Powell
111 MILLENNIUM	Luis Royo
18 EIGHTEEN MAGAZINE	
1980'S GLAMOUR: 20TH CENTURY PIN-UPS	Ian Penberthy
200 UNCENSORED SEX ACTS MAGAZINE	
2PAC VS. BIGGIE	Jeff Weiss/Evan McGavery
30 SOMETHING MAGAZINE	
300: THE ART OF THE FILM	F
50 NIGHTS IN GRAY	Weldon Owen
500 FAIRY MOTIFS	Myrea Petit
75 CONVENTION SKETCHES VOLUME 10	William Stout
8 WAYS TO TELL YOUR FORTUNE	Sarah Bartlett
A CHILD OF A CRACKHEAD	Shameek A. Speight
A CLASH OF KINGS	George R. R. Martin
A DICTIONARY OF MARTIAL ARTS	Louis Fredic
A GAME OF THRONES, THE GRAPHIC NOVEL, VOLUME FOUR	
A GAME OF THRONES, THE GRAPHIC NOVEL, VOLUME THREE	
A GAME OF THRONES: THE GRAPHIC NOVEL, VOLUME ONE	George R. R. Martin
A GAME OF THRONES: THE GRAPHIC NOVEL, VOLUME TWO	George R. R. Martin
A GUIDE TOUR OF HELL, A GRAPHIC MEMOIR	Samuel Bercholz
A HISTORY OF WESTERN ART, FIFTH EDITION	Laurie Schneider Adams

Excerpt from
California's Banned
Book List

A book might arrive at a prison in Alaska and be censored, and the next day another copy could arrive and make it through the mailroom without any issues. There was no standardization within the prison systems in some states, much less any mechanisms for appeal.

As we worked, we pushed out information on Twitter to try to boost the issue into the inboxes of journalists. We looked for opportunities for exposure where the content of books on the list was either clearly so mundane that their exclusion was laughable, the content had been obviously targeted by the prison system due to political material, the list itself was absurdly long, or a number of censored authors were prolific on Twitter—and we knew that we could count on them to amplify our tweets. With the assistance of Twitter (eternal gratitude to #librarytwitter), we attracted the attention of several journalists, including journalists in Kansas and Florida who published excellent articles excoriating the lengthy and unfair lists that had been implemented in their states. In response to the negative publicity in Kansas, the Department of Corrections (DOC) promised to review and reduce the list's contents.[11] Other journalists began to pick up on the project and duplicate the work, resulting in coverage about bans on computer books in Oregon.[12]

To date, however, we still lack a comprehensive list of censored materials across the country, and we therefore have not yet been able to move forward in making broader changes to carceral censorship. Here are the recommendations that I would make for substantial progress to happen in this area:

1. Each prison system must make a rational, clear set of guidelines for minimal censorship that applies to every prison mailroom and provide consequences when staff refuse to abide by those standards.
2. Information about book rejections must be collected and made publicly available, such as how Washington and Pennsylvania already make their lists available on their websites.
3. A publication review committee must be created to review rejections in every prison system.
4. The incarcerated person and the sender of the book must be allowed to appeal a rejection, and ample time must be given for an appeal.
5. The staff who run the libraries must be separate from the staff employed by the DOC to ensure that trained librarians aren't under the thumb of the DOC who are judging books.

For all of its issues, the Washington DOC already takes these steps: a notification form for censored materials is provided to both the incarcerated person and the sender; both parties can appeal; and the DOC holds a monthly meeting with three state government staff members (including one librarian)—and all librarians are employed through the secretary of state rather than the DOC.

Prison books programs face constant battles in ensuring access to quality reading materials. We will never have enough staff to keep up with shifting book regulations at the 3,134 jails, 1,833 state prisons, and 110 federal facilities currently warehousing people in this country. So long as sites of incarceration exist, it's likely that censorship will also exist as another mechanism to control the bodies and minds of those inside. If we cannot eradicate censorship, we need to make this an unignorable issue until such time as we can abolish prisons. And to do that, we need help from people who care about access to books and the rights of people who are incarcerated. We need the help of librarians and educators and anybody in the political machine who wants this to end. We need a broad coalition of incarcerated people and their loved ones and other advocates. We need you, dear reader.

NOTES

1. "Literature Locked Up: How Prison Book Restriction Policies Constitute the Nation's Largest Book Ban," PEN America, September 2019, https://pen.org/wp-content /uploads/2019/09/literature-locked-up-report-9.24.19.pdf.

2. JPay's fees vary depending on location. Percentagewise the fees are generally highest for deposits of $0–20. For example, on February 17, 2021, it would cost $4.70 to make a $0–20 deposit via the telephone using JPay at the Bent County Correctional Facility (Colorado). JPay, https://www.jpay.com/Facility-Details/Colorado-State-Prison-System/Bent-County -Correctional-Facility.aspx.

3. "ACLU of Arkansas Calls on Benton County Sheriff to Restore Access to Reading Material in County Jail," American Civil Liberties Union, January 27, 2021, https://www.aclu.org /press-releases/aclu-arkansas-calls-benton-county-sheriff-restore-access-reading-material -county-jail.

4. Jimmy Jenkins, "Don't Kill My Vibe: Arizona Alleges Kendrick Lamar CD Ban is Unconstitutional in Appeal to 9th Circuit," 91.5 KJZZ, February 11, 2021, https://kjzz.org /content/1658464/dont-kill-my-vibe-arizona-inmate-alleges-kendrick-lamar-cd-ban -unconstitutional; and *Edward Lee Jones Jr., v. S. Slade et al*, United States Court of Appeals for the Ninth Circuit Court, no. 20-15642.

5. Jeanie Austin, Melissa Charenko, Michelle Dillon, and Jodi Lincoln, "Systemic Oppression and the Contested Ground of Information Access for Incarcerated People," *Open*

Information Science 4, no. 1 (July 1, 2020): 169–85, https://www.degruyter.com/view/journals /opis/4/1/article-p169.xml.

6. *Prison Legal News v. Florida Department of Corrections*, United States Supreme Court, no. 18-355, https://www.supremecourt.gov/DocketPDF/18/18-355/67506/20181019133857149 _No%2018-355%20Amicus%20Brief%20of%20Prison%20Book%20Clubs%20Supporting %20Petitioner.pdf.

7. Maggie Watson et al., "Banned Books in the Texas Prison System: How the Texas Department of Criminal Justice Censors Books Sent to Prisoners," A Texas Civil Rights Project 2011 Human Rights Report, Austin, Texas, 2011, https://www.prisonlegalnews.org /media/publications/texas_civil_rights_project_prison_book_censorship_report_2011.pdf.

8. *Prison Legal News v. Florida Department of Corrections*, Brief amicus curiae of Prison Books Clubs, Supreme Court of the United States, no. 18-355 (October 2018), https://www .supremecourt.gov/DocketPDF/18/18-355/67506/20181019133857149_No%2018-355%20 Amicus%20Brief%20of%20Prison%20Book%20Clubs%20Supporting%20Petitioner.pdf.

9. Sabrina Conza, "Oregon's Excessive Public Records Fees Deter Investigative Reporting," Reporters Committee for the Freedom of the Press, November 13, 2020, https://www.rcfp .org/oregon-high-public-records-fees/.

10. Tennessee Public Records Act, Tennessee Code § 10-7-503 Section 2.

11. Sherman Smith, "Corrections Secretary Eliminates Banned Book List for Kansas Prisons, Deploys New Policy," *Topeka-Capital Journal*, August 21, 2019, https://www .cjonline.com/news/20190821/corrections-secretary-eliminates-banned-book-list-for-kansas -prisons-deploys-new-policy.

12. Rachel Alexander, "Oregon Prisons Ban Dozens of Technology and Programming Books over Security Concerns," *Salem Reporter*, June 18, 2019, https://www.salemreporter.com /posts/891/oregon-prisons-ban-dozens-of-technology-and-programming-books-over -security-concerns.

UNTIL THERE IS A WORLD WITHOUT PRISONS: BOOKS FOR LGBTQ PEOPLE Melissa Charenko

LGBT Books to Prisoners is a donation-funded, volunteer-run organization based in Madison, Wisconsin. Like many prison books programs, LGBT Books to Prisoners provides free books directly to individuals who are incarcerated across the United States. It is the largest prison book program focused on lesbian, gay, bisexual, transgender, and queer (LGBTQ) people. LGBT Books to Prisoners aims to acknowledge and work against the oppressive functions of the prison system. By giving those who are incarcerated control of what they read, we seek to shift some power back into incarcerated people's hands. We provide access to knowledge of an individual's choosing so that individuals can learn and grow as they desire. In so doing, we believe that our work affirms the dignity of all individuals.

In March 2019, volunteers at LGBT Books to Prisoners received an email from one of the largest sheriff's departments in the United States. The corrections officer writing the email worked at a detention facility, which, the email said, had a special unit that houses "all biologically born female gender inmates including all members of the LGBTQIA communities." The officer said that they, along with one other person, were the "primary source for our LGBTQIA inmates especially those whom identify as trans gender." The officer was researching ways to provide better services for this population. She asked LGBT Books to Prisoners to submit samples of books that would give the facility's captain "an opportunity to vet the material source . . . so we can utilize you as a resource accommodation for our LGBTQIA community." LGBT Books to Prisoners responded to the request from the sheriff's department offering to send books directly to any LGBTQ person who was incarcerated

Back of an envelope received by LGBT Books to Prisoners

at the facility. We provided order forms to distribute and offered to follow any of the facility's content guidelines and to adhere to other restrictions. We chose not to send books to the facility to vet because we send thousands of unique titles each year, matching an individual's request for books as closely as possible with the donated books on hand. We couldn't send a library's worth of books that would be destroyed if deemed unacceptable.

Within a few weeks, we had received over thirty scans of order forms from the corrections officer, some of which you can see in figure 3.2. Before distributing the order form, the officer had modified it, removing several genres of books. The forms continued to list LGBTQ books, self-help, language-learning books, and *libros en espanõl* as possible genres an individual might request. Before photocopying the order form and distributing it, the officer had removed fiction, nonfiction, history, and dictionaries. She had also added a note stating that "all content must be LGBTQIA related" and that sexual content and nudity were "not ok."

LGBT Books to Prisoners followed up with the officer about the requests. Many of the requests asked for books on transitioning. We asked whether the nudity and sexual content guidelines applied to educational or medical books. For those seeking information on transitioning, we hoped to send *Trans Bodies, Trans Selves: A Resource Guide for the Transgender Community*, which remains the leading text by and for transgender people.[1] Prisons often reject this book because it contains information on sexual and reproductive health, sexuality, and intimate relationships. In 2016, for example, LGBT Books to Prisoners received a letter, reproduced in the figure below, from the Missouri Department of Corrections rejecting the book because it "contains inappropriate sexual behaviors," and there was penetration on two pages.

Although the flagged illustrations are from an educational section on safer sex that stresses the importance of consent as well as methods to prevent contraception and sexually transmitted infections, the department denied a written request from LGBT Books to Prisoners asking that the censorship be overturned.[2]

What kinds of books do you want? Please specify:
(Note: We cannot send magazines or calendars.)
☐ LGBTQ books. Specify: ______
☐ Education books ______
☐ Fiction ______
☐ Non-fiction ______
☐ History ______
☐ Self-help books ______
☐ Dictionary (English) ______
☐ Other dictionary ______
☐ Paper to write on ______
☐ Libros en español ______
☐ Language learning books ______
☐ Easy-to-read books ______
☐ Other: ______
Please tell us more about the types of books you want:

What are the prison's restrictions on books?
☐ Softcover only? ☐ New only?
Hardcovers w/ covers removed? OK ☐ Not OK ☐
☐ Rules about LGBTQ content?
☐ Rules about sexual content or nudity?
☐ Maximum number of books per package: ______
Please explain:

What kinds of books do you want? Please specify:
(Note: We cannot send magazines or calendars.)
☒ LGBTQ books. Specify: Transitioning, relationships, misc...
☒ Self-help books misc, Transitioning etc...
☐ Libros en español ______
☒ Language learning books Hebrew, Spanish
☐ Easy-to-read books ______
ALL CONTENT MUST BE LGBTQIA RELATED
What are the prison's restrictions on books?
☒ Softcover only? ☒ New only?
Hardcovers w/ covers removed? OK ☐ Not OK ☒
☐ Rules about LGBTQ content?
☒ Rules about sexual content or nudity? NOT OK
☐ Maximum number of books per package: ______
Please explain: MUST BE ABLE TO FIT INSIDE ONE PROPERTY BAG UPON RELEASE OR TRANSFER

What kinds of books do you want? Please specify:
(Note: We cannot send magazines or calendars.)
☒ LGBTQ books. Specify: Activism biography (Harvey Milk) Nautical/Sailing History
☐ Self-help books ______
☐ Libros en español ______
☐ Language learning books ______
☒ Easy-to-read books SUDOKU
ALL CONTENT MUST BE LGBTQIA RELATED
What are the prison's restrictions on books?
☒ Softcover only? ☒ New only?
Hardcovers w/ covers removed? OK ☐ Not OK ☒
☐ Rules about LGBTQ content?
☒ Rules about sexual content or nudity? NOT OK
☐ Maximum number of books per package: ______
Please explain: MUST BE ABLE TO FIT INSIDE ONE PROPERTY BAG UPON RELEASE OR TRANSFER

What kinds of books do you want? Please specify:
(Note: We cannot send magazines or calendars.)
☒ LGBTQ books. Specify: Any Allowed
☐ Self-help books ______
☐ Libros en español ______
☐ Language learning books ______
☐ Easy-to-read books ______
ALL CONTENT MUST BE LGBTQIA RELATED
What are the prison's restrictions on books?
☒ Softcover only? ☒ New only?
Hardcovers w/ covers removed? OK ☐ Not OK ☒
☐ Rules about LGBTQ content?
☒ Rules about sexual content or nudity? NOT OK
☐ Maximum number of books per package: ______
Please explain: MUST BE ABLE TO FIT INSIDE ONE PROPERTY BAG UPON RELEASE OR TRANSFER

What kinds of books do you want? Please specify:
(Note: We cannot send magazines or calendars.)
☑ LGBTQ books. Specify: All, Transgender Shots for Females who want to Become Men. Lesbian.
☐ Self-help books ______
☐ Libros en español ______
☐ Language learning books ______
☐ Easy-to-read books ______
ALL CONTENT MUST BE LGBTQIA RELATED
What are the prison's restrictions on books?
☒ Softcover only? ☒ New only?
Hardcovers w/ covers removed? OK ☐ Not OK ☒
☐ Rules about LGBTQ content?
☒ Rules about sexual content or nudity? NOT OK
☐ Maximum number of books per package: ______
Please explain: MUST BE ABLE TO FIT INSIDE ONE PROPERTY BAG UPON RELEASE OR TRANSFER

What kinds of books do you want? Please specify:
(Note: We cannot send magazines or calendars.)
☒ LGBTQ books. Specify: ______ ALL TRANSITIONAL RELATED
☒ Self-help books ______
☐ Libros en español ______
☒ Language learning books ______
☒ Easy-to-read books ______
ALL CONTENT MUST BE LGBTQIA RELATED
What are the prison's restrictions on books?
☒ Softcover only? ☒ New only?
Hardcovers w/ covers removed? OK ☐ Not OK ☒
☐ Rules about LGBTQ content?
☒ Rules about sexual content or nudity? NOT OK
☐ Maximum number of books per package: ______
Please explain: MUST BE ABLE TO FIT INSIDE ONE PROPERTY BAG UPON RELEASE OR TRANSFER

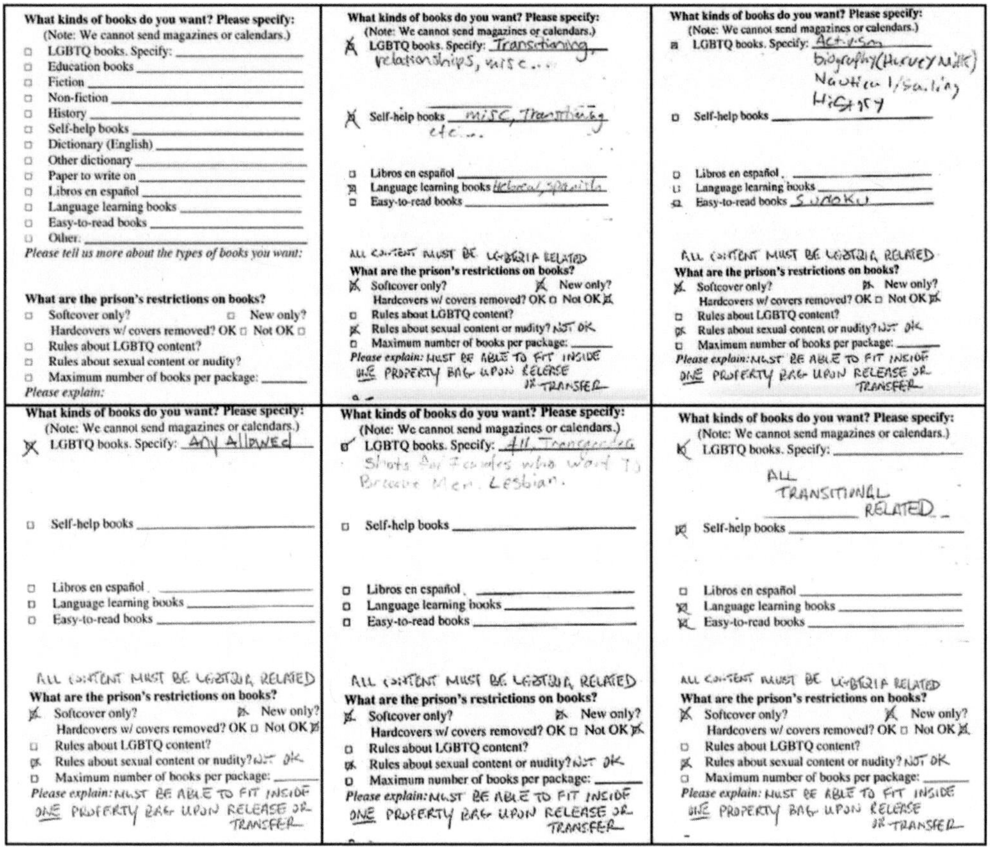

Excerpt of the LGBT Books to Prisoners' order form. Original form in top left, five examples of modified and completed order forms, with several order forms identical to the one on the bottom right.

LGBTQ Books to Prisoners grew out of Wisconsin Books to Prisoners (WIB2P) and the work of volunteer Dennis Bergren, who began volunteering with Wisconsin Books to Prisoners in 2006. He was a former high school language teacher who had a passion for learning. Bergren, who came out as gay late in life after years of feeling alone and imprisoned in his body, noticed that WIB2P was receiving lots of requests for LGBTQ materials. He asked if it would be okay to begin adding more gay books and, by spring 2007, began responding to requests for LGBTQ materials. As more and more people heard that the program offered books that affirmed their identities, people began writing for books from all over the country. Bergren began a separate chapter, LGBT Books to Prisoners, which sent reading materials to LGBTQ people nationwide. For years, this was largely a one-person operation with Bergren's house, and life, transformed by books to prisoners. Bergren provided most of the funding for the project. The ground floor of his home began to fill with books, and he kept binders of each letter he received, alphabetically organized with notes about what books he had sent. Dennis wanted to make sure that no person would ever receive the same book twice (unless they wanted a replacement for a well-loved favorite) and so that he could send more of the same if someone mentioned that they enjoyed the last books they received. Bergren once said that he devoted "probably close to seven or eight days a week" to books to prisoners, which is likely an underestimate. The letters from incarcerated people contained in the binders contain many personal notes to Bergren; he had clearly developed strong relationships with hundreds of people. Long after he stepped down from LGBT Books to Prisoners in 2013 due to failing health, people continued to write to Bergren thanking him for his many letters and books—and friendship—over the years. Dennis Bergren passed away in 2015.

Because of these kinds of experiences and the officer's frequent references to vetting any books we might send, we wanted to double-check that the books would make it to their intended readers. We asked the officer if *Trans Bodies, Trans Selves* was permissible and whether a non-LGBTQ book might better fit for the individual requesting "abuse-related" books. The officer responded:

The book about abuse is fine. I would say use your best judgement however most of our inmate [*sic*] currently housed here are extremely sheltered in regard to our LGBTQ community. They really don't know much about it, are happy we

STATE OF MISSOURI
DEPARTMENT OF CORRECTIONS
CENSORSHIP NOTIFICATION

**Jefferson City
Correctional Center**

OFFENDER NAME & DOC NUMBER

The Missouri Department of Corrections has reviewed materials sent to you. Pursuant to our review of this material, we conclude that the security of this institution will be at risk if the material is delivered to you within this institution because the material:

1. constitutes a threat to the security, good order or discipline of the institution;

2. may facilitate or encourage criminal activity; or

3. may interfere with the rehabilitation of an offender.

THIS CONCLUSION IS BASED UPON THE FACT THAT THE MATERIAL (SELECT ALL REASONS THAT MAY APPLY)

contains inappropriate sexual behaviors, sexually explicit materials and pictures

ADDITIONAL COMMENTS

Penetration pages 377 & 387; sexually explicit

Sexually explicit

MATERIAL SENT BY
Rainbow Bookstore Co-op, 426 W Gilman Street
Madison WI 53703

DATE RECEIVED
4/5/2016

TITLE
Trans Bodies, Trans Selves by Laura Erickson-Schroth

PUBLICATION DATE

AUTHOR

SERIES/ VOLUME NUMBER
2014

PUBLISHER
Oxford University Press, 198 Madison Ave
New York NY 10016

STAFF MEMBER

DATE
April 11, 2016

STAFF MEMBER

DATE
April 11, 2016

MO 931-3485 (12-14)   DISTRIBUTION: ORIGINAL - CLASSIFICATION FILE
COPIES - OFFENDER CENSORED MATERIAL; CENSORSHIP COMMITTEE CHAIRPERSON; SENDER (ON PUBLICATIONS ONLY)

Censorship of
*Trans Bodies, Trans
Selves.* Redacted to
protect privacy.

are supporting, and want to be properly educated which is why we are asking for LGBTQ specific books to help them along. Just an FYI ALL books are vetted prior to the inmates receiving. Nudity, gang related, too erotic, etc. will not be given to the inmate and that›s just our policy standard.

The officer promised to research whether *Trans Bodies, Trans Selves* would be allowed, but never wrote back with a decision. This example illustrates key problems for LGBTQ people in prison. The officer wanted to be a resource for the LGBTQ population, but the prison system and the staff administering it are poorly equipped to meet the needs of LGBTQ people. The officer at the jail was unaware of even the most basic text for transgender people and needed to have any books sent to the prison captain for approval. What training the captain had for determining the appropriateness of LGBTQ books remained unclear, especially because vague restriction policies are often used to deny resources, even as staff and the people in prison requesting this information acknowledge that these resources are needed.

This lack of awareness of, and active bans on, resources for LGBTQ people exist despite the disproportionate numbers of LGBTQ people who come into contact with the criminal justice system.[3] Nearly one in ten transgender people reported that they had been incarcerated at some point in the past year in the 2015 U.S. Transgender Survey.[4] When the 2008–9 National Transgender Discrimination Survey asked transgender people whether they had been incarcerated at any point in their lives, 16 percent of respondents answered in the affirmative. Among Black transgender people, 47 percent reported being incarcerated at some point in their lives.[5] Similarly, federal data on gay, lesbian, and bisexual people suggest that GLB people are three times more likely to be incarcerated than the general population and that over 40 percent of incarcerated women are lesbian or bisexual.[6] Yet carceral facilities often do not have relevant resources for this population. LGBTQ people often do not have access to gender-affirming clothing and self-care products. They continue to be housed based on sex assigned at birth, rather than gender identity or expression. Most do not have access to LGBTQ-affirming books; a survey of LGBTQ people in prison reported that only 20 percent had access to LGBTQ-affirming reading material.[7]

Most facilities are not interested in providing these resources; homophobia and transphobia run rampant in prisons.[8] Politics of punishment or "rehabilitation" focus on producing productive citizens who conform to society, reducing information that does not follow conventional gender binaries and heteronormative ideals.[9] Budget restrictions limit books even further. Institutions often only begin to provide books to incarcerated people. Prisons have been forced to provide books because of court decisions and statutes, such as a Supreme Court decision (*Bounds v. Smith* 1977) that stipulated that all prisons must provide "meaningful access to the courts through people trained in law or through law library collections." But many have fought these cases or do not fulfill their legal obligation. For LGBTQ people, statutes such as the Prison Rape Elimination Act (PREA) are particularly important. PREA demands that confinement facilities prevent, detect, and respond to sexual abuse. Since LGBTQ people face the highest rates of abuse while they are incarcerated, "protecting" this population through special housing units or solitary confinement are some of the ways that PREA influences the

MELISSA CHARENKO

I HAVE BEEN IN PRISON FOR ALMOST 9 YEARS NOW, AND ALL BUT ABOUT 8 MONTHS OF THAT TIME I HAVE BEEN IN SEGREGATION (SOLITARY CONFINEMENT). BACK HERE WE HAVE VERY LIMITED ACCESS TO THE PRISON LIBRARY. WE ARE ALLOWED TO HAVE BOOKS, BUT WE'RE NOT ALLOWED TO GO TO THE LIBRARY. THEY WILL BRING YOU BOOKS BACK HERE, BUT THAT SERVICE IS NOT VERY RELIABLE AT ALL. TO GIVE YOU AN IDEA, I SAW THE LIBRARY WORKERS THIS PAST THURSDAY, AND THAT IS THE FIRST TIME THEY HAVE BEEN BACK HERE SINCE EARLY DECEMBER. WELL, TODAY IS MARCH 5TH. WE HAVE SEEN NO BOOKS IN ALL THAT TIME.

experiences of LGBTQ people.[10] These measures result in more punishment and restrictions against some of the most vulnerable people. Occasionally, PREA compliance might mean providing resources to LGBTQ people. The officer requesting books from LGBT Books to Prisoners was in charge of one of these special housing units, and she was the facility's PREA compliance officer. She did "PREA risk screenings" during intake interviews, where she handed out LGBT Books to Prisoners' order forms to those who might benefit from books.

Even when facilities are interested in providing gender-affirming material—whether out of recognition of the benefits of this material, in response to their legal obligations, or because of public backlash—many carceral facilities routinely limit LGBTQ content. In the opening example, LGBT Books to Prisoners could provide books to those in detention based on our "best judgment" that the book would most closely match a person's request, but the facility staff would use their own judgments to decide whether the person would ultimately receive the books. The officer suggested that once the books were vetted, they would only be provided as a "resource accommodation," rather than as standard materials for all those incarcerated. The language the officer used to describe the vetting process—supposedly part of a standard policy that might ban sexual or "too erotic" content—was ambiguous. Many policies like these allow Harlequin romance novels but ban books that depict homosexual relationships. For instance, the Illinois DOC listed "homosexuality" as a reason why a book may not be allowed into its prisons.[11] Many other policies perpetuate implicit and explicit biases against LGBTQ people: Texas bans "deviant criminal sexual behavior," and its rejection lists flag homosexual content. New Hampshire has banned a publication about the experiences of LGBTQ incarcerated people because it depicts "unlawful sexual practice."[12]

In addition to censorship, the fact that the officer had modified the order form suggests another way in which carceral facilities police the information that incarcerated people can receive. The officer seemed to be selecting genres of books based on what was best for this supposedly uninformed population. The officer had noted that the people in the special unit didn't know much about LGBTQ identities and felt that it was the facility's job to "properly educate" them. But on individuals' order forms, they could clearly express topics that interested them, whether it was hormone shots or true stories of lesbian relationships or fiction or history books. People in prison can clearly speak for themselves about what they most need, but the prison system regularly seeks to limit their voices.

Several order forms had been filled out by the officer. They are all in the same handwriting as the script restricting sexual content that appears on all order forms. The request on these order forms was all the same: "all transitional related" books. Perhaps the incarcerated individuals told the officer filling out the form that this is what they wanted, but compared to the diversity on the rest of the other forms, this explanation is hard to believe. Once again, the state was choosing the kind of resources people would receive.

Denying the agency of an LGBTQ person in prison can be particularly harmful. Not every transgender person prioritizes or desires social, legal, or medical transitions, such as gender-affirming surgery, hormone therapy, pronoun changes, alteration of appearance, or a legal name change.[13] But by determining that "transitional related" books were most needed, the officer had decided that a trans person was one who surgically transitioned, which is perhaps unsurprising in a system that enforces gender binaries. The order forms filled out in different handwriting, along with the letters that LGBT Books to Prisoners receives from incarcerated people, speak to the diversity of transitioning experiences. Some may want information on medical procedures, but others want information about coming out to friends and family, changing their names, religion and the queer experience, or erotica. LGBTQ experiences are varied, but the carceral system is unable to deal with that diversity.

In contrast to the restrictive, paternalistic carceral system that limits information and decides what information is appropriate, LGBT Books to Prisoners directly responds to individuals' requests. We trust a person to know what books they would like, whether they wish to learn about a process such as transitioning or to relax with a crossword book. We try to be informed about LGBTQ books and resources in ways that most jails and prisons are not. Some of our volunteers are librarians with expertise in LGBTQ content, and many of the volunteers have or are pursuing degrees in gender and women's studies or queer studies. Many of our volunteers are members of the LGBTQ community. We have read the books ourselves and regularly recommend and discuss appropriate books for a particular request. Since the organization receives regular deliveries from LGBTQ book awards, authors, and publishers, we also have diverse resources on hand for those who request them. We will buy some of the most requested resources, including gender and sexuality workbooks. Given our knowledge, we at LGBT Books to Prisoners attempt to fulfill each request as directly as possible, matching each order with the most appropriate books and writing a personal note explaining the choice.

LGBT Books to Prisoners receives letter after letter from those who have been sent books by the organization. The letters explain the importance of this personalized, community-building approach. A gay man incarcerated in New York State wrote:

> I received love in the form of books from you guys and ladys. I just want to say thank you for showing us that we mean something. What you do reminds me that I am human and not some foreign creature. Thank you so much for your generosity, and most importantly your love!

This letter reflects the solidarity networks that form across the prison walls, with books and letters that reiterate an individual's humanity and that their sexual orientation, gender identity, and experiences are valued. There is pride in being part of this community, as the back of the envelope at the opening of this chapter suggests. This solidarity helps people create community within the confines of prison. As this letter explains,

> I want to say thank you from the bottom of my heart for the work you all do. Thanks to your group we have started a sort of pass around library among the LGBTQ here. . . . There is a small handfull [sic] of us but we stick together. Like on a Saturday night, a few of us meet out at Recreation for Pinochle. A few of us that identify as Christian do bible studies. A couple of the group work out. When new people come onto the compound that are open we show them around and help them find their "click" that they feel comfortable in. As for the ones to [sic] scared to acknowledge what they are openly, we quietly help build their spirits so they come to know they are accepted.

This letter suggests something quite different than the email exchange with the corrections officer. The letter writer was building community despite the lack of resources from the state or the perceived safety concerns of being out in a violent system. The letter writer further notes the diversity of identities,

lgbtbookstoprisoners.org

Postcard used for fundraising

interests, and comfort levels among the small group of people who identify as LGBTQ. Only providing LGBTQ content because someone is LGBTQ denies the full spectrum of human experience, which is why LGBT Books to Prisoners will send someone queer fiction, a celebrity memoir, a notebook, and a dictionary if these are the books that someone has asked for. Someone else may receive books on their Mayan heritage and a language-learning book if they express this preference. The LGBTQ identity might not be paramount. We see people as people and understand intersectionality.

While LGBT Books to Prisoners is primarily oriented toward building community and upholding an individual's humanity by sending books of their choosing, we envision and work toward a world without prisons. The prison industrial complex perpetuates oppression and inequalities through punishment, violence, and control. Some of the oppression and inequality within the prison industrial complex is targeted at LGBTQ people, making

Card received by LGBT Books to Prisoners

Melissa Charenko, with books

Book packages ready to ship

Donations

prison abolition an LGBTQ—and much broader—issue.[14] As one person in prison wrote to LGBT Books to Prisoners, "I have been retaliated against because of my homosexuality. . . . It needs to be out there that LGBTQ prisoners need to be proud of who they are and to take a stand against unfair and cruel treatment." We amplify this sentiment by arguing that everyone needs to take a stand against the violence perpetrated by the prison industrial complex.[15]

While we work to dismantle the prison industrial complex and envision a world without cages, we continue to connect with those currently experiencing violence. As one incarcerated person reflects about his experiences in prison and receiving books from us:

> I get along ok socially for the most part but it's like stepping back in time with the way the LGBTQ community is viewed and treated. My sexuality is viewed as negative and is a constant joke among inmates AND staff. I have a good sense of humor, so I can laugh at some of the teasing, but then there's also that moment it seems to cross a line and then I realize they're serious and then you start to feel isolated. So having gay literature helps me feel a little less alone and gives me something I can connect with.

We will foster these connections until there is a world without prisons.

NOTES

1. Laura Erickson-Schroth, ed., *Trans Bodies, Trans Selves: A Resource Guide for the Transgender Community*, 2nd ed. (2014; New York: Oxford University Press, 2022).

2. Jeanie Austin, Melissa Charenko, Michelle Dillon, and Jodi Lincoln, "Systematic Oppression and the Contested Ground of Information Access for Incarcerated People," *Open Information Science* 4, no. 1 (2020): 169–85.

3. Joey L. Mogul, Andrea J. Ritchie, and Kay Whitlock, *Queer (In)Justice: The Criminalization of LGBT People in the United States* (Boston: Beacon Press, 2011).

4. Sandy E. James, Jody L. Herman, Susan Rankin, Mara Keisling, Lisa Mottet, and Ma'ayan Anafi, *The Report of the 2015 U.S. Transgender Survey* (Washington, D.C.: National Center for Transgender Equality, 2016): 184–96.

5. Jamie M. Grant, Lia A. Mottet, and Justin Tanis, *Injustice at Every Turn: A Report of the National Transgender Discrimination Survey,* (Washington, D.C.: National Center for Transgender Equality & National Gay and Lesbian Task Force, 2011), 163.

6. Ilan H. Meyer, Andrew R. Flores, Lara Stemple, Adam P. Romero, Bianca D. M. Wilson, and Jody L. Herman, "Incarceration Rates and Traits of Sexual Minorities in the United

States: National Inmate Survey, 2011–2012," *American Journal of Public Health* 107, no. 2 (February 2017): 267–73.

7. Jason Lydon et al., *Coming Out of Concrete Closets: A Report on Black & Pink's National LGBTQ Prisoner Survey* (n.p.: Black & Pink, 2015), https://www.blackandpink.org.

8. Terry A. Kupers, "The Role of Misogyny and Homophobia in Prison Sexual Abuse," *UCLA Women's Law Journal* 18, no. 1 (2010): 107–30; John Nguyet Erni, "Legitimating Transphobia: The Legal Disavowal of Transgender Rights in Prison," *Cultural Studies* 27, no. 1 (2013): 135–59.

9. Rehabilitative standards may deny books and periodicals altogether; see Megan Sweeney, "*Beard v. Banks*: Deprivation as Rehabilitation," *PMLA* 122, no. 3 (May 2007), 779–83.

10. Lydon et al., *Coming Out of Concrete Closets*; Patricia Elane Trimble, "Ignored LGBTQ Prisoners: Discrimination, Rehabilitation, and Mental Health Services during Incarceration," *LGBTQ Policy Journal* 9 (2018–19): 31–38.

11. Lee V. Gaines, "Non-Profit Sues IDOC over Censorship of LGBTQ Publications," Illinois Public Media, National Public Radio, November 2, 2018, https://will.illinois.edu/news/story/non-profit-sues-idoc-over-censorship-of-lgbtq-publications.

12. James Tager, "Literature Locked Up: How Prison Book Restriction Policies Constitute the Nation's Largest Book Ban," *PEN America Report*, September 2019, https://pen.org/wp-content/uploads/2019/09/PEN-America-Literature-Locked-Up-Report-9.23.19.pdf.

13. Ian T. Nolan, Christopher J. Kuhner, and Geolani W. Dry, "Demographic and Temporal Trends in Transgender Identities and Gender Confirming Surgery," *Translational Andrology and Urology* 8, no. 3 (2019): 184–90.

14. Dean Spade, *Normal Life: Administrative Violence, Critical Trans Politics, and the Limits of Law* (Durham, N.C.: Duke University Press, 2015); Eric A. Stanley and Nat Smith, eds., *Captive Genders: Trans Embodiment and the Prison Industrial Complex* (Oakland, Ca.: AK Press, 2015); Eric A. Stanley, Dean Spade, and Queer (In)Justice, "Queering Prison Abolition, Now?" *American Quarterly* 61, no. 1 (March 2021): 115–27; Ryan Conrad, ed., *Against Equality: Queer Revolution, Not Mere Inclusion* (Oakland, Ca.: AK Press, 2014).

15. Angela Y. Davis, *Are Prisons Obsolete?* (New York: Seven Stories, 2003).

KNOWING STUDENTS INSIDE
Lauren Braun-Strumfels

Driving past Edna Mahan Correctional Facility for Women (EMCF) is an entirely ordinary exercise. So ordinary, in fact, that most of us pass right by, never knowing what happens when you turn left off of the two-lane Hunterdon County road and continue to the end of the shaded drive, where the prison's small guard house and dingy visitors' trailer sit. It is easy not to know what lies beyond the guarded entry, to never really know the 378 women who today occupy the drab halls of this prison, and that is the point.

From the fall of 2013 until 2019, I made that left turn, traveled that quiet road, and entered the gates of the EMCF as part of a vanguard of colleagues bringing an entire associate's degree in liberal arts (AA) to students incarcerated in the state of New Jersey. My colleagues and I were part of the liberal arts program at Raritan Valley Community College (RVCC) through what was once called NJ-STEP (New Jersey Scholarship for Transformative Education in Prisons, which continues at Rutgers University–Newark) and is now RISE (Returning and Incarcerated Student Education). Teaching inside was an invitation to let go of my preconceived notions and to recognize the humanity of the students sitting in front of me.

Initially I worried my students might have significant deficiencies in reading, writing, and study skills. As a community college professor for twelve years, I was used to balancing the needs of a spectrum of academic competencies in a single classroom. Not only was I proven wrong, but I found in my first course in "max," or maximum security, the most gifted writers I have ever encountered in an introductory history course. The women who had been inside the longest—something I only sensed based on the tattered

Road signs for Edna Mahan Correctional Facility

and faded appearance of the mandatory state ID they had to wear pinned to their prison scrubs—wrote the most insightful analytical essays I have had the pleasure to read from a student, ever. In the classroom they could feel human again, for three hours stepping outside the confines of a dehumanizing system.

Teaching U.S. history inside brought my limited views on incarcerated people to the surface and pushed me to dismantle them. In their place I have a much more nuanced view of the members of our society whom we lock up. They are us, and we are a part of them. When I first went inside, like most new instructors I've met, I had questions about my personal safety. What would happen if something went down? Soon I realized that my students were actually my protectors, my defenders. They valued our time together and the freedom of the classroom so much that nothing bad could ever come to pass. I started to appreciate the time we had alone and realized that having a corrections officer in the room during class—an idea I entertained in the earliest days—would pierce the delicate bubble of safety we built together in each class meeting. Once, on the first chilly fall day of the year, the radiators started leaking water onto the floor directly under the chalkboard. What started off as a nuisance quickly became a minor flood. My students sprang into action, using the very limited furniture in the classroom first to try to absorb and then to hold back the pooling water. They steadfastly refused to let me help clean it up. I noticed how much they cared about keeping me safe and preserving my ability to carry on with our lecture and group discussion. For my students, it was an embarrassment that seemed to show how little the state cared about them and their learning spaces. To fix the problem that stood in the way of our teaching and learning on that day was an act of defiance in the face of powerlessness. They would not be diminished, erased, or ignored.

I never researched my students' reasons for their incarceration. They were now enrolled in my class, and that was all I needed to know. My experiences in "real college" courses, as my students called them, offer a window into the dynamics of higher education in prisons, its meaning and purpose, the ways that we as people on the outside can better know and support those on the inside. Incarcerated people are, by and large, forgotten behind prison walls. When we do think about them, and I am speaking as a person who had never been inside or even known someone personally who had been incarcerated before I came to teach at Edna Mahan, we think in clichés and generalizations. Teaching U.S. history inside a prison forced me to reevaluate my views on prison and punishment. I saw that while I was not a hard-line defender of tough sentencing laws, I also harbored views that essentially supported the idea that a person who commits a criminalized act should pay with the loss of their freedom. Writing that phrase now seems so harsh. Because I taught three hours a week for fifteen weeks, for more than seven years, students who happened to be incarcerated rather than sitting in my class on campus humanized the people I previously saw as undifferentiated, apart, ghost-like, broken. Or whom I never thought about much at all.

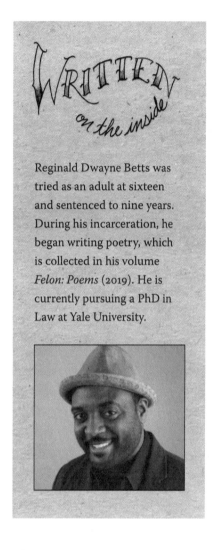

Reginald Dwayne Betts was tried as an adult at sixteen and sentenced to nine years. During his incarceration, he began writing poetry, which is collected in his volume *Felon: Poems* (2019). He is currently pursuing a PhD in Law at Yale University.

I WANT TO TELL YOU ALL THANK YOU! PRISON IS 24 HOURS-A-DAY. AND ON MOST UNITS IT'S VERY REAL. BUT LET ME TELL YOU WHAT A BOOK CAN DO. I JUST FINISHED READING A BOOK THAT TOOK ME TO A SMALL TOWN IN ITALY. A PLACE I HAVE NEVER BEEN AND DOES NOT LOOK LIKE I WILL GET TO GO. OH BUT I DID GO TO THAT TOWN——IF ONLY BY WORDS. YOUR VOLUNTEER-RUN ORGANIZATION PUT THIS IN MY HANDS. I CAN'T TELL YOU WHAT THESE BOOKS DO TO US. THEY OPEN OUR MINDS. AN IF ONLY THRU OUR MIND——WE GET TO LEAVE PRISON. OH YES GOOD ENDING OR BAD I'M STILL IN PRISON. BUT YOU GAVE ME A TOOL TO DREAM——TO LEARN TO OPEN MY EYES AND MY MIND. TO MANY TIMES PEOPLE LOOK AT US AS MESS UP. THAT IS A FACT.

TRUST ME I LIVE WITH MY PAST. BUT THANK YOU ALL FOR SEEING PAST THAT. TO ME AND MY FELLOW INMATES YOU ARE ALL VERY MUCH APPRECIATED. PLEASE KEEP UP THE GREAT WORK.

In the prison classroom, all of us are teachers and learners. The EMCF classroom is not like an ordinary college class; in an all-female classroom, we can explore women's history as our history; also, we create our "campus" among us each week, and this reminds me that learning can take place anywhere for anyone, under any circumstances—even inside a maximum-security prison. What I have seen incarcerated students do in the classroom has also invigorated my teaching and mentoring of on-campus students in dramatic ways. I craft my teaching to challenge students to take an interpretive stand, ask and answer deeper questions, and communicate with scholarly authority—skills and habits of mind that do not come easily to many students both inside and outside the prison. Bearing witness to the intellectual bravery and commitment to learning that our incarcerated students possess has inspired me to push my on-campus students to reach for deeper levels of intellectual and personal growth. The community college was founded on the principle of democracy in education—that every person is capable and deserves the dignity of a life of the mind. It was inside the prison classroom that I truly saw this mission come to life.

The history of our prison program reflects in microcosm the larger struggle over the purpose of prison education and what can happen when even well-intentioned people from the outside elevate their own needs over those of the incarcerated. The community college is in many ways ideally positioned to teach people in prison because of its institutional focus on underserved students. (Former RVCC president Casey Crabill acknowledged early on that women at EMCF were in "our catchment area" and were thus "our students," just like any other person living in Hunterdon County.) Yet the stigma that still haunts community colleges, labeling them as "less than" institutions or as places to get training but not the "real" education of a four-year college, presented challenges for our program that started as a collection of voluntarily taught courses by Princeton and other schools with little clear curricular grounding. The program actually needed RVCC's established curriculum to become a degree-granting program that reflected disciplinary standards of excellence. The faculty founders of what would become NJ-STEP, Deborah Corbett, professor of psychology emeritus at RVCC, and Johanna Foster, associate professor of sociology at Monmouth University, had a commitment to an intellectually rigorous liberal arts degree program—and not a credential-focused or a random set of courses—that helped infuse the program with a faculty commitment to excellence that created the kind of learning spaces that could be truly transformative for our students.

It took just over a year to go from the initial idea to bring college credit courses to women at EMCF to enrolling the first cohort of students. Establishing and then running a comprehensive degree program required the support of numerous college administrators. My experiences also suggest that the philosophy of a degree program should be carefully, and continuously, articulated. While some early players pushed for a credential-focused degree, the program at RVCC emphasized the power of the broad liberal arts degree and the importance of bringing active scholars in their fields into the prison classroom. Well-intentioned people on the outside may assume that incarcerated people would benefit more from career education, and these are overwhelmingly the types of programs offered in prisons today. We are not doing students a favor by teaching vague "courses" untethered to the framework of an academic discipline. My direct experiences with students on the inside show that to deny them the life of the mind can further reproduce the inequities of the system in which they are incarcerated. If prison education is to counteract the degrading and humiliating treatment incarcerated people face on a daily basis, let the students decide what they want. Give them the tools to discern what they value, and take them seriously as leaders, as knowledge creators to whom we should listen.

Lauren Braun-Strumfels.
Photo by Paul Pastrone

Institutional pushback came in surprising ways as the initial consortium formed to bring credit courses to EMCF changed in membership, and new or departing institutions fought for ownership. These struggles did not serve the needs of the students themselves but were motivated by leaders' ideas about what incarcerated students needed to learn or, at an even more basic level, by the desire to "own" the students for credit purposes. Even though incarcerated students pay no tuition, after being excluded from the ability to obtain federal PELL grants for twenty-six years, only in December 2020 did Congress restore this funding. Ethically, it was a major win: no longer would incarcerated people be denied access to public dollars to fund their college education particularly when multiple studies show that education lowers recidivism by 48 percent.

From my perspective as a faculty member going inside to teach a history course required for the AA degree, institutional tensions manifested around me and sometimes frustrated my work. Access to textbooks provide an excellent example. As the program passed between institutional partners working with my college, control over the physical books students depended upon also shifted. As faculty members we used our relationships with supportive textbook publishers such as W. W. Norton to obtain donations of recently retired editions. These books then had to be stored and moved at EMCF from "max" to "grounds" by corrections officers, and in some cases across the New Jersey prison system as our degree program expanded. This meant that books got lost, the wrong books got delivered, and chaos often ensued. Twice in one year I taught an entire course with half of the students using one version of the book that ended at chapter 6. The version that I and the other half of the class had included twelve chapters. Some of the textbook problems stemmed from who managed the book closet (and before we had a storage location, this was sometimes the trunk of someone's car). Who controls access to the physical books is incredibly important. While there is no template for doing this work, it was really important to have faculty, or former faculty, closely involved in the administration of the program. Because they knew the fundamentals of how college courses functioned, they could facilitate the back-end support that enabled us in the classroom to teach with fewer challenges. Initially our prison program got off the ground because of the social and cultural capital of passionate advocates who used their social ties to advance the program. Yet the day-to-day work of administering a successful liberal arts degree program is decidedly less sexy and in many ways more important work. Students on the inside deserve the same quality education as students on the outside. Community colleges, with a mission and infrastructure focused on underserved students, are perhaps best positioned to bring degree programs to people incarcerated nearby.

The physical conditions of my classrooms also left much to be desired. Before COVID, my students and I met to learn in the classroom we called the fishbowl, sandwiched at the nexus of four hallways, across from the gymnasium, in clear sight of the guard booth and just down the hall from the double set of automatic locked doors. Over eight years I cycled between the fishbowl, in EMCF's "max" or maximum-security section where almost 75 percent of the women are held, and the cinderblock, vaguely 1950s spaces in minimum security "grounds." Our very first class was a survey of U.S. history from its beginnings to 1877, but there would be others. Coming together in these drab physical spaces gave us the freedom to be something else, to see in ourselves and each other a struggle to be free. The study of the American past became a window onto the dynamics of oppression that my students knew too intimately, in the structure of the prison system and the intersections of their lives before incarceration.

Basic aspects of teaching are more complicated in the prison classroom. I had no access to a photocopier and had to bring everything I wanted students to read beyond their textbooks into the facility with me in a clear plastic tote bag. Our classrooms consisted of tables, plastic outdoor chairs, a blackboard, and, when I remembered to bring it, chalk and an eraser. Absolutely no cell phones, computers, or internet-connected devices were allowed. Click pens were also banned. Sometimes I was told I couldn't bring my car keys and had to leave them with my driver's license at the visitors' trailer. Eventually I was able to obtain a Department of Corrections (DOC)-issued ID, which facilitated my entry to teach, but before that I had to hope that each day I came to teach my name was on a visitors' list provided by the director of education. A handful of times my name did not appear, no one answered the phone to confirm, and I was denied entry, my students and I losing the opportunity to meet in class that day. If I arrived too close to the start of class, I could be denied entry. If an officer or prison official was frustrated with something someone else did in the program, I could be denied entry. I learned to never take for granted the vagaries of the entry process that granted me the only access I had to my students.

For any prison program that relies on instructors from the outside, cooperation with DOC is absolutely essential. Yet, DOC operates by its own philosophy and protocols. Each facility had its own director of education. A delicate balance had to be struck. We depended on the trust of DOC—from upper levels down to the individual officers staffing the doors—to let us in to teach. We also had to tamp down our natural desire to be respected and in charge, as academics, in spaces outside of our classrooms. As instructors we had to act deferentially to DOC personnel in the halls. At times I was forced to question my own instincts as a college professor. Once I asked a student to retrieve a documentary film and screen it for our class. On the outside, selecting a student to facilitate such an important task would be seen as high praise and recognition of their leadership. Inside, this request led the student to face the threat of disciplinary action, the loss of some privileges, and a special role that she enjoyed. Dumbfounded, I wanted to make it right; but she asked me not to intervene in the internal politics. As an outsider I would only cause more harm to her by speaking up. This incident showed me not to expect the world inside the prison to follow the same rules as the world on the outside.

People demonstrating support for the women incarcerated at EMCF

In the summer of 2021, Governor Phil Murphy ordered EMCF closed following a series of damning reports of abuse of prisoners going back decades at the hands of corrections officers. Over a two-year period from 2016 and 2018 six officers and one staff member were charged with sexual assault or related crimes, and evidence has emerged of a harrowing night of violence carried out by officers in January 2021. By the time this book comes out in print we may know more about the conditions women incarcerated at EMCF had to endure. I had only a glimpse into the lives of my students on the inside, but that window, however brief and limited, changed the way I see everything else.

BIG HOUSE BOOKS V. HALL
Beth Orlansky and Robert McDuff

In 2017, South Mississippi Correctional Institution (SMCI) stopped allowing incarcerated people free books unless they were religious books. SMCI continued to allow paid books of any type to be sent directly to imprisoned people. The Mississippi-based prison book program Big House Books was directed to mail all books to the prison library, where, it was said, the books would be available to all imprisoned people. Through this policy change SMCI effectively banned all free, secular books from any source.

Big House Books mailed Charles Owens, who was incarcerated at SMCI, a book that was returned by the prison undelivered. Mr. Owens filed a complaint about the undelivered book and was informed by a prison official, in writing, that "you can no longer get the Big House Books [or] any books that are free unless it is religious materials." Mr. Owens was told that free books are allowed only if they are religious on other occasions as well. Free books are a lifeline for many incarcerated people, and although he, and other people incarcerated at SMCI, were able to receive paid books in their cells, Mr. Owens was unwilling to be denied access to free books. This is when Mr. Owens and Big House Books approached the Mississippi Center for Justice (MCJ) about representing them in a lawsuit against SMCI to regain the right to receive books.

The MCJ opened its doors in 2003 with a simple mission: dismantling the policies that keep Mississippi at the bottom of nearly every indicator of human well-being and that deny African American and lower-income Mississippians the opportunity to advance themselves. As a home-grown public interest law firm, the center advances racial and economic justice through an approach that combines legal services with policy advocacy,

Reading books is good for everyone, including people in prisons, and under the Constitution, prisons cannot prevent them from receiving books. The Mississippi Department of Correction's general policy of allowing people in prisons to request and receive free books from Big House Books is commendable. Apparently, there has been a misunderstanding at a couple of the prisons and we look forward to that being ironed out soon.

Rob McDuff, attorney for Big House Books in press release

community education, and media outreach. The MCJ partners with national, regional, and community organizations to develop and implement campaigns designed to create better futures for low-income Mississippians and communities of color in the areas of educational opportunity, financial security, health care, affordable housing, and other vital issues—such as rights for incarcerated people.

Despite the fact that Big House Books and other recognized distributors had sent free materials to SMCI imprisoned people for years, prison officials had begun to apply the Mississippi Department of Correction's (MDOC) policy 31-01-01 (line 32) to prohibit the distribution of free books: "Publications—Pre-paid soft cover books, subscriptions and newspapers sent from the publisher, distributor or vendor." The mail department at SMCI used this language to prohibit free books from being sent to imprisoned people in 2017. Clearly, the intention is to preclude imprisoned people from receiving publications COD; there is no reason for SMCI or MDOC to care if the price for the publications is $0.00.

MDOC policy limits the number of books allowed in an individual cell to five at any one time, and the initial response to the Mississippi Center for Justice's letter to MDOC about the policy indicated difficulty in enforcing the five-book limit when inmates received books directly from Big House Books and other distributors. Traditionally inmates had donated excess books to the library or shared them with other inmates, keeping the number of books in individual cells down to five or fewer.

On April 26, 2018, the Mississippi Center for Justice and pro bono partner DLA Piper filed suit on behalf of Big House Books and two people

JUST WANT TO SAY THANK YOU VERY MUCH FOR GETTING BACK WITH ME WITH MY REQUESTS. I THINK WHAT YOU GUYS DO IS A TRUE BLESSING BEING ABLE TO GET BOOKS IS GREAT FOR ME BECAUSE RIGHT NOW I AM GETTING MY GED, SO TO GET EDUCATIONAL BOOKS IS GREAT AND IT IS GREAT TO ASK FOR A GOOD FICTION BOOK TO GET MY MIND OUT OF THIS PLACE. BUT I AM ONE WHO LIKES TO READ AND TRY TO LEARN WHY I AM IN HERE AND NOT JUST PLAY GAMES ALL THE TIME. BUT MY FUNDS DOESN'T ALLOW ME TO GET BOOKS THAT I WOULD LIKE SO HAVING YOU GUYS IS A BLESSING.

incarcerated at smci, challenging this bizarre practice of limiting reading materials to paid books and free religious books.[1] The complaint sought relief under 42 U.S.C. § 1983, challenging this new policy as discriminatory on the basis of religious content in violation of the First and Fourteenth Amendments to the United States Constitution. The suit sought declaratory relief and an injunction requiring MDOC and its commissioner, as well as smci and its warden, to remove this unconstitutional restriction on books for imprisoned people.

Almost immediately after the suit was filed, lawyers from the Mississippi attorney general's office reached out to the Mississippi Center for Justice to discuss a change in policy. The state's lawyers agreed to recommend that the commissioner of corrections send a directive to the effect that Big House Books is a recognized distributor and that MDOC-imprisoned people would be allowed to receive its books. We worked with the attorney general's office to propose specific changes to MDOC policy to make this clear. As a result, the commissioner changed the policy with the following memo:

TO: MDOC Institutions
from: Commissioner Pelicia E. Hall, Esq.

RE: *Big House Books*
Please refer to SOP 31-01-01, page 13 of 16, lines 601–608, which states "Publications will come directly from a recognized publisher, distributor, or authorized retailer. Secondary markets such as eBay and auctions sites are not authorized retailers or distributors. Used books are authorized provided they are shipped directly from a recognized publisher, distributor or retailer. Further, donated and free books are authorized provided they are distributed from a

Rubin "Hurricane" Carter was imprisoned twice for crimes he did not commit. During his second imprisonment, he wrote *The 16th Round: From Number 1 Contender to Number 45472* (1974). The book documents the racism Carter experienced growing up and then in the justice system. His case received national and international attention, with Bob Dylan writing a song about Carter's innocence called "Hurricane." Despite the media attention and public support for his innocence, it took twenty years for the wrongful conviction to be admitted following a petition of habeas corpus. The 1999 film *The Hurricane*, starring Denzel Washington, tells Carter's story.

recognized publisher, distributor or retailer." Also, the phrase in SOP 31-01-01, stating "incoming publications will be pre-paid," shall be deleted from page 13, line 607, leaving the remaining language intact. Finally, a sentence will be added on page 13 after line 609, which wills [*sic*] state, "Donated books and free books are authorized provided they are shipped directly from a recognized publisher, distributor or retailer." Big House Books Distributor is permitted to send both new and used books to inmates consistent with MDOC Policies/Procedures Rules/Regulations and the MDOC Allowable Items list for all inmates.

Other charitable organizations may petition the MDOC through the Deputy Commissioner of Institutions or designee(s) to be reorganized [*sic*] as a used and new book distributor under this SOP 31-01-10.

Violation of MDOC rules by any organization may result in suspension or termination of an organization's ability to distribute books to inmates within the MDOC. Furthermore, violations of MDOC rules and/or policies/procedures by MDOC employees may result in suspension or termination.

On August 7, 2018, almost exactly a year after the policy went into effect, plaintiffs Charles Owens and Jess Green reported successful delivery of books from Big House Books. "Reading books obviously helps people in prisons, and it also helps prison officials who are trying to maintain a positive environment," said Jackson attorney Rob McDuff, who brought the case with the Mississippi Center for Justice as part of MCJ's George Riley Impact Litigation Project. "Big House Books performs an important service by sending free books to those who can't afford to pay for them. We are pleased that MDOC fixed the problem that caused us to bring this lawsuit in the first place." After the Big House Books case was resolved, the Mississippi Center for Justice continued to get a few calls about situations where jails were restricting reading materials. The MCJ filed a second suit against the Forrest County Jail, which only allowed delivery of Bibles to imprisoned people. That suit was also resolved favorably for broad distribution of reading materials.

While MCJ had the legal experience and ability to quickly reverse a restrictive policy of MDOC, MCJ would not have known about the problem without the courage of affected people who recognized a wrong and sought a solution. Big House Books provides a valuable service to incarcerated persons through distribution of reading materials, and individuals such as Charles Owens and Jess Green rely on this organization to improve their living situation. Because Mr. Owens, Mr. Green, and Big House Books failed to accept a new policy and sought assistance, MCJ was able to intervene on their behalf.

Charles Owens's mother expressed the importance of this case in an email written to the Mississippi Center for Justice after MDOC changed the policy, and free books were flowing once again:

> I just want to say Thank you for helping my son, Charles Owens and his cellmate, Jess Green, challenging this ridiculous Book Ban on Free Books. Now that I've retired and on a fixed income, I cannot buy reading material like I could buy for my son before. Yet, when a human is locked in a cell for 22 to 24 hours per day, everyday, Books are important to them. Reading becomes a necessity rather than a leisure activity.
>
> This Case has more importance than I think many realize.
>
> Thank you for fighting this fight.

NOTE

1. Big House Books, Charles Owens and Jess Green v. Pelicia Hall, Commissioner of the Mississippi Department of Corrections; Mississippi Department of Corrections; Jacquelyn Banks, Superintendent of the South Mississippi Correctional Institution; and South Mississippi Correctional Institution (S.D. ms 3:18-cv-259-dpj 2018).

AN ONGOING CASE OF PRISON LIBRARY CENSORSHIP
Rebecca Ginsburg

From November 2018 to February 2019, the Education Justice Project (EJP), the Illinois-based college-in-prison program that I direct, was subject to a series of increasingly aggressive acts of censorship. We responded by mounting a campaign that drew the attention of elected officials and the media. For a while, we believed we had won. Four years later, though, I am not so sure.

As the situation is ongoing and sensitive, I stick close to the facts in this account, without much editorializing or analysis. That said, the facts are so extraordinary that little commentary is needed.

Background

I've been part of EJP from its beginning—I'm one of its founders. EJP began offering programs at Danville Correctional Center, a men's medium-security state prison, in 2008. By 2018, we had received multiple awards for our prison education programming, which includes for-credit courses, tutoring, English as a Second Language, a computer lab, guest lectures, workshop series, an anti-violence program, a mindfulness group, and a student-run newsletter. Incarcerated EJP students earn University of Illinois credit, and several have earned bachelor's degrees upon release. We also produce the state's most comprehensive reentry guide, which the Illinois Department of Corrections (IDOC) accommodatingly distributes to all prisons in the state.

EJP's relationship with IDOC, with respect to our college-in-prison program, has been more difficult. Creating critical, democratic learning environments

A class at Danville Correctional Center

that encourage students to question authority and honor their own knowledge runs counter to the principles upon which penal incarceration in general rests and to those that IDOC employs in running its facilities. Confinement and control are core values. Sometimes the friction between EJP and IDOC is productive, in that it requires us to reflect on and be intentional about our role and mission. At other times, the friction can be destructive of our efforts to provide dignified learning environments at the prison.

EJP operates according to the regular University of Illinois schedule. Just as on campus, course instructors select their books and readings, prepare their syllabus, and write up their course assignments in advance of a given semester's courses. Unlike the traditional campus, though, we must submit those materials to the prison about two months before the start of each semester for "clearance." This refers to the process by which prison officials provide permission for any given—texts, materials, and even individuals—to enter the facility.

Danville frequently changes the process for requesting clearance. In fact, by November 2018 we had been subject to six different processes within the previous four years, all of which we complied with. Being able to bring educational materials into the prison is a basic necessity for us. Our students take upper-division university courses, and their academic success depends on access to books and other resources. We've long been aware that other states have less onerous clearance requirements. For example, instructors in Georgia and Indiana can exercise discretion in bringing in materials; no advance approval is required. In Oregon, advance approval is required, and the clearance process takes up to two weeks. In Mississippi, the warden-provided approval takes up to one week.

The process that existed in November 2018 was the following: EJP staff were required to provide a memo to F.A., the assistant warden of programs, listing the materials we wished to submit for approval. The memo had to be submitted at least seven days in advance. Upon receiving approval to proceed, we would drop off the actual physical materials (e.g., books) so that they could be reviewed. The assistant warden asked for two weeks to approve materials, but in practice she often took longer. That was why, following the protocol that was applicable at the time, in November 2018 we submitted a memo requesting permission to bring to the prison materials that we wished to distribute to students on January 10, 2019.

Course Books Denied

Our November 2018 memo included a list of books intended for spring 2019 courses. Ms. A. signed it, but before doing so indicated that she would not consider five of the books on the list for clearance review. That is, she had determined based on their titles and authors that she would not allow EJP students access to those books. They included *The Color or Law: A Forgotten History of How Our Government Segregated America*, by Richard Rothstein; and *Why Government Is the Problem*, by Milton Friedman.

Please see the end of this chapter for a full list of all denied materials.

Former Black Panther and UC Santa Cruz Distinguished Professor Emerita Angela Davis edited *If They Come in the Morning: Voices of Resistance* in 1971 while incarcerated. Davis included the library in her description of the abominable conditions. "To talk a little about the library, they have a collection of adventure stories and romances which they have designated the library. It is important to realize that although the prison population is 95 per cent Black and Puerto Rican, I found only five or six books about Black people and literature in Spanish is extremely scarce."

We did not contest Ms. A.'s decision, nor did we elect to supply a statement of "how the concern of safety and security of prison staff and volunteers would be protected in bringing the sensitive issues in these books to the forefront of offenders's (*sic*) minds would be addressed," as we were invited to (email from Lance Pittman, November 11, 2018, quoting email from the prison chaplain). It was election season, and wardens in Illinois are appointed by the governor. We had seen questionable behavior before on the part of wardens during the anxious period when they were waiting to learn whether they would keep their jobs.

We also took comfort in knowing that denied books are sometimes later approved. We knew this not because we made a point of testing the system, but because there were many "natural experiments" that affirmed this. For example, we would see that a book that had been denied for our use being taught in another program at the prison, or we would realize that a book that had been denied approval for course use was already in our library at the prison, indicating that it had been earlier approved. We knew that the approval process was unpredictable and fluid. We decided to submit the rest of the books for clearance.

On November 26, we learned that most of the materials for which we had requested clearance had been approved. However, the assistant warden had denied nine titles, including

> *Narrative of the Life of Frederick Douglass, an American Slave,*
>   by Frederick Douglass
> *The Souls of Black Folks*, by W. E. B. DuBois
> *Public Housing Myths: Perception, Realty, and Social Policy,*
>   by Nicholas Dagen
> *Little Book of Victim Offender Conferencing,* by Lorraine Amstutz.

Again, we did not respond nor, this time, were we invited to. The impacted instructors, teaching classes on American literature and public policy, created work-arounds for their courses.

All Course Materials Seized

At the beginning of each semester EJP holds a convocation. The students organize these events, select the speakers, and use the occasion to welcome one another and us to another fruitful year of learning and growth. Instructors distribute course books and syllabi.

EJP staff prepared the usual tubs of books, readers, and syllabi to bring into the prison for the convocation scheduled for January 10, 2019. They contained the materials that the assistant warden had cleared back in November and, of course, none of the books that she had denied. We had submitted the memo to bring in these materials on December 19, and all was in order.

When staff entered the facility with the tubs, though, they were told that they could not bring the materials back to the hall where the convocation was being held. The materials were being seized. The convocation went on as scheduled, but no course materials were distributed.

The next day, four days before the first day of class, the prison suspended EJP programming. The head warden, V.C., told me they were conducting an investigation. As it's standard practice for IDOC not to identify the subject of a given investigation, that was all the information he provided. Internal Affairs (IA) staff interviewed some of our staff about many matters, including our new Diversity and Inclusion Initiative. On January 24 Mr. C. told me by phone that the investigation was over. On January 25, he called me to tell me that we could resume programs, but that I was locked out of the facility and our materials would not yet be returned. I was not provided an explanation for either.

The books, all previously approved, that the prison continued to hold included all course readers and *Leaves of Grass*, by Walt Whitman; *Notes on the State of Virginia*, by Thomas Jefferson; and *Adventures of Huckleberry Finn*, by Mark Twain.

About three weeks later, on February 16, Ms. A., the assistant warden, stated in an email that she was directing our course instructors to sit down with IA staff "and go through each one of the readers to remove any unacceptable material." Incredibly, each of our instructors agreed to this, although we let them know that they could choose not to teach the course and that we would understood if they so elected. Instead, each met with IA staff and agreed to physically remove specified pages from their readers. The articles that were impacted included "Affective Economies," by Sara Ahmed; "Urban Crisis and Black Politics," by James Jennings; and "Los Angeles: America's 'White Spot,'" by Charlotte Brooks.

Soon after, IA returned the books and the vandalized readers, and we distributed them to students who had by this time been taking classes almost a month without access to readings.

Library Targeted

Meanwhile, an even more serious situation was developing. On January 28, EJP's director of academic programs, Lance Pittman, arrived at the prison to find yellow tape covering the doors to EJP's three rooms at the prison, including the two rooms that housed our community library. This was an important resource to EJP students and instructors, containing over four thousand volumes, including circulating fiction and nonfiction books and a reference section. EJP students serve as library workers, responsible for cataloging, shelving, and weeding books in addition to developing governing policies regarding the library and organizing library-based programming. EJP alumnus Johnny Page describes the community library as "a fortress of solitude" within the chaotic atmosphere of the prison.[1]

Mr. C. had recently allowed our program to resume, but the yellow tape prevented use of EJP's community library or computer lab, the other impacted room. Lance Pittman observed IA staff going through the library shelves and carrying cardboard boxes of books away from our library. "When I got into the rooms later, it was clear that certain sections were more heavily targeted. I saw them take a big red book called *Critical Race Theory* for example, and as many as half the books from that section of the bookshelf had been taken"[2]

The library pre-raid

Working within the System

We had not assertively contested the assistant warden's refusal to consider specific titles for clearance, her denial of so many of the titles that we did submit (more than had ever previously been denied at one time), or the seizure of our cleared course materials. Instead, we sought clarification about these actions, in polite terms.

I wrote emails to both wardens requesting timelines for resuming programing and the return of our previously cleared materials. I sought to help them understand the core value of books to an educational program. For example, I told the assistant warden, F.A.:

> I wasn't sure if you realized the implications of removing all these materials from the prison. In order to provide U of I course credit to Danville students, we must offer classes at the same level and of the same quality as comparable courses on campus. This is challenging sometimes, as the EJP students don't have internet access. But at least we can offer rigorous readings. (email, February 8, 2019).

I asked how she would like to proceed.

I wrote to the head warden, V.C., a couple of days later:

> This semester we operated per procedures of the past 4 years: course materials were approved in advance by Danville staff. They were then conveyed by EJP members, per memo, to the facility on the day of convocation, to be distributed to EJP students. Danville staff have had possession of our for-credit materials since January 10. I appreciate your moving this situation forward.[3]

There were multiple emails to both of them and communications to other individuals whom I hoped could provide clarity or advocate for our program. Unfortunately, they did not appear to move the situation toward resolution. Neither, by the beginning of March 2019, had we received an explanation for the removal of the books from EJP's library at Danville Correctional Center, nor had we received the books back. The prison would not even provide a list of the titles it was holding. I was still locked out of the prison without explanation.

While all that was bad, there was worse. My supervisor on campus was unresponsive. That implied that university administration did not intend to become involved. EJP's "situation committee" agreed that we needed to change gears.

Taking a Public Stand

We decided to take two steps. First, we agreed to consult Illinois's other college-in-prison programs. The Illinois Coalition for Higher Education in Prison had a legislative subcommittee concerned with state policy. The dangerous precedent this situation posed for our state's prison education programs was obvious. We decided to jointly form a campaign. The "Freedom to Learn Campaign" would not only seek clearer guidelines and transparent policies around prison censorship and the clearance of instructional materials but would also take on the other shared concerns of Illinois's college-in-prison programs. These included protections for incarcerated students, access to office space at prisons, and smoother pathways to university enrollment upon release. Freedom to Learn reached out to likely allies such as library associations, unions, civil liberties organizations, campus organizations, and books to prisoners programs. We created a website and began consulting with currently incarcerated students regarding campaign priorities.

Second, we contacted the media. This was not a step we took lightly, as no agency welcomes bad publicity. We were concerned that an embarrassed IDOC might retaliate against our program or, more devastatingly, against EJP students. That's why the support of our state representative, Carol Ammons, and our state senator, Scott Bennett, were so essential. Both expressed

Some of the books seized

concern over the removal of books from our library. When I showed Carol Ammons the list of the books that prison staff had removed from the shelves, she quickly noted what was obvious about the censorship of our library: it targeted books that concerned race. When the prison finally turned over the boxes of books that it had removed from our library, we could see that of the over two hundred titles that prison staff had boxed up, most addressed the Black American experience, including

The Negro People in American History, by W. Z. Foster
Race Matters, by Cornel West
Strange Fruit: The Biography of a Song, by David Margolick
Roll Jordon Roll: The World the Slaves Made, by Eugene D. Genovese
*Black Feminist Thought: Knowledge, Consciousness, and the Politics of
     Empowerment*, by Patricia Hill Collins

Other titles included

Visiting Day, by Jacqueline Woodson (a children's book)
Discipline and Punish: The Birth of the Prison, by Michel Foucault
The Rise and Fall of Gay Culture, by Daniel Harris
Life and Death in the Third Reich, by Peter Fritzsche

We reached out to impacted authors we knew to make them aware. Lee Gaines, the Illinois Public Media reporter who first broke the story, went even further and interviewed some of them for one of the three pieces that she wrote about the incident.[4] There was a front-page story in our local paper and in the *Chicago Tribune*, and other outlets picked up on it as well, so many that I lost track of our media mentions.

The Tide Turns

Even before the news stories were published, reporters' Freedom of Information and interview requests alerted the Department of Corrections that they were going to be held to account. The incoming Democratic governor took office, and the political environment in Illinois started to shift. On May 9, 2019, Mr. C. called and asked me to provide a list of the books that his staff had removed from the EJP library so that they could review them and determine whether it would be suitable to put any back in the library. Mr. C. also told me that my lockout had been lifted and encouraged me to return to the prison. I declined to provide the list—didn't they have their own copy?—and

I explained that I would return to the prison when the books were back on the shelves.

At this point, our goal was no longer simply returning the books to the library so EJP students could access them. It was launching a statewide campaign to draw attention to problem of censorship for incarcerated people and the other challenges faced by incarcerated scholars. I realized, as I assume Mr. C. did, that the news stories would have less "punch" if the books were back on the shelves. In addition, I doubted the integrity of the process by which the books would now be "reviewed," more than three months after their removal.

I also knew what was coming. On July 8, 2019, Carol Ammons hosted a subject matter hearing in Chicago on censorship in prisons. Both I and the incoming IDOC director testified, as did a former EJP student, Michael Tafolla, and EJP's community librarian, Holly Clingan. It was the first time the new director, Rob Jeffreys, had appeared before the legislature, whose members expressed confusion, surprise, and anger at the removal of books about slavery and civil rights, American classics, and children's books from EJP's library. He assured them that this would not happen again. The following day, he ordered all books returned to their shelves on the EJP community library.

Epilogue: Not Over

The Freedom to Learn Campaign continued to work closely with Carol Ammons, who represents the district containing the University of Illinois, and introduced a resolution calling for the creation of a task force on higher education in prison. It was charged with recommending legislation to the governor that will make Illinois a national leader in higher education in prison, including ensuring incarcerated students access to instructional materials and strengthening the appeals process when such materials are denied. (There had been no formal appeals process available to EJP.) The resolution passed in October 2021. We look forward in the next few years to working with legislators to create a stronger, more protective environment for the growing number of college-in-prison programs and their students.

And EJP's community library?

On October 7, 2020, while our program was suspended due to COVID, the assistant warden emailed me to ask whether an EJP staff member could come to the prison to oversee the consolidation of EJP's two library rooms into a single room. She told us the prison needed one of the rooms for another purpose. EJP students and I quickly boxed up the books and moved furniture. COVID was at its height, and I did not want to spend any more time in the prison than was necessary.

When our program resumed in August 2021, there was finally opportunity to arrange the books properly on the shelves. As to be expected, the only way to fit bookshelves that had formerly lined the walls of two rooms into a single room was to place one row of shelves directly in front of the other, with no space between them. After all, we needed to keep the middle of the room open for use by library patrons and other programs. In any case, security regulations do not allow us to place the tall wooden shelves anywhere other than around the perimeter of the room, so sight lines aren't compromised. This meant that about one-third of our library collection was inaccessible.

I don't know whether this is censorship. After all, there was no interference on the part of the prison as to which of our books were placed in the back shelves, where no one could reach them. Even if it is not technically censorship, though, squeezing our library had the effect of restricting incarcerated individuals' access to books and the ideas contained within them. As importantly, it was an assertation of power on the part of the prison administration. It is hard for me, at least, to avoid interpreting this as IDOC's response to our successful and public efforts to have the seized books returned to the EJP library. Technically, all of our books were back on the shelves. However, over a thousand of those books were invisible, about one-quarter of our four thousand volume collection. No one could see them, let alone use them.

Since October 2020, I've communicated my concerns to the assistant warden, the head warden, and other IDOC administrators. Our students need access to an academic library. In fact, course accreditation requires it. Administration's responses have varied from "I'll look into that" to "I'm afraid we can do nothing." The effort is ongoing, and the number of people involved is widening.

As of this writing, in March 2023, our library remains confined to a single room. By moving several bookshelves from that room to our nearby computer lab, we've managed to spread out our collection and provide students access to all our volumes at the prison (even though this has put a squeeze on space in the lab). However, literally thousands of books that have been purchased or donated to our program over the past few years remain in boxes at our offices in Champaign because there is nowhere to put them at the prison. Nonetheless, I am determined. We continue to be creative with space

I DON'T HAVE FAMILY THAT WILL SPEND THEIR TIME OR MONEY TO SEND ME BOOKS TO READ. THEY FALSELY BELIEVE— LIKE THE MAJORITY OF THE PUBLIC— THAT THE STATE WILL AND DOES TAKE CARE OF MY EVERY NEED. THIS JUST ISN'T TRUE.

and have found generous funders whose support will allow us to purchase furnishings so we can squeeze books into unlikely spaces.

I am reminded that censorship is promethean and an act of power. Sometimes people employ censorship to restrict access to particular ideas, such as those related to Black history and rights struggles. At other times, those in control restrict access to knowledge less for ideological reasons related to content than simply because they can.

NOTES

1. Illinois House of Representatives, Censorship of Reading Materials in the Prison System: Subject Matter Hearing (Testimony of Holly Clingan of the Education Justice Project), July 8, 2019.

2. Lance Pittman, email to author, January 28, 2019.

3. Rebecca Ginsburg, email to V.C. and six others, February 12, 2019.

4. Lee V. Gaines, "'It's Heartbreaking': Authors Criticize Removal of 200 Books from an Illinois Prison Library," NPR Illinois, June 6, 2019, https://www.nprillinois.org/politics/2019-06-06/its-heartbreaking-authors-criticize-the-removal-of-200-books-from-an-illinois-prison-library.

THE CASE FOR CONTRABAND EDUCATION AND RADICAL PEDAGOGY IN PRISON

James King

> The paradox of education is precisely this—that as one begins to become conscious one begins to examine the society in which he is being educated. The purpose of education, finally, is to create in a person the ability to look at the world for himself, to make his own decisions, to say to himself this is black or this is white, to decide for himself whether there is a God in heaven or not. To ask questions of the universe, and then learn to live with those questions, is the way he achieves his own identity. But no society is really anxious to have that kind of person around. What societies really, ideally, want is a citizenry which will simply obey the rules of society. If a society succeeds in this, that society is about to perish. The obligation of anyone who thinks of himself as responsible is to examine society and try to change it and to fight it—at no matter what risk. This is the only hope society has. This is the only way societies change. —JAMES BALDWIN, "A Talk to Teachers"

Whether it's Malcolm X, Eldridge Cleaver, or George Jackson, prisons have loomed large in the mythologies of some of America's human rights advocates and greatest thinkers. To call prisons incubators for radical thought runs the risk of romanticizing or sanitizing their role, and to say prison birthed these intellectuals would further that particular brand of American violence that sent them to prison in the first place. At the root of what is often called the Black radical tradition of self-education in prison is the basic desire of Black Americans to heal, by purging themselves of the internalized violence of white supremacy. The first learning objective is, always, what does it mean to be Black in America? Also on the syllabus: Who were we

Malcolm X

before we were enslaved, and why does America remain so committed to denying equal opportunities to the Black community?

Most frequently, education in prison happens in spite of the prison. The reasons for this are numerous. For starters, it is never lost on any person being held in captivity that the prison's first priority is always the incarcerated person's compliance with their captivity. Implicit in demanding this compliance is that the person being incarcerated deserves their captivity and thus all of the violence meted out by the prison that is necessary for it to function effectively. This desire for compliance will frequently lead to the suppression of certain texts that are deemed dangerous or potentially inciting because they undermine or confront the lie that incarceration is deserved. As the Equal Justice Initiative notes, *Narrative of the Life of Frederick Douglass* by Douglass; *The Souls of Black Folks* by W. E. B. DuBois; *Just Mercy* by Bryan Stevenson; *Dreams of My Father* by Barack Obama; *The Bluest Eye* by Toni Morrison; *She's Come Undone* by Wally Lamb; *Kindred* by Octavia Butler;

and *Mosby's Medical Dictionary* are among thousands of books banned by state and federal prisons in America."[1] What many of these banned books have in common is that they either help contextualize the Black experience in America or are merely authored by notable Black authors.

Still, like cell phones and other items considered contraband, books that the prisons prohibit often make it into the hands of incarcerated people anyway. Like spotting overlooked treasures in a distorted version of *Antiques Roadshow*, the most valued texts will have covers removed, notes upon notes in the margins, with whole pages and chapters highlighted and re-highlighted.

By force, people who are incarcerated learn a basic aspect of critical thinking; always question your sources. The prison has an easily seen conflict of interest, and therefore, the prison and anyone who partners with it fall under suspicion. This dynamic is often subtly reinforced as programs that send books into prisons comply with any explicit rules regarding banned texts or subjects

Kindred by Octavia E. Butler (Headline, 2018)

or follow the general trends of the book publishing industry, which regard white authors and white American perspectives on history or social life as the default, even though those rules and American trends often erase the very people and perspectives of the people being held captive within our prisons.

Fortunately, learning often occurs outside of what is officially being taught. For example, children learn constantly, yet our current educational systems do not often account for this fact. In my own childhood, I learned several lessons between the time I woke up and when I first walked into the classroom a few hours later. I studied my parents' interactions, tried to glean my place in our social hierarchy, learned the rules of my neighborhood, as well as the lessons taught by my peers on the school bus, all before my butt first

IN MY TIME IN SOLITARY, I HAVE LITERALLY WATCHED MEN GO CRAZY IN HERE. MOST OF THESE GUYS DO NOTHING TO STIMULATE THEIR MINDS. SO, I TRY TO MAKE SURE THAT I EXERCISE MY MIND AS MUCH AS I EXERCISE MY BODY, AND SINCE WE DON'T HAVE TVS BACK HERE, I READ. I READ AS MUCH AS I CAN.

hit that wooden desk seat. Often those lessons were huge, and hard to stop thinking about, even when the teacher wanted me to focus on the sounds *e* and *i* make when they follow each other in a word. That my grade school teachers often acted as if their classrooms were the epicenter of my education created conflicts within me. For example, how can I focus on diphthongs when, just this morning, I learned that violence is an acceptable way to resolve conflict or that the same people who care for you will sometimes be the first to hurt you?

All of that to say, people enter prison with a fully developed, hard-learned set of beliefs. In America, for a Black person, that may look something like this: *There are fewer opportunities for people who look like me. When speaking to white folks, I can't speak the way my parents speak, it will make them uncomfortable, underestimate me, consider me stupid. The fact that I am black scares people, even cops with guns. My life is not valuable, so I may have to risk it to survive, or to provide. My pain is a sign I am not strong enough. I need to get tougher. Prison is a rite of passage...*

For many, these teachings become deeply ingrained, and the lessons of prison are very effective at reinforcing them. The person who experiences shame, or low self-worth, will find those experiences affirmed by the ways they are treated in prison. Meanwhile, the potential educator who declines to acknowledge the incarcerated person's relationship with both the prison and the ways the educational system has failed them participates in a version of learning that is forced and dysfunctional at best.

Education occurs within community, often continually, and even in the most extreme cases, say an isolated monk in a cave learning from nature, the monk is still *learning from*. At the same time, the most skilled teacher cannot teach without the cooperation of their students. As has often been said, before I care about how much you know, I have to know how much you care. I have to trust you, and without that trust I, as the student, will have the agency to disbelieve, or refute, anything a teacher explains. You cannot really teach me if I do not want to learn from you.

Though prisons often discourage anything but the blandest, assimilationist education, I, and many others, however, who have been incarcerated, experienced a deep yearning to know if the lessons we'd

The author, James King

Lorenzo Kom'boa Ervin wrote "Anarchism and the Black Revolution" (1993) during his imprisonment. A civil rights activist and former Black Panther, Kom'boa Ervin first read anarchist theory in the late 1970s. His essay is considered foundational for anarchist thought and has been reprinted extensively. It has recently been expanded into a full-length book, published in 2021. He is the author of many other works on anarchism as well.

internalized about our identities, capabilities, and worth were actually true. I'm speaking of the tradition within prison, in which so-called Black radical intellectualism has formed as a site of resistance against the state violence that Black people experience, and that sometimes culminates in going to prison in the first place. As a result, we gravitated toward teachers and books that acknowledged, explained, and brought clarity to our experiences of being marginalized, then criminalized, in a nation of extreme wealth.

Prisons are often more explicit versions of the white supremacist capitalist patriarchal culture that America embodies. So, when a Black person in prison learns, for instance, that their ancestors had a history prior to being enslaved, and that America hasn't yet come to grips with their original sin, that education feels radical. It requires courage to be held in captivity for violating the penal code, and to state that the penal code is illegitimate, because it wasn't created with input from all of society. To announce that the laws that protect property and wealth also institutionalize inequity and marginalization.

To follow this thought to its logical conclusion, whenever a person takes a public stand against oppression, it is considered radical by the people who are benefiting from the oppression. One can easily argue that Malcolm X, for

Louisiana State Penitentiary in Angola, Louisiana, August 18, 2011.
Photo by Gerald Herbert, Associated Press.

instance, is far more of an advocate for freedom and the American ideals of liberty and justice for all than George Washington or Thomas Jefferson, who both participated in violently suppressing Indigenous people and enslaving Black people, but only Malcolm has ever been considered a militant radical *in this country.*

Ultimately, terms such as "Black radical" and the role prisons have played in the intellectual development of some of America's most courageous freedom fighters are further evidence of the cultural violence America continues to commit against marginalized people in this nation. Until we learn to divorce ourselves from the inclinations to minimize the courage, vision, and righteousness of the brilliance our prisons and legal system have failed to suppress, or the equally damning inclination to romanticize and mythicize the people who have made these contributions to this nation's assumed desire to live out its ideals and values, we will never account for what is actually happening. People within our prisons are choosing their own educators *as they should*; they are learning collectively *by avoiding the mistakes they have experienced within our educational systems*; and they are modeling a form of educational learning that is producing the type of thinkers we need more of to create a more inclusive future. *Perhaps it's time we ask them to teach us as well.* But first, let's free them.

NOTE

1. "Banning Books in Prisons," Equal Justice Initiative, January 7, 2020, https://eji.org/news/banning-books-in-prisons/.

ORIGIN STORIES

DRAWING BY WILLIAM ROSENCRANS

INTERVIEW:
LORENZO KOM'BOA ERVIN
AND THE MOVEMENT'S BEGINNINGS
Interview by Dave "Mac" Marquis

Maybe we can start with some general questions about books on the inside and then we'll move to specifics. Can you tell me a little about your observations regarding people's access to books on the inside during your incarceration?

When I was first locked up there really weren't books being allowed on the inside. There was a total ban on controversial or radical literature. That all changed when Martin Sostre brought his lawsuits against the New York State Prison System in federal court. In fact, that is where I first met Sostre in 1969 when he was in New York City at the federal house of detention. He was suing the officials over a number of issues, but the main issue was the right to receive Black and revolutionary literature, and of course other literature as well. In those days, when I went to prison everything was considered contraband by prison officials except for the Bible. Even a copy of the Constitution was considered contraband [and] could be seized—and was seized—by prison mail officials.

When I met Martin Sostre and talked to him myself, one of the things he pushed onto me, and he was a forceful individual, was that in order for his lawsuit to have the kind of national impact it should have, he needed prisoner paralegals willing to fight for prisoners as a class to receive unapproved literature, and especially Leftist political literature. He said he needed prisoners to bring their own lawsuits, to bring their own campaigns and protests so forth inside the prison system all over the country. When I left him, and then went down to Georgia for my criminal trial, and later was put in the

Lorenzo Kom'boa Ervin

penitentiary, I followed his script. I worked with some other prisoners to bring a series of lawsuits inside the federal prison system, and it was that way that we defeated the ban on revolutionary literature. We [prisoners throughout the U.S.] defeated them in court in various parts of the country. I remember working with a prisoner named George Blue. George was a jailhouse lawyer and radical activist; he later became an anarchist as well. He was in the Atlanta Federal Penitentiary with me, and we had an extensive campaign to get the lawsuits filed to force the prison officials to allow the literature in. Then I carried out one of the other things that Martin Sostre suggested and that was to start study groups as a way of reaching prisoners with these books and ideas, radicalizing them further. We started contacting all the radical publishing houses that we could, all those that we had the addresses for. I started writing them asking them to send literature to myself and other prisoners so that we could create a radical prison library that would be independent from the institution's library.

Do you remember any of the books? I know you said radical, but a couple of specific titles might help.

The first anarchist book I read was *The Unknown Revolution* by Voline. Other books that were popular at the time, *Black Rage*, *Soul on Ice*, books by James Baldwin, and other Black authors of that time. We're talking about the time of the Black Power movement, a revitalized Black poetry movement, and a series of writings that prisoners were involved in. George Jackson's book would come later . . . this was before the Attica Rebellion . . . right at the end of the 1960s. . . . There was a variety of literature that we were able to eventually get in starting in 1970—it was almost like a crush of literature. They couldn't stop it, because they didn't have any rules on how many books you could receive or the nature of any of that stuff. They were reeling from the lawsuit, especially from Martin Sostre's lawsuit, which was changing law all over the country in relation to prison literature.

We were able to get all this literature in, but what do you do with it? You want to let people read it; you want to have guided discussion groups. Cultural societies and all kinds of groups grew out of this plentiful supply of literature that we were getting in. The prison officials couldn't stop it.

This idea that there was this moment when there were no rules about the number of books you could receive because of these lawsuits is really interesting. It is almost like there was moment when you able to do this in a way that could not be done now. How did you organize the radical library? Did each person have some books in their cell, mostly in one person's cell, or did you just put the books in the main library? How did that work structurally?

We didn't put anything in the main library because we didn't trust the officials. They wouldn't receive it anyway. I was writing to radical publishing houses all over the country; eventually we started writing commercial publishers asking for "hurt" or copies of books that they couldn't sell. So the list of publishers was the main thing because our program

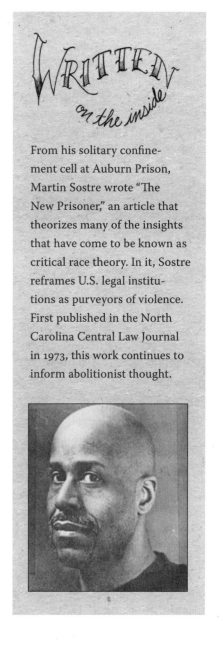

WRITTEN on the inside

From his solitary confinement cell at Auburn Prison, Martin Sostre wrote "The New Prisoner," an article that theorizes many of the insights that have come to be known as critical race theory. In it, Sostre reframes U.S. legal institutions as purveyors of violence. First published in the North Carolina Central Law Journal in 1973, this work continues to inform abolitionist thought.

was not a books through bars program coming from the outside inside. This was the prisoners organizing themselves to contact publishers and asking for books. We explained why we needed the books and what they meant to us.

It was also a way of teaching people to read—a considerable segment of the prison population couldn't read. One of the things I used to do was to teach prisoners how to read in the prison Education Program. I can remember one of the first prisoners I taught telling me that it felt like a huge rock was lifted off of him and the veil of ignorance was removed. He said that he would never be taken advantage of by anybody again because now he could read, write, and understand what people were saying to him. I remember that. Learning to read had an effect on a lot of prisoners, and it changed people's thinking, changed them from being gangsters and engaging in criminal activity to understanding how political and social movements work. The basics of education opened so many doors for a lot of these people. I know people who got out of prison and went to college. They were the first person in their family, maybe in their whole neighborhood that went to college. Access to books had a tremendous impact in terms of the confrontation of orthodoxy by coming into contact with new ideas. It is important to remember that all of this was happening during the time of the civil rights movement, the Black Power movement, the anti-war movement, the New Left, and all these groups were out there, and they were strong, comparatively speaking. A lot of people, including prisoners, were influenced by these movements. But many prisoners had no educational training to help them understand what the ideas these movements were pushing meant. They were emotionally connected to things happening in the street, but they didn't necessarily thoroughly understand it. So when we came along and the ideas that we spread that were in those books and also through talking with people literally blew their minds. That is what radical books and ideas can do.

One of the things that was an important part of Sostre's lawsuit was to prevent officials from punishing you because of your political or religious beliefs. You could be talking with another prisoner about a set of ideas, and the prison officials could grab you and put you in solitary confinement and say that you were violating prison rules or threatening prison security. We broke that up and made them change their prison regulations. Sostre's lawsuits successfully challenged this practice that prison officials could just grab you and put you in solitary without any due process. He won a basic set of rights for prisoners that even in disciplinary process, that the officials had to abide by. This prevented a lot of unnecessary locking up of people in solitary confinement for years and years under egregious conditions. This even opened the door for people to talk with one another about controversial political ideas just like you could in the street. So it made a huge difference. The book opened a lot of doors and a lot of minds. It even allowed us to set up prison cultural studies groups and book clubs.

When folks could not get books from the prison library, and they could not get them from your sources of writing publishers directly, were family members or other organizations sending books inside?

Yeah, but that happened later. We are talking about a different stage. We are talking about the stage of free books for prisoners and programs that we organized ourselves. We reached publishers themselves, and the publishers sent books voluntarily. Of course, family members would try to get books in, but prison officials would use various stratagems (to limit this). Even though prisoners had the right to receive the books, it was who they received them from. They could only receive from publishing houses, that was their first rule. Of course, we crumbled that up with a series of lawsuits. It was only later that radical groups and families . . . that people on the outside were able to send books in. That happened only later. There was years of organizing that had to go forth just to get literature in.

Of course, there was an unevenness to how this played out. Some prison systems, especially in the South, would try to hold out to the last. The prisoners in these states would have to file their own lawsuits, but by this time

I WANT TO THANK YOU AND YOUR CREW FOR YOUR KINDNESS TO ME, AND THE OTHER FELLAS AND LADIES WHO ASSIST YOU IN BRINGING A LIL BIT OF WISDOM AND ENLIGHTENMENT AND WANDERING DREAMS TO FOLKS INSIDE THESE LONELY BOXES . . .
YOU ARE SIMPLY A DELIGHT AND I WRAP Y'ALL IN A
BIG BEAR HUG FROM MY HEART.
PLEASE EXTEND MY HAND AND WORDS OF GRATITUDE TO ALL YOUR SUPPORTERS, ESPECIALLY THE FUNKY LADY WHO HELD THE DANCE—THAT'S LOVE FOR ALL GOD'S CREATION PERSONIFIED! I RECEIVED THE BOOKS AND POETRY GUIDE. WILL LET YOU KNOW HOW I FARE WHEN I'M DONE!
THANK YOU FOR YOUR SWEETNESS. MUCH LOVE, LOYALTY AND RESPECT, B

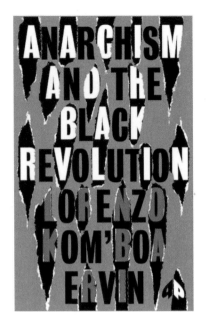

Anarchism and the Black Revolution: The Definitive Edition (Pluto Press, 2021)

we had created a prisoner's lawbook that showed prisoners how to put together a lawsuit to sue prison officials to allow books inside. We had various methods. We had to fight for groups and organizations from the outside so that they could get their material inside because prison officials would claim it was from a source that was troublesome to them or whatever the case may be. . . . We had to go to court on that. We had to fight incessantly, we organized, and we fought. Martin Sostre had given us so much information, and the legal guide that George Blue, myself, and others had put together was sent to prisoners throughout the country, certainly all over the federal prison system where I was locked up. It started making a difference, and once we started rolling, it opened the door for a lot of other things to happen, like cultural studies programs for African Americans and other peoples of color especially. It opened the door for religious groups, including the Nation of Islam, who had been fighting for years for the right to have meetings and use the Qur'an. Martin Sostre originally came out of the Nation of Islam, and one of his first lawsuits was centered on the right to give the Nation the right to worship according to their beliefs and to receive publications from the Nation of Islam. New religions, like the Church of the New Song, founded in San Quentin, spread all over the country, along with various traditional religious faiths, that had been forbidden by prison officials.

Martin Sostre was an individual who, with his legal work, really changed the prison system and won important rights for prisoners. I am not saying everybody got out, and they all lived free or whatever. He certainly created the conditions for prisoners to live as human beings and enlighten themselves in a way that hadn't happened before. Before, they used to beat down prisoners and kill them; they would dehumanize you, lock you up whenever they felt like it; they could seize whatever literature that you had that they felt was in violation of their code or their beliefs. Sostre showed us how to fight back, and myself and others picked up on it. I had met with him directly, and he taught me a great deal. . . . He taught me to go into study of law and become a jailhouse lawyer, counseled me on how to follow up his lawsuits, especially the ones related to radical and Black literature.

You had some support from the outside through the Anarchist Black Cross. Were they able to send materials?

I started receiving anarchist literature in 1969 and 1970. I was just getting it for myself and whatever study group I could set up. There was no organizing about my case until a little later; people didn't know anything about me. The first anarchist group to deal with my case . . . was around 1969 or 1970. I was the first American prisoner adopted by them. They were able to send me literature, but they also did a lot to publicize my case worldwide. This was essentially how I was able to create an autonomous defense committee, The Free Lorenzo Movement . . .

You wrote a famous piece of anarchist literature while inside, *Anarchism and the Black Revolution*. What were your influences during that time, and can you talk about the writing process?

The first book I read was the one by Volin on the Russian Revolution. I read other books on the Spanish Revolution. . . . I received a lot of literature; I can't remember all of it at this time. I got a lot of Black literature, the Black Panther Party and many radical protest movements were still in existence. Just as Sostre expected, the literature we got and read influenced myself and others. We started organizing inside the prison. Of course, when you start organizing inside the prison you know that you are going to run into fierce repression by the authorities.

Do you want to talk about Terre Haute a little bit?

Yeah, I can talk about Terre Haute. I was taken out of Atlanta Penitentiary in 1970 and was sent to Terre Haute. I was there for several years, but when I got there, I quickly noticed that it was really a racist place—it used to be called "the Ku Klan jail." It (the region) was the headquarters for the Ku Klux Klan during the Klan's second revival in the 1920s. It was a racist place with a racist reputation of violence and murder against Blacks. When I got to the prison, I found out that there was a long history of racial terrorism against the Black prisoners there by both the guards and the white prisoners. It was a vicious place, but it was also at a historical moment when Black Power and the civil rights movement had dominated American society for at least twenty years. So there was a new Black consciousness, especially among young Black people. We were not afraid of the Ku Klux. I came out of the South, became a civil rights activist, and I was not afraid of the Ku Klux Klan. We were not intimidated, we started organizing, and we were able to use the

Martin Sostre

Sostre lawsuits and other lawsuits we filed to force the government to allow Black people and other peoples of color to form cultural studies programs. Of course, at the same time on the outside that is what college students were fighting for. Black studies was a real big issue in 1969–1970. We were able to get allies in even the prison towns; this and the filing of lawsuits forced them to allow us to set up our own programs inside the prisons. In Terre Haute, it was called the Afro-American Cultural Studies Program and ultimately had hundreds of prisoner members.

That changed things drastically in terms of the prison struggle. Black studies had, at the center of its program, political education and cultural studies. The cultural studies were focused on studying books, culture, and history. We got a lot of books in the prison that would never have been allowed before; we ordered books like mad from book companies all over the country. Companies were sending us books on all manner of subjects, and we had a huge library of Black literature, radical political ideology, and various fictional and nonfictional subjects. I estimate we had several thousand books.

[Because of the lawsuits] the officials didn't feel like they could do anything about it . . . but they monitored us.

One of the curious things that happened after a while is that some white radicals and antiracist activists were starting to come into the prison system, and they were not going to be intimidated by the Klan. They were not in unity with the Klan and these other organizations that had been able to intimidate both white people into towing the line and to terrorize Black people. So [the Klan] was losing their base of support. When white people started reading the books [in the library we started] and started talking about what was happening in this prison, this worked to ideologically defeat the Klan. When the Klan tried to rise up in violence on one occasion, they were met with a lot of force from multiple sides. White radicals hit them—those that we had been sending literature to and having antiracist discussions [with], Mexican prisoners, other people of color, and Black prisoners, who at this time were the leaders of the prison movement, hit 'em. So, we defeated them ideologically, and eventually we defeated them physically. We drove them out of existence, and all these racist guards that had been going along with this stuff for years were driven out—they retired or what have you. All this came about because of books, literature, just the fact that people were able to read literature and have political discussions. People were able to connect what was happening in the streets to what was happening in prison. It changed that prison. I mean, I don't know about forever because I haven't been back, but it changed it for a long time. . . . The Klan did not run it anymore.

Just for clarity, when you say that you were able to establish these cultural studies programs and Black studies programs, was this done wholly on the inside? Were you given space to do this by the prison, or was this something that you just did on your own, and you were not interacting with the authorities at all?

Well, we forced them to grant it to us. They did not stand in when we were conducting our business or anything like that. We started talking about white racist cops, and they didn't want to be there. They weren't going to tell us we couldn't say it; they just weren't going to be there to hear it.

Were these sessions in the yard? Where were they?

We got a space in the education building where we had our own room. We would meet every week. It was really something. That was brought about because of our ability to get literature, to hear about things in streets, and to be able to have political discussions on the inside. I mean, we did political discussions in the yard and elsewhere in addition to our meetings. . . . The fact that we could read what these revolutionaries were saying, including George Jackson and others, even the Attica prisoners in 1971. By this time, George Jackson's book was the major book of the period for revolutionary politics. It was the kind of book that almost gave you a certain kind of guidance about what revolutionaries should be doing on the inside. I mean, we were trying to survive, don't get [me] wrong, but we were also trying to understand that we have a responsibility to transform ourselves and to educate ourselves so that we can go out in the community and do good by the community instead of just going out and dealing drugs or robbing or whatever. People went through that reeducation process, and some people were changed forever. Of course, some people just did it when they were in prison, and when they got out they might have gone back to doing what they were doing before, I don't know. But the thing is, they got access to the literature, and they got access to new ideas that altered some people's thinking completely. So, the cultural studies program would not have been possible, I don't think, if we had not won the lawsuits leading up to it to obtain books.

We had an auxiliary group on the outside of students from Indiana State University, who occasionally attended our meetings. We had some Black students come every week and meet with us, and we would have joint discussions. It had a real serious impact. We went from the reading of literature to a cultural and a political understanding and then to organizing. We started organizing on the inside for survival and self-defense . . . so that by the time the officials tried to stop us, there was a group on the outside protesting against them.

About how long did this last?

It lasted a long time; I was part of this group for about five years. . . . The books were the tool that changed everybody's thinking. Radical literature, the discussions. . . . I'll be quite honest, we did not intend for it to be some kind of interracial thing. We didn't intend for it to be that way, but it happened that way in terms of the outside supporters, and even a number of prisoners. All kinds of prisoners started reading from the Black library. The prison officials tried to stop it from happening, and I said OK, we'll go to court, and you can tell that to the judge, and they backed away. We started giving the literature out to anybody that asked for it. . . . It wasn't just Black literature; it was radical literature, and from a hell of a lot of different sources. . . . People started rethinking things; you go to prison, you're in solitary confinement, and you have nothing to do but think. You get a book, you dissect it and try to think about what the author is saying. It has more of an impact on you because you are in an isolated life and death situation . . .

One thing about Terre Haute that is really important to understand is that when the rebellion took place, and white people rose up, as well as Black people and Mexicans . . . almost the whole population against the Klan, that was the one thing that made me understand the power of the word, the power of literature, the power of revolutionary ideas. That was the one thing that made me understand it. I saw these things. No white people had ever risen up on behalf of Black people in the prison before. . . . It wasn't because they were all racists, but they were afraid to stand up against the racist guards and prisoners. They could be stabbed and killed; that happened there. . . . But when we got organized it meant the prison officials had no control over us anymore because they couldn't use the Klan to intimidate people anymore. . . . They could not run that prison as a racist hell hole anymore . . .

Is there anything else you want to talk about regarding the importance of books inside or books to prisoners programs now that these programs exist on the outside?

Well, there is a different dynamic to what I am talking about. This was part of the prison struggle, the prisoners themselves organized this movement, and we were the ones that called for free books for prisoners. What we did with it ultimately, in terms of the cultural studies programs, which were in prisons across the country . . . by having the literature and the ability to discuss politics . . . won more rights than even exist in prisons right now to be quite honest. . . . The book, the radical book had a hell of a lot to do with it. . . . This is the high point of the radical prison struggle in this country, the 1970s, and it was led by Black prisoners. Especially George Jackson in California and the Attica Brothers.

I still think, even to this very day, that if a radical movement is going to develop inside prisons once again, it is going to have to be a movement based around political theories, literature, and the book, in addition to a protest over oppressive conditions. Because that opens the door to other things and can help [it] become a full-fledged movement. Even today, if the prison officials try to stop you—it is difficult to stop. I've seen it with my own eyes, how difficult it is to stop. No army can stop an idea whose time has come. The authorities still haven't figured it out. It is just that it is a different kind of prisoner consciousness right now than it was back then. They don't see any radical tendencies on the outside, whereas we were surrounded by the civil rights movement and other movements in the 1960s and 1970s. . . . They don't see the possibilities like we saw back in the day; it makes a difference.

But, it is starting to happen right now. I have spoken to many prisoners who have distributed my own book for years and continue to distribute many prisoner zines of my writing and that of other activists. One of those is Anthony Rayson of the South Chicago ABC literature [Zine] Distro, who has literally distributed thousands of zines, books, and pamphlets that he and his small collective of volunteers has created by hand and then distributed to prisoners all over North America. It's amazing what he has done, and I am in awe of him and those who continue to do this work. But I want to create a book through bars program named after Martin Sostre specifically, to distribute literature to prisoners, since all of this started with him. Love and struggle to his revolutionary spirit, and may we learn from his example.

ASHEVILLE PRISON BOOKS PROGRAM: AN ORAL HISTORY
Dave "Mac" Marquis in Conversation with Sarah West and Annie Masaoka

The Asheville Prison Books Program was conceived in the late 1990s when Sarah West and Jen X were walking home late one night from a punk rock show, lamenting the lack of prisoner support organizations to volunteer with in Asheville, North Carolina. Sarah volunteered with the PBP in Boston (Jamaica Plain) for a little over a year before relocating to Asheville, giving her some very helpful experience to draw from in getting the program running. It is possible Jen volunteered with a PBP program on the West Coast as well. This conversation could have been random, or it could have been driven by the DIY politics of the show, which the two women desired to see more concretely put into action. At this time, Asheville was in the process of becoming a well-known way station for punks. It was still possible to live inexpensively, which gave people free time to create art, music, or engage in activism.

Once the idea was hatched, other people expressed interest in supporting it, and the search was on for a space. Our first location was just outside of downtown at a punk house that dedicated space to activism, The Pink Haus. It was a great location, centrally located, and most importantly it was free thanks to the generosity of The Pink Haus collective. A little while later we had to move the program to a moldy basement location in a neighboring town, Woodfin. Moving PBPs is a lot of work, mostly on the back end when it comes to getting the new space ready, building the shelves, and organizing the books, etc. . . . Thankfully, we were all still highly motivated. Woodfin proved to be a little too out of the way for a lot of people, and a basement full of moldy books does not make for the best working environment. When we got the chance to move the program back to Asheville and close to downtown, we jumped at the opportunity.

ASHEVILLE CITIZEN-TIMES

COMMUNITIES

232-2935 or JStevenson@CITIZEN-TIMES.com

ASHEVILLE

Group starts book program for inmates

Organization connects prisoners with outside world

By Barbara Blake
STAFF WRITER

There's a group in Asheville that believes prison inmates deserve the chance to improve their minds and their attitudes, and they're providing the books to help the inmates do it.

Calling themselves "Prison Books," the small group of young people began the book-donation service for inmates in the Southeast a few months ago, based on the 25-year-old "Books to Prisoners" project headquartered in Seattle, Wash.

Sarah West, an Asheville artist who moved here from Boston six months ago, helped launch Prison Books after working with a similar – albeit larger – group in Boston. When she moved south, she found it was the one thing outside of her work that she missed the most.

"It really touched me in a differ-

Jennifer Kates, 19, left, a member of the new Prison Books organization that sends books to prison inmates who request them, explains the group's mission to Kendra Sarvadi, 25, a new member of the volunteer organization.

JOHN COUTLAKIS/CITIZEN-TIMES

"It really touched me in a different way. We get letters back saying, like, 'It's amazing to know there are people on the outside that think about us, because we feel so forgotten-about and lost.'"

WANT TO HELP?

To donate books to the Prison Books organization, drop them off at the "Pink House" at 201 Broadway, or call 236-0949. To donate books to Craggy Correctional Center, call 645

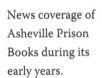

News coverage of Asheville Prison Books during its early years.

The new location was in the basement of an editor for the local radical newspaper, the *Asheville Global Report*. This was a great landing spot, though the lack of bathroom was a concern, but once again the price was right . . . free. The location meant that people passed through on their way to and from other events or locations in town. In some ways it was an alternative to bar culture—you could show up and drink beer although you worked, and nobody batted an eye. In fact, most people were happy so long as you shared. People were respectful enough to know that while you could have a drink, it was not a place to get wasted. There was an expectation that you were there to work. Not all volunteers were from our small subculture, though. In fact, some of our most consistent volunteers were senior citizens who tended to come during the official work hours. A few of us spent a lot of time in the shop, and it was during the nonpublic hours that the music tended to get a little louder and the conversation a little more ribald as we packaged orders.

Some folks from Austin with PBP experience moved to town as things were getting up and running, and they made a great addition. No one can remember where we got our first batch of letters from, but it is likely they came from a long-running PBP, such as Boston. We set up some book donation locations and with the help of some sympathetic employees we got a local secondhand bookstore, The Reader's Corner, to sponsor us. These first few years were notable because we did not wait until we had everything figured out or until we had the most desirous circumstances; we just did the best we could with what had. We knew we would make mistakes, and we did, but we felt driven to support folks on the inside.

Eventually, it was time for us to move again. A group of activists had been working to create a central location to house several community organizations in town. They landed a spot in the heart of downtown, in a space dubbed the Asheville Community Resource Center (ACRC). The ACRC housed a show space (The Magpie), a reading room, the *Asheville Global Report*, the Asheville Bicycle Recyclery, a trans and women's health collective, a community gardening organization, and Asheville Prison Books. These were the halcyon days of anarcho-organizing in Asheville, and the city had become a destination for activists in no small part thanks to the efforts of the groups housed in the ACRC. Being an activist destination had its perks for groups such as Prison Books—mostly it kept us full of volunteers.

So many volunteers have similar stories about getting involved: read and answer your first letter, and you are hooked. And make no mistake, the physical letter is important here. There is a connection through the handwriting (often great penmanship) and the art with which incarcerated people often adorn envelopes that makes these communiques more than the request itself. Many volunteers express an initial astonishment at the lack of access to books on the inside or at the conditions described in the letters. Other folks are moved by the many requests for dictionaries, which indicate a genuine need that many people don't realize exists. Dictionaries are the most requested book, and they are emblematic of a larger thirst for knowledge.

PBPs are also a great spot for book nerds to really dive into their nerd-dom. Sarah recalls with fondness going to the semiannual public library book sale. There you could get boxes and boxes of books dirt cheap. Here book nerds put their skills to use, knowing that the first edition of a book could be sold to a local bookstore for significantly more money than the purchase price, and therefore that book would help us purchase lot more dictionaries . Every volunteer's strength was an asset, and we all had our little labors of love. One volunteer eagerly took every request from someone on death row or doing life. They did their best to get these folks exactly what they wanted. Other folks only wanted to answer letters from women. One or two volunteers were only concerned with making sure we had enough radical literature, usually in the form of zines. Some folks found the search for books overwhelming, and they preferred to package the books. It all worked; we were all happy to work with one another to make the program as strong as it could be.

During this time, we served the entire Southeast, and (as best we can recall) we were the only program in the Southeast at that time.[1] Serving incarcerated people in nine to twelve states meant hundreds of prisons. We were aware that it was too much, but there was no one else. Not only was the demand high, but because PBPs hadn't started effectively sharing resources yet (the internet was in its infancy—yes, that old), we had to do a lot of background work just to be able to mail packages. We spent a lot of time creating comprehensive restrictions lists. This meant calling prisons for every returned package and talking to someone in the mailroom to determine why the package was returned and if there was a way to avoid that in the future. We also put together a prisoners' resource list. Although there were resource lists circulating, some versions were out-of-date, and incarcerated people would routinely let us know what listings were incorrect. This meant regularly tracking down free resources for people currently inside as well as people who would soon be released. Although there are support organizations that offer free legal work, letter writing, and transition services for

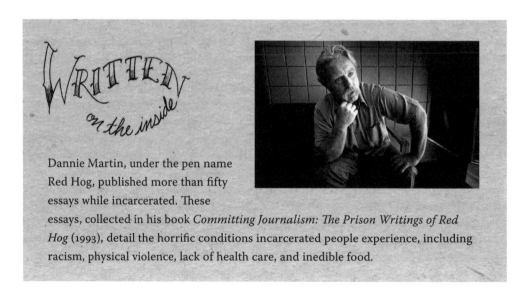

Dannie Martin, under the pen name Red Hog, published more than fifty essays while incarcerated. These essays, collected in his book *Committing Journalism: The Prison Writings of Red Hog* (1993), detail the horrific conditions incarcerated people experience, including racism, physical violence, lack of health care, and inedible food.

people leaving prison, most people do not know about them, and prisons often don't tell people about resources they're entitled to or can access. People are sometimes given up to $40, and the prison will call a cab to take them somewhere. For this reason, resource lists are the second most requested item after dictionaries. Not only did we have to spend time researching and compiling up-to-date listings of these resources, but we also had to spend money to print them. Fortunately, an employee at a copy shop run by a large corporate entity was in solidarity and gave APBP unlimited free copies. Of course, that meant we had to make copies at 2 a.m., but that was a small price to pay. You can always work for or against justice, whatever your paid employment. APBP survived and thrived because people like this copy shop employee recognized the need to support justice.

It was all a lot of work, and there were a lot of other things that we just did not have time for or were not informed about. For instance, we did not get nonprofit status. We lacked the confidence to navigate what we thought was an overwhelmingly bureaucratic process. It turns out that it was not as difficult as we believed it to be, and in retrospect we had internalized some of the societal forces that told us we were incapable.

By the time the ACRC was fully up and running, many of the original organizers had left town or were only minimally involved. Annie Masaoka and Mac spearheaded APBP's operation, though they did manage to wrangle Sarah back in from time to time. In many ways the ACRC space was a dream come true. It was big enough to for us to have a massive library, and the location meant plenty of volunteers. That said, we could never work fast enough. The more books we sent out, the more requests we received. We were perpetually months behind, and it could take a toll on us. Sometimes there was a feeling that we were failing people inside who had come to depend on us. Sometimes we had no money, and so we would just keep packaging books, there would be 10–20+ mail bins full of books stored under the shelves waiting for us to raise money for mailing—something we were never particularly good at.

Our fundraising ran the gamut. One of the first fundraisers was supposed to be a punk rock benefit show, but some volunteers made a convincing case to have a dance party with a DJ instead. We couldn't believe the turnout; we raised several hundred dollars and exposed the program to a wider variety of people. We did have many punk show benefits afterward, but we did our best to cast a wider net.

Sadly, the ACRC got evicted, and we had to pack up the program once again. By this time, we were all burnt out. We packed up and stored everything in a punkhouse basement. We couldn't find a new space, and there was no one that really wanted to take the project on. After a few months Patrick Kukucka came along and got the project back on its feet again with the help of other volunteers.

Asheville Prison Books is still up and running, making it one of the longest running collectives in Asheville. We know that our efforts helped spawn the Tranzmission Prison Project, which provides incarcerated members of the LGBTQ+ community with free books and letters. To the best of our knowledge, some of our former volunteers founded several other PBPs in North Carolina. Some of our most consistent problems revolved around funding and volunteers. We usually had either volunteers or money, but rarely both. Many of us would not have suffered burnout if we were properly funded or even had a semipermanent location. Some people just assumed that we were paid because we might spend thirty hours a week doing Prison Books, but truth be told, we often felt like Prison Books was our job, and the things we did for money were more of an inconvenience. It was a labor of love. Unfortunately, in our society that sort of effort is unsustainable as you realize you need health care or perhaps you no longer want ten roommates. . . .

PBP work is easier now. The NPRL (National Prisoner Resource List) is online, and anyone can download it. There are tons of programs, and most only fulfill letters from up to three states—although some are nationwide. (There is a full list of PBPs at the end of this book.) There are restriction lists online that are crowdsourced, and there is the listserv where your PBP can ask people for help and advice. Bruno, from the Bay Area PBP, will even send you boxes of curated, amazing books for stocking your shelves. Of course, even with these resources it's still work. But with these resources you realize you are part of a community of people, working for the same goal. Community is what sustains PBPs and the people who devote themselves to it.

Of course, the end goal is that all beings are free, but until then, many of us will be prison booking somewhere, in some way, with the vision of that freedom urging us on.

NOTE

1. There are now over ten programs based in the Southeast. Some of them, like Open Books Prison Book Project (Pensacola), can directly trace their origins back to Asheville. See Aaron Cometbus and Scott Satterwhite, *A Punkhouse in the Deep South: The Oral History of 309* (Gainesville: University of Florida Press, 2021), 61.

Asheville Global Rept
P.O. Box 1504
Asheville, NC 28802

Dear AGR;

I am saddened to learn that _AGR_ will cease print publishing.

As a man on Death Row, w/ no access to the internet. The _AGR_ was a wonderful resource for me as a writer and commentator, and indeed I've cited it specifically as a source;

I did not pay for my sub, but a friend of mine did (Data: ~~~~~~~~~~~~~~~~~~~~

You guys and gals produced an extraordinary product of Alternative journalism.

It is damned near criminal that your voice has been stilled by the postal rate hikes!

All Best —
Mumia Abu-Jamal
(#AM-8335)
175 Progress Dr.
Waynesburg, Pa
15370

APPALACHIAN PRISON BOOK PROJECT ORIGINS Ellen Skirvin

On Spruce Street in Morgantown, West Virginia, near the state university and next door to the public library is the Aull Center, a building over a century old that primarily houses local history and genealogy records. If you venture inside and upstairs, tucked away in a modest back room, you will find the place where the Appalachian Prison Book Project (APBP) does much of its work. Bookshelves and crates are stuffed with an array of paperbacks. The books are in good condition, but it is clear they have been read and loved. Handwritten labels organize sections such as "Sci-Fi," "Poetry," "Law," "LGBTQ+," "Westerns," "Dictionaries," and "Vampires." Near the window, someone wraps a book in brown paper and writes an address in sharpie on the front, another person sits on the ground cross-legged sorting through a section of books, while someone else takes a letter from a stack and begins to read the words: "Dear APBP."

The idea for this project began in 2004 when Katy Ryan, an English professor at West Virginia University (WVU), taught a prison studies graduate course. Katy had been visiting and corresponding with friends in prison for years and wanted more people on the outside to recognize the essential voices behind those walls. Her graduate students read fiction, essays, memoirs, and poetry across 150 years of writing and were inspired by the continuous mention of books as a source of power and freedom inside prisons. Katy told them about the lack of organizations that sent free books to people incarcerated in the Appalachian region. This realization led to further research and conversations about the many prisons and jails in Appalachia both far and near to WVU's campus. West Virginia, Virginia, Tennessee, and

Volunteers working at Appalachian Prison Book Project.
Photo by Raymond Thompson Jr.

Kentucky all have incarceration rates higher than the national average, and the United States already locks up more of its citizens than any other country.[1] The class wanted to do more than lament these facts. They wanted to take action but had virtually no experience in organizing volunteers around this work. Although none of them had volunteered at a prison book project before, they decided to start their own anyway.

They tapped into the surrounding community for help and involved Morgantown locals and university members through the collection of paperbacks and fundraising. Even after the prison studies class ended and some students graduated, the effort continued. More people contributed in whatever way they could—many of them working other full- or part-time jobs or taking classes in fields that had little to do with creating and running a project like this. They started calling themselves the Appalachian Prison Book Project and eventually secured a donated workspace at the Aull Center. After two years of preparation, they sent their first book to a person in prison.

Since then, the growing number of letters we receive reveals a vast need for books inside prisons and jails in Appalachia. People request dictionaries,

GED textbooks, how-to books, hiking guides, sci-fi novels, religious texts, and the list goes on. APBP began because of a love of reading and the power and freedom it offers. Every letter is a reminder of this:

> It truly gladdens my heart to know that people like myself are not forgotten, and that there are still organizations out there that think about us and care about our well-being.
> —Alexander

> I will be sharing this book with others as soon as I finish reading. I've had the book all of an hour now and there is already a waiting list.
> —Paul

> So far the books you have sent has been very helpful: the one helped me obtain my GED!
> —Steven

APBP learned a lot from a network of other prison books projects across the United States, exchanging information and resources about trends in book bans in prisons or other restrictions. We currently send books to people imprisoned in six states: West Virginia, Virginia, Tennessee, Kentucky, Ohio, and Maryland, where we feel we can make the greatest impact. Although APBP takes pride in its small and humble beginnings, we continue to grow and achieved 501(c)(3) nonprofit status in 2012.

I have been volunteering with Louisiana Books 2 Prisoners for years, and I still remember the time that we got a letter asking for a Tagalog-English dictionary. We were sure that we wouldn't have any such thing but dug through the language books and—oh look!—found exactly what that person wanted. It felt great to be able to provide a perfect match for someone's interests, especially with something that seemed so unlikely to be in our donation-based library.

ONE TIME at PRISON BOOKS.

We have no full-time staff and are powered by volunteers—many of whom are WVU students. In the beginning of each academic year, we host a "book wrapping" party for new freshmen, where they have a chance to meet seasoned volunteers and learn about our mission. APBP also trains new volunteers almost every week. After training, a volunteer can drop by the Aull Center at any time to read a letter, match a book to a request, or prepare a package to be mailed. There is no shortage of work. The letters keep coming. We receive about two hundred requests per week.

Students often mention that they enjoy the quiet off-campus respite at the Aull Center, where they can take a break from college life to fulfill a simple yet meaningful act. Sometimes they show up alone

Books selected and ready to be packaged. Photo by Raymond Thompson Jr.

and listen to music while volunteering. Others bring a group of friends or meet fellow volunteers who become friends. Undergraduate and graduate students also get involved with APBP through internships, work-study programs, teaching opportunities, or leadership roles in the student organization.

Kristin DeVault-Juelfs describes her introduction to the organization in 2017 soon after she transferred to WVU to pursue an undergraduate degree in social work:

> I applied to the position with a vague job description in hopes that it would turn out to be something fun. I was the first official non-volunteer worker they had hired through the university. I knew I liked reading and books, I liked social justice, and I needed a job. While my work with APBP was definitely something fun, it was rewarding, educational, thought-provoking, passion-inducing work. My first day was the day of a letter-sorting event in which we categorized every letter ever received by APBP by month/date. Never one to be much of a "joiner" in groups and activities, I jumped into this headfirst. Over the years, I had countless opportunities to reach out to the community, advocate and educate fellow students, plan fundraisers with my wonderful fellow student organization members, host wrapping parties, wheel carts of books to the post office on foot, attend community mixer events as an APBP representative, and so much more.

APBP's library. Photo by Raymond Thompson Jr.

Many WVU students attribute APBP with helping them realize and acquire their academic and career goals, whether describing their experiences in a personal essay for an application to law school or in an interview with the American Civil Liberties Union. But working with APBP is more than a line on a résumé for students; it shifts their perspective about people who are imprisoned across America and empowers them to work toward a more sustainable, restorative, and empathetic world.

Because of the commitment and passion of the APBP community after a decade of work, we felt we had enough support to expand our mission. In 2014, we engaged with experts and held a multiday Educational Justice & Appalachian Prisons Symposium at WVU. Hundreds of people, including public officials, people previously incarcerated, students, artists, and educators, participated. The first panel featured a group of men who were able to leave prison temporarily to speak at the event.

Soon after the symposium, APBP started its first book club in a prison. Our goal was to make creative and intellectual connections in a place that isolates and often deprives people of educational resources and collaboration. Since then, about one hundred imprisoned people have participated in APBP book clubs and creative writing workshops organized by volunteers. Each APBP book club is composed of about fifteen incarcerated members and five volunteers, including WVU English faculty. The group decides on what to read for each meeting. Some groups have compiled original writing and artwork into collections titled *Holding onto Sand* and *Women of Wisdom*, which are published on the APBP website.

The impact of the book clubs led us to expand our mission further. In 2017, Katy taught a WVU English course inside a federal prison in West Virginia through the Inside-Out Prison Exchange Program. Inside-Out brings college students inside prisons to learn alongside students who are incarcerated. One outside student, Keith, reflected that he had learned more in the Inside-Out class than in the past three years at college. Ric, one of the inside students, said: "*This class made me feel human again.*"

In the fall of 2019, APBP reached out to community members and raised funds to provide tuition support to incarcerated students in a Pennsylvania prison earning WVU's credit-bearing Inside-Out class. During the class, one of the inside students, Craig, wrote about how people on the outside's participation in a program like Inside-Out is an expression of love:

> Love is late nights spent red penning thoughtful responses to provocative papers. Love is getting on the bus for a ninety minute ride before Dunkin Donuts morning brew has finished percolating. Love is processing hundreds of request slips, hounding counselors for vote sheets, prepping call outs, and securing gate passes. Love is getting your work done early even though you've got four other classes and you can feel the hot breath of midterms on the nape of your neck.

Craig's words ring true for so many of us at APBP. Whether we are carrying bags of books to the USPS, housing hundreds of extra donated books in our basement, traveling with other volunteers to participate in a book club inside a prison, or spending a day in the Aull Center fulfilling requests, we all hope to create a better world—a world where this work is no longer needed. Until that happens, we can't help but share the work of APBP with others.

When Kristin DeVault-Juelfs participated in her work-study with APBP, she enjoyed welcoming friends and family into each project she worked on. Now as a long-time volunteer and former board member, she reflects on the impact of sharing APBP with others:

> I brought APBP letters home for the weekend, opening and processing them with my mother and sister, pausing to look at a drawing or notice a mutual interest we had with the writer. When I volunteered for a new project, my fiancé Austin was there to help, whether it was carrying heavy books or offering his car to help us move supplies. When another work-study position opened, I threw Austin into the running. He was hired as our designated "numbers guy," filling a vital role in the organization with his science and number-oriented

mind. Working with APBP has very much been a family endeavor for us in this way. Forming bonds with other volunteers, student workers, board members, and our readers through years of many emails, phone calls, vented frustrations, shared successes, and a common goal, APBP is our home away from home.

It is difficult to fathom the number of people who have supported APBP and our mission. They range from family members of volunteers to USPS workers to Morgantown residents donating a beloved book collection to people who recommend APBP to others inside prison. They don't have to be someone who visits the Aull Center regularly to make a difference, but after someone contributes in a small or grand way, they often feel like they are a part of something much larger than themselves, because they are. With each new person who learns about APBP or another prison book project is also a conversation about mass incarceration, the potential to shift someone's perspective, and progress toward action and change. We hope to continue expanding our mission, not only to provide more educational opportunities and resources to those inside prisons and jails, but to educate the people on the outside about the full range of people behind those walls. There is still so much work to do.

NOTE

1. Emily Widra and Tiana Herring, "States of Incarceration: The Global Context 2021," Prison Policy Initiative, September 2021, https://www.prisonpolicy.org/global/2021.html.

COMMUNITY

THE GENESIS OF COMMUNICATIONS IN THE NATIONAL PRISON BOOK PROGRAM MOVEMENT Andy Chan

As best as can be determined, secular prison books programs in the United States, which have proliferated in the twenty-first century, have their roots in a small number of radical groups that formed in the early 1970s on opposite sides of the country. The Prison Book Program in Cambridge (later Boston, then Quincy), Massachusetts, was established by the Red Book Store Collective in 1972 and was "initially committed to distributing politically progressive literature."[1] The roots of Books to Prisoners (Seattle) are somewhat murky but were laid in the early 1970s in Seattle by activists who formed the community that also established the anarchist book store, Left Bank Books, in the tourist heart of Seattle, Pike Place Market (which remains there almost fifty years later).[2] The Seattle activists' goal was to support radical political prisoners, many of whom languished in the correctional system in the wake of the late 1960s radicalization, through sending them otherwise impossible to obtain reading materials.

The missions of these groups morphed to reflect growing aspirations, recognizing a more general deficit of access to reading materials so obviously apparent in the massively expanding national prison system. It is no accident that the growth timeline of these programs roughly mirrors the growth of the U.S. prison population. The example of these programs inspired similar organizing in the Bay Area (in 1981), Philadelphia (1988/89), and beyond.

The extent to which these early groups communicated is uncertain, although no long-standing communication network existed. Activists drifted freely, particularly along the West Coast, leaving open the possibility that people who volunteered with one program might later find themselves volunteering at a different program. In short, while there may have been occasional contacts between two groups, there was no multilateral networking and no coordination. With so few groups, with small capacities and under-the-radar profiles, there was no apparent pressing need for national coordination.

No single precipitating event motivated the effort to create multilateral national communications. But by the mid- to late 1990s, the growth of interest in prisoner issues across the country made some things apparent. Established programs were answering the same questions over and over from embryonic groups, and there was no indication that the need for help or advice on how to get a prison books program started was going to stop. It also became clear that a critical mass of regionally dispersed groups meant the question of equitable national coverage could be examined. It just didn't make sense for multiple groups to serve the same populations and leave other populations or areas unserved.

Unsurprisingly, state and federal Departments of Correction and politicians looking to profit (financially or electorally) through the expansion and control of the prison industry have almost always been the exclusive gatekeepers of prisoners' access to reading materials. By the mid- to late 1990s, prison activists began to sense that they were approaching a time when a critical mass of groups could—with sufficient collaboration and solidarity—begin to tip the scales away from the arbitrary censorship and total control of prison systems by challenging them through the courts and otherwise. These activists were not naively emboldened by the recent proliferation of their numbers; rather they were coming to realize the advantages their solidarity presented. Specifically, they realized that what was successful in one state might be successful in another, or that a challenge to a federal prison anywhere might help similar challenges to federal prisons everywhere.

The element that made collaboration on a national scale an easily realizable goal was technology: a cost-free and barrier-free email listserv. Today, it can be hard to conceptualize how time-consuming national organization from scratch was before email and the internet. A dedicated organizer would have to research who all the potential players were through phone calls to radical friends, trawling through DIY (do-it-yourself) zines, and asking local crusty guru activists. Contact to interested groups in other cities would often only be possible via snail mail to post office boxes that were checked every other week, creating a time lag of sometimes a month or more.

Books to Prisoners in Seattle started using a listserv, onelist, for internal discussion around 1998, and the utility of this technological tool was immediately apparent. Given the passage of time, I don't recall if a light bulb flicked on over my head, or if everything just slowly came together, but some time in 1999 I started emailing groups that had email addresses and sending out letters to groups that did not, suggesting the creation of a national prison books program listserv. The response to this call was gratifyingly positive, and no doubt the idea had been germinating in other groups. The list switched platforms a few times in the early years, finally settling on Riseup in 2006, where it has been housed ever since.

As hoped for, the establishment of the national prison books program listserv meant rapid access to a wealth of experienced activists and led to an immediate outpouring of information sharing. It was now easy to distribute restrictions lists that groups had painstakingly developed through trial and error over years. This helped newer groups waste less money on postage and demonstrated how inconsistent prison systems were. It was now possible to alert everyone quickly about new prison restrictions, again saving a lot of postage and frustration. Newer groups were able to pick up valuable fundraising ideas and organizational tips.

The national prison books program listserv illustrated the value of countrywide communication and collaboration and directly led to the next level of organization—the first national prison books program conference.

[bookstoprisoners] GLJ

 ⬜⬜⬜@hotmail.com
Tue 6/20/2000 8:33 PM
To: bookstoprisoners@egroups.com

Georgetown Law Journal is currently donating copies of its mammoth Annual Review of Criminal Procedure - which every jailhouse lawyer should have. Only problem is it weighs over 3 pounds so it ain't cheap to send. To ask about getting some copies email Nerissa Phillips at
PHILLIPS@wpgate.law3.georgetown.edu

Andy

Resource-sharing email from the early days of the national listserv

Nascent thoughts about something resembling a national gathering were already swirling in 2001. Philadelphia's Books Through Bars and Self-Education Foundation (notably through activists Nicole Meyenberg and Barbara Hirshkowitz) were instrumental in workshopping the idea into a realistic proposal. Putting together a national gathering, for the first time, for a collection of under-resourced, micro-budget, all-volunteer groups, run mostly by anarchists and various shades of lefties, was no small mountain to climb. The Self-Education Foundation granted the effort funds that subsidized travel and paid for dorm-style accommodations, without which a truly national conference would not have occurred.

The first Prison Book Program Conference took place in Philadelphia September 19–21, 2003, attended by about forty-five representatives from seventeen different groups from the United States and one from Canada. This was the first opportunity for the vast majority of participants to put faces to the names that had been providing insights and tips on the listserv for a few years at that point. The conference agenda covered many of the key areas that had cropped up in listserv conversation threads: fundraising, restrictions, outreach tools, coordination and planning. Real-time in-person conference discussions allowed for fuller and richer development of ideas and plans. Even ideas that met with mixed support, such as regionalization, resulted in some bilateral agreements.[3] More than anything, though, the feeling of shared purpose and solidarity was palpable.

High expectations of accelerating momentum in organizing were tempered in the following months, an acknowledgment that inertia and the myriad

I'M A INDIVIDUAL THAT HAS NO FINANCES TO SUPPORT MY MIND'S WEEKLY FIX OF BOOKS. BESIDE THE PRISON LIBRARY STAFF IS LAZY AND REALLY DON'T CARE WHAT WE REQUEST BUT JUST GIVE YOU ANYTHING THEY WANT TO GET THE JOB DONE OR IF WE ASK TO BE PUT IN LINE FOR BOOKS OTHER INMATES' FAMILIES SEND THEM IT TAKES MONTHS TO GO DOWN THE LINE IF IT'S A NEW AUTHOR. SO I'M ONLY ABLE TO REACH OUT TO PEOPLE LIKE YOU THAT ARE READING THIS LETTER AND HAVE A CARE FOR A PERSON YOU DON'T EVEN KNOW BUT FIND IT IN YOUR HEART TO HELP ME TO BECOME FREE. I COULDN'T READ, LET ALONE WRITE ABOVE A THIRD GRADE LEVEL, BUT I PUSHED MYSELF WHILE I'M DOING THIS TIME. . . .

Attendees at the September 2003 Philadelphia Prison Book Program Conference

distractions of daily life can be hard to overcome, especially when the majority of those involved in this work do it in their spare time while holding down paid jobs and other responsibilities. However, the Philadelphia conference set the tone for greater collaboration and spawned follow-up conferences in Urbana-Champaign in 2007 and Boston in 2019. The pandemic, of course, made it difficult to follow up on the most recent of these conferences.

Almost twenty-five years later, the national prison book listserv continues as the communication center of the movement. If usage patterns are at all indicative, its utility has grown over time. With a current membership of over two hundred people who represent dozens of groups, large and small, its no-frills simplicity has limitations, but it benefits from the requirement that participants only need to be willing to use email in order to access the knowledge and experience of scores of committed activists. Web-based communications apps and platforms have been suggested and piloted as ways to improve national-level collaboration—but they have generally failed as they have, on balance, yet to provide a sufficiently better communication experience to gain the critical mass of users necessary.

Prison Book Program Conference Agenda

Friday, September 19
4-6   arrive at Chamounix Mansion
6   dinner
7:15ish   Introductions (who you are, where you're from, why do you do
           this work, approx. 3 minutes/person)

Saturday, September 20
8am   Breakfast
9-10:30   Fundraising basics & Fundraising intermediate
             Break
10:45-12:45 Prison restrictions & Focus on special issues (women, prison
             libraries, art projects
12:45-1:45   Lunch
1:45-3:45   Tools we use in our work & Outreach/Public Education
             Break
4-6   White Privilege discussion
6:30   pop in cars and head for the Klein Gallery
6:30   dinner and gallery tour
8:00   return to Chamounix, hang out & relax

Sunday, September 21, 2003
8am   Breakfast
9-10:30   Project coordination part 1
             Break
10:45-12:30 project coordination part 2 (focus on planning)
12:30-1:30   Lunch
1:30- 3:15   Visions for the future
             Break
3:30-4:15   Evaluation
4:30   Departure

Chamounix Mansion (215) 878-3676 3250 Chamounix Drive in West
Fairmount Park
Nicole's cell phone 8am to 11pm
Housing: Kim and Tom   Transport: Jarf
Program & everything else: Barbara and Nicole

September 2003
Philadelphia Prison
Book Program
Conference agenda.

The efforts that created multilateral conversation between prison book programs would have been valuable enough if all that had been achieved was sharing of insights and information on book restrictions across the United States. However, the listserv has also enabled national-level activist collaboration that has reversed reactionary efforts to limit access to books. Rapid dissemination of information, response planning, and activist mobilization were all made possible through the listserv.

Perhaps the greatest demonstration of what the listserv has helped prison book programs achieve is the series of mobilizations against increased prison

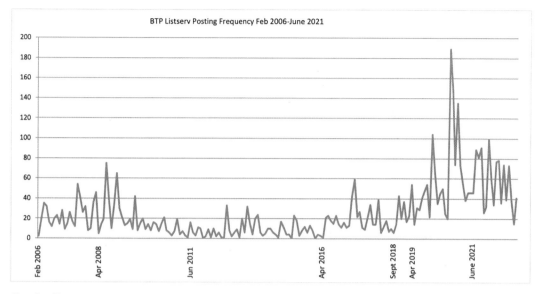

Graph of listserv postings

restrictions in 2018 and 2019. Among others, Departments of Correction in New York, Pennsylvania, and Washington State introduced different types of new limitations, or outright bans, on nonprofit prison book programs sending books to prisoners in their states in this period. Posts on the list increased significantly during the organizing against these bans, demonstrating the importance of the list in helping to fight them. The information sharing ensured that departments of correction and their political masters were blasted with complaints from across the country, that successful strategies from earlier fights were shared, and that messaging was consistent to the press and to state institutions. New York, Pennsylvania, and Washington Departments of Correction were stunned by the backlash against the new restrictions that they had imposed on books. In short order, each state walked back—in whole or in part—their restrictions, and this is due in no small part to the nationwide awareness and pressure that the prison book program network created.

Going forward there are still many areas for improvement regarding collaborative efforts: an embryonic Books to Prisoners Alliance seeking greater national coordination and collective fundraising competes with the natural tendency of many prison book groups to operate entirely independently;

more time and resources will need to be thrown into responding to new book restrictions as they pop up, not to mention beginning the fight against long-standing restrictions in states such as Michigan and New Mexico; the much-prophesied death of the printed book hangs like an ominous cloud in the distance; funding remains a constant headache.[4] Good communications remains a key element for success for prison book programs and the prison book program listserv has been the backbone of these communications.

NOTES

Thanks to Bruno and Tom with Prisoners Literature Project in the Bay Area, Madeline with Books Through Bars in Philadelphia, Left Bank Books veterans Sylvie and Lynne, Books To Prisoners stalwart Kris, and NYC Books Through Bars founder Vikki for their assistance.

1. "Our Story," Prison Book Program, https://prisonbookprogram.org/about/our-story.

2. The author received snippets of firsthand BTP history from founding collective members of Left Bank Books: with Lynne Thorndycraft in 2021 and in an informal chat with another (possibly Jo Maynes) in 2003.

3. While some prison book programs respond to requests from anywhere in the United States, many only serve a small number of states, or just one. Regionalization was an effort to bring increased services to underserved regions by assigning a group to serve a particular region. General agreement was hampered by several insuperable issues including the widely varying capacity of attending groups and their more or less overt political stances. Not all discussions were equally successful or beneficial. The white privilege session featured racial caucusing that was quite awkward, not least as some participants in the caucus for people of color felt unprepared or questioned the need for racial caucusing at all.

4. This most recent conceptual iteration of a national organization was born out of discussions at the 2019 Boston Books to Prisoners National Conference. An Exploratory Committee for the Alliance was formed in May 2021.

THE NATIONAL CONFERENCE
Jodi Lincoln

For a long time, communication and collaboration between prison book programs existed almost solely in the online email listserv. Groups were able to share updates on prison restrictions and information about publishers and authors who were looking to donate books as well as other resources such as zines. While the listserv has been an important resource for years, PBPs didn't actually know the people behind the email signatures, and the opportunities to learn from each other through emails is limited.

Starting in 2017, there was chatter here and there on the listserv about the possibility of creating a more formal collaboration. Peter Esmonde, a core volunteer at the Prisoners Literature Project in Berkeley, California, was one of the people involved in these first conversations and kept the momentum going, reaching out to groups individually to assess need and interest. Peter leveraged his connection with the Vireo Foundation Fund to acquire funding for a national conference, explicitly with the goal of bringing groups together in person, in order to strengthen relationships and further collaboration.

About ten years earlier, there was a PBPs conference in Urbana, Illinois. The 2007 conference focused a lot on sharing practical advice between PBPs on how to raise money, coordinate volunteers, and manage logistics. The full pressure of prison censorship and the transition to tablets had yet to emerge. Although that conference was well attended, a conference wasn't initiated every year due to the volunteer nature of prison book groups, and by 2017 long-standing PBP folks and newcomers were ready for another meeting.

In January 2018, the Vireo Foundation Fund sent out a request for proposals (RFP) to groups around the country to host a Books to Prisoners National

Image of logo for the Books to Prisoners National Conference

Conference the next year. They were offering a large grant to support a conference that would "foster sharing of best practices around provision of free learning materials to U.S. prisoners and . . . encourage productive alliances and partnerships among non-profit books-to-prisoners groups."[1]

The Prison Book Program in Quincy, Massachusetts, had a couple of volunteers who were very interested in responding to the RFP. Erin Wentz and Emma Lathan applied. Six months later, Vireo announced that the Prison Book Program had been selected to host the conference and was receiving a $18,000 grant. So began a rigorous ten-month planning process by the Quincy group.

Emma and Erin realized early on that the $18,000 wouldn't cover the full cost of the conference, especially with the intention of making it free for attendees and helping to cover the cost of travel as needed. Prison Book Program volunteers were ultimately able to get enough donations over the next year to fill the cost gap.

SO WHOEVER READS THIS, EVERYONE NEEDS A HELPING HAND, A SHOULDER TO LEAN ON, A BOOK TO OCCUPY YOUR MIND. IBP NEEDS HELP IN COLLECTING BOOKS, COVERING POSTAGE, AND EVERYDAY ACTIVITIES BECAUSE THESE PROJECTS A'NT EASY. IF I HAD THE MEANS I WOULD DO EVERYTHING I COULD BECAUSE I KNOW WHAT THESE PEOPLE HAVE DONE FOR ME AND THERE A'NT NO AMOUNT OF THANK YOUS THAT CAN EVERY MEASURE TO THE GRATITUDE I HAVE FOR YOU. I CAN'T WAIT FOR THE NEXT TRIP TO FAR DISTANCE LANDS YOU'RE ABLE TO SEND ME. THANK YOU FOR EVERYTHING YOU HAVE DONE FOR ME.

One of the first things Emma, Erina, and coworker Marlene Cook did for the conference was to send out a survey to the Books to Prisons listserv asking folks what they wanted out of the conference. It asked respondents to list what they would be most interested in learning about and had them share their interest level in attending different kinds of sessions. They proposed a sample program in their application and pulled from that to make sure folks wanted to attend those sessions. Many of the sessions originally proposed ended up being workshops and panels offered at the conference. One of the most important parts of the survey, though, was geared toward figuring out who was willing and able to run these sessions.

Suddenly it was time. On Friday, April 5, conference attendees began arriving at the Unitarian Universalist Association building in the Fort Point district in Boston. Volunteers from the Quincy chapter welcomed folks with warmth, joy, and dinner! Behind the scenes they were scrambling, and Erin recalls anxiously waiting for the name tags and programs to get there while people were starting to arrive. They handled it like professionals, and I had no impression they were off pace. Almost one hundred people showed up at the conference from twenty-eight different PBPs and some allied groups such as Black and Pink.

That first night was mostly mingling and a showing of *13th*, a film about how the modern-day prison system directly grew from slavery. A moving and educational film, it grounded the conference in the understanding that the people we send books to are victims of a racist and unjust system that exploits and harms everyone it touches. Book tables were also set up at the conference and became a great cornerstone in the entrance of the conference. Multiple tables were filled with books in PBPs most requested genres—law, business, pagan, abolition, and more. When our groups have the funding to purchase books instead of relying on donations, it's great to be able to fill our empty shelves with books that are requested all the time. I remember taking pictures of some of the titles and putting them on our wish list to purchase in the future. I found out about the Nolo Legal Research and Business books there and regularly purchase them for the Pittsburgh Prison Book Project. Throughout the conference it was great to be able to stop by for a quiet moment to check out these wonderful titles.

Saturday the conference really kicked off with the first break-out sessions. Two years later, reviewing the conference schedule for the purpose of writing this chapter, I'm filled with a rush of memories and am drawing the connections from what I learned to things we did at my own organization. Attending the "Getting Feedback from People Who Are Incarcerated" session helped the Pittsburgh Prison Book Project (Book 'Em at the time) commit to regularly sending out surveys to the people we sent books to. It's important for any organization to assess their work and get feedback from clients and stakeholders. This can be hard for PBPS because we are physically separated from the people to whom we send books, and the system is designed to make communication difficult. Sending out surveys to all our contacts worked well, and we asked questions about how long it took for people to get their books, general satisfaction, and areas for improvement. One important piece of feedback we got was that people didn't like getting books from the middle of a series without the first books, especially with fantasy or action adventure. Using this feedback, we changed how we organized and sent books, making sure to bundle series together on the shelves so volunteers would pull them together and keeping books without the beginning of the series separate. Surveys we did during COVID were very enlightening about the conditions people were facing inside and the increased barriers to library access people had while on lockdown.

"Fundraising and Donor Development" was held in a conference room that was far too small for the number of people who ended up attending that session. We squeezed ourselves on top of each other, standing like sardines in the corners and in between chairs to listen to Jamie, Shelby, and Marlene talk about how they keep their groups thriving and not just surviving. They shared some fantastic ways to engage donors and strategies for going after grants and larger donations. Our organization has always just "gotten by" and not put a ton of effort into fundraising, and the session really made me think about how to increase our individual giving and leverage other sources. It's paid off.

A main topic of conversation at the conference was the recent ban by the Washington State Department of Corrections on people in Washington prisons from receiving free books from Books to Prisons groups. The ban had just been announced a few weeks before the conference, and Books to Prisoners in Seattle was extremely active in the public pushback and engaging other groups around the country. This was one of the challenges that the conference was supposed to help us work on, and it not only helped teach a lot of people about this and similar issues but also built support for the pushback in Washington.

Andy Chan from the Seattle group and I were actually already planning a session, "Tracking and Responding to Prison Restrictions," before the Washington State ban was announced. I had been on the front lines of the successful pushback against the ban on people getting books in Pennsylvania only a few months earlier in the fall of 2018. With that experience, I was going to discuss the strategies for challenging book bans and how to build the necessary networks to be successful. Andy had been planning on mostly talking about how to keep internal records and track the different restrictions in different prisons and jails. However, when the Washington DOC ban happened, Andy was in the weeds organizing efforts in Seattle to change the policy. It was clear to us that focusing our session on these larger book bans and how to challenge them was needed. These recent statewide bans are a threat to all of us and the people we serve, so everyone was asking the questions:

When is this going to happen in my state?

Is there anything we can do to prevent these policies BEFORE they happen?

Why do the telecommunications companies suck so much?

The spread of tablets is just going to make this worse . . . How do we best organize together?

The topics explored in sessions poured into our conversations throughout the conference and ended up being some of the most important moments. These chats were held over lunch, walking in the hallway to a breakout room, or at the brewery before catching the plane home. Erin said that her favorite part of the conference was the energy, watching people meet one another and immediately bond and start sharing. There were so many familiar names that I had seen on the email lists and groups that we followed on social media, and now we finally got to meet in person. Everyone there had shared struggles but also shared joys working to achieve a better society.

Most importantly, we recognized that the collective power of all our organizations and our networks was bigger than any of us acting on our own. In 2018, people connected to groups in Massachusetts and California called the Pennsylvania governor during our phone zaps to increase the public pressure; they shared our local stories on social media, which helped raise awareness and get national coverage of the ban. Only a few days after the conference, we found out that the Washington DOC was backing down from their ban as well. We were proving that we can make a difference and saw successful strategies, but it also felt unorganized, desperate, and extremely grassroots. There wasn't the infrastructure to be proactive—just reactive.

We realized it didn't have to be that way. It would take work, but the people in the building and their co-volunteers at home would be just the kind of people to make it happen. These were the conversations Peter Esmonde had wanted to happen when he first pushed for a conference.

But then boom! The conference was over. Folks piled into cars and planes to head home to their groups, bringing new knowledge, excitement, and to-do lists. Part of my to-do list was creating a shared Google Drive so people could share resources. It's been used to upload zines, PDFs we print, and all sorts of information that could be useful to other groups. In their post-conference rundown with Peter, Marlene and Emma enthusiastically brought up the conversations about an alliance among PBPS and the interest across

We were nine months to a year behind in our letters. We were one of the only programs serving incarcerated people in ten-plus states. We had a good location, sporadic fundraising, a lot of books, and regular volunteers, but we just could not keep up. We decided to combine a fundraiser with a packing party. We would do it March of Dimes style and ask people to donate for every hour in a twenty-four-hour period that a person packed. I was one of three primary organizers. The three of us decided that we would do the entire twenty-four hours, so we loaded up on coffee, energy drinks, trucker speed (ephedrine), and all varieties of legal stimulants. We started with coffee at 7 a.m. on a Saturday. People came and went throughout the day. By evening we had exhausted our supply of energy drinks and had moved on to the trucker speed. We picked up a steady stream of volunteers throughout the evening, though I suspect some people came just to gawk. So long as they packed books while gawking, we were cool with it. People came and went; spirits were high, and books were being wrapped. By midnight we had moved on from coffee and were raiding the energy drinks with abandon. Some folks were trying to keep up with us, but they all fell by the trucker speed wayside. It is a good thing nobody dropped by between 3 and 5 a.m.; we were in that phase where you have ceased to make sense to anyone who has not been by your side for the last twenty hours. We finally made it all the way to 7 a.m., though I don't think I was able to sleep for several more hours. It was not the healthiest thing I have ever done, and it did not work so great as a fundraiser, but I will be damned if we did not make it through six-plus months of letters.

ONE TIME at PRISON BOOKS...

the board on moving forward with that. Together, Peter, Marlene, and I along with Michelle Dillon and Joan Ross from the Seattle group started coordinating and reaching out to groups around the country to try to find out how an alliance could benefit groups. What are their needs and struggles?

The feedback we got from groups around the country noted a few main goals that people would like to see from a larger alliance group. Many groups spoke of a common website that would be able to provide information to the public but also include internal resources for groups. There are dreams of an interactive map and database that would show which groups cover which states, indicate what restrictions each area has, and list our ally groups around the country. The website could also host a forum and shared documents platforms for groups.

The other large, identified need was for a place for groups to strategize, plan, and find funding for other common initiatives. At the core of this would be a committee focused on challenging restrictions and hopefully being proactive and combating prison telecoms' infringement on the rights of incarcerated people to access information. The group could also be a tool to help create greater diversity among PBPs and provide technical and financial support to groups in need.

With the need for an alliance clearly expressed by conference attendees and groups around the country, we started to work on the next steps. Groups from the listserv were invited to online Zoom meetings that started in September 2019. The process of the alliance has been slowed since the COVID pandemic impacted all aspects of our world in 2020 and 2021. Despite the challenges we are all facing in our communities and personal lives, Books to Prison group leaders met when we could to push the alliance forward. Goals were developed and the network built up piece by piece. As of November 2021, the alliance is hiring a consultant to assist the group in developing a two-year work plan and budget. The consultant is being pulled in to help the alliance establish organizational structures and governance and identify missed opportunities and other strategic partners. The alliance is currently launching into the next steps, realizing many of the ideas that came out of the national conference.

NOTE

1. Vireo Foundation Fund, email to bookempgh@gmail.com, June 28, 2018.

INDEPENDENT BOOKSTORES AND PRISON BOOKS PROGRAMS
Patrick Kukucka

The role of a bookstore's sponsorship for prison books-related projects has been an important part in the success of many different groups. Although bookstores are generally for-profit ventures (albeit very narrowly), most independent bookstores are started in order to play an active role in the local community and to share a passion for books. Prison books programs seem to find a niche with local independent bookstores, usually secondhand ones.

A bookstore sponsorship can offer several services. When I began my work with the Asheville Prison Books Program (APB), The Reader's Corner, a used bookstore on the edge of downtown, partnered with us. The Reader's Corner became the mailing address for APB. We would pick up mail there once a week and use them as a return address. That perhaps was the most important aspect of the partnership, as many prisons have strict and seemingly arbitrary rules about what can and cannot be accepted. Having the return address from a legitimate bookstore immeasurably helps the packages get to the recipients. Some facilities today only accept books from big third-party companies such as Amazon, which restricts access to literature and printed material to only those who can afford to pay. The Reader's Corner also offered some storage in their basement and generally created a consistent hub and address for the program, which had to change spaces four or more times during our relationship with them.

When The Reader's Corner closed, the bookstore I worked at, Downtown Books & News (DBN), offered to allow us to use it as a mailing address. We also set up a system for different bookstores and other shops in town to collect donations for the program. After a while with DBN sponsoring us, we

I WOULD LIKE TO KNOW IF YOU HAVE ANYTHING ON DEATH BY EXECUTION. I HAD TWO BROTHERS WHO WAS EXECUTED. ONE WAS EXECUTED IN 1977 BY A FIRING SQUAD AT THE UTAH STATE PRISON. MY OTHER BROTHER GOT THE DEATH SENTENCE IN 1990. I WOULD VERY MUCH LIKE TO GET A BOOK ON EXECUTION.

had to change spaces once again. So, we put together a proposal to clean up an unused backroom in the building and begin using that as the volunteer space. This has continued for years and helped create a sustainable and consistent room for APB and another program in town, Tranzmission Prison Project. One problem PBPs have is finding a space to keep the books and to use as a workspace. The concept of paying rent rather than using the money on postage and supplies is dismaying. DBN offered the space rent-free, which I believe stabilized APB and allowed it to grow, find volunteers, and thus better support incarcerated folks.

Downtown Books & News in Asheville, North Carolina

Firestorm Café in Asheville, North Carolina, also supports Asheville Prison Books and Tranzmission Prison Project

After opening my own bookstore, I realized that with so many books on the market, space is also a commodity. Rather than turning away some of the books we do not need, we filter them and donate to the current prison books programs, as well as to the local Friends of the Library. Another bookstore in town, Firestorm Books & Coffee, has also been a huge supporter of the programs and has provided space for monthly packing parties and volunteer recruitment. They also have a direct link on their website listing the most requested books in prison; it includes nonfiction, reference, and blank notebooks. The books can be purchased and directly donated to APB. These relationships are important. Bookstores not only serve as places to buy books but also provide access to reading material for people in the community.

Collaboration Ideas

The following ideas are suggestions for how bookstores can collaborate with, support, and sponsor a prison books program:

- Place a donation jar (with a small info sheet about your pbp) near the register.
- Keep a stack of free bookmarks near the register that give info about your PBP and where and how people can donate used books.
- Establish a donation book drop or box somewhere in the store where customers can drop off used book donations. If the store doesn't want to purchase a customer's used books, it can then suggest that the customer donate these books to the program.
- Set up a "buy a book for someone inside" shelf, stocked with paperbacks frequently requested by prisoners. Customers can pick up a book, buy it, and leave it at the bookstore.
- Create a prison books wish list, curated by the bookstore staff, and post it on the store website, allowing browsers to purchase books for folks inside.
- Allow the PBP to sell T-shirts and other fundraising swag at the bookstore.
- Host packing parties if the store has space.
- Host authors to give book talks on books that address imprisonment and abolition.

INTERVIEW: ROD CORONADO ON BEING LOCKED UP AND NATIVE
Interview by Dave "Mac" Marquis

Can you talk a little about your general observations about books on the inside. . . . Did the prisons you were in have libraries? What were those libraries like? Did you and other people have access to them?

The libraries were always really thin. I never really heard, via other incarcerated people, about PBPs. It was always something that I always felt like I was exposing people to because they did not have those resources or connections with people on the outside. Those resources weren't known to the general population. It's evidence of the negligence of prisons that there aren't better systems for educating people, especially when they want to be educated. The focus of education in most prisons that I was in was the GED. Folks could work on their GED, but as far as expanding their knowledge about what they personally desired, they were pretty much left to fend for themselves, unless they had a connection on the outside that could provide them with reading materials. So, the people I shared PBP info with benefited from those programs. They wrote their own letters and got on the list to receive books. I was interested in the kinds of books that contained radical, political, or historical material, and they were never on the shelves in the prison library. So, to be able to receive those materials from PBPs and to share them with the other incarcerated people was the only way to get those resources. It was never easy for folks to find reading material on specific issues they were interested in.

Rod Coronado

Did you see other people getting books from the outside?

That wasn't something I really witnessed. I was in prison for four years for my first stint, and I received a tremendous amount of mail from supporters. This illustrated to me how little mail other people got. They were just hoping for a letter, let alone a book or a package or something. Many people were lost, completely undernourished when it came to reading material. Sharing books became something that I would do because I always had lots of books in my library, particularly books on Native American and political history. People knew that, and so they would come to me, and I would lend them books. I regularly had to send books out since I was only allowed so many books in my locker at a time. I tried to keep books that other people would be interested in, but I had my own interests too, and I was reading a lot during this time. I loved reading and learning about things, so this became a very politicizing and empowering time for me, whereas I could see for all the incarcerated people around me that it was way more routine, and doing time was hard.

Can you talk about the process of lending books out? Most PBPs assume that our books go through multiple hands on the inside.

As an Indigenous person I was in with the Native crowd, and amongst ourselves we shared a lot of material. I took it upon myself to really educate and share with the Indigenous population everything that I was receiving. This was the time of the Zapatista rebellion and the Túpac Amaru [rebellion]. I was sharing information about the Indigenous struggles that I was reading about because I had progressive people on the outside that were getting me these materials. It was really powerful to share those with Indigenous peoples that had really sheltered opinions about Indigenous sovereignty. It was really empowering, not only for me, but for other people as well. I saw that as my role since I was the recognized political prisoner, and people sent me things. I felt like those resources weren't just for me—they were to be shared. It was a great way for me to build friendships and show solidarity with other people. I even shared material with people who held beliefs that I was opposed to. I lent things out to anyone so long as they returned it.

Did you see incarcerated people challenge restrictions on getting books?

I didn't see much of that. As Native people we spoke a lot about that our rights to sweat lodges and tobacco and things that people fought long and hard for. We spoke of that. As far as other people challenging the system, to get more learning material or books, I didn't see any of that. The second anybody starts instigating any type of organizing, boom: they're transferred, shipped out. I kept a low profile and advocated for animals.

Amongst the Native community, I would put together a weekly cut-and-pasted, photocopied little zine drawn from the materials I was getting. It would just be two or three pages with quotes and stories. I got assistance from a sympathetic Native staff person. I would only circulate it amongst the Native people since we didn't want to get the staff person in trouble. We would, of course, have gotten in trouble too. I was nervous about that kind of thing because I was doing time close to my family, and I didn't want to get transferred.

Did you all have any sort of study groups, informal as it may [have] been, about the material you were providing them?

Yes. As Native prisoners we had one night a week in the chapel for our own meetings. Somebody would buy a pack of cookies, somebody else would buy some coffee and creamer, and we would sit in circle, and I would hand

Rod is the subject of the documentary *Operation Wolf Patrol* (2021) covering Rod's nonprofit, Wolf Patrol, a conservation movement founded on the principles of biocentricity and Indigenous cultural preservation.

out the newsletter. We would read over it, talk about it, and maybe sing some songs. There were one or two other incarcerated Native people that really got a lot out of it, and they would help me host it. For me, that was very politicizing, to see someone who had never been exposed to this sort of material and watch them go through that next step of helping other people. That made me feel as if I was reaching my duty as an incarcerated Native person. . . . These are all people who, when they finish their time, are going to go back [to] rural locations, on remote reservations, where they probably won't have any exposure to these ideas. I'd like to think that seeds were planted, and maybe they had the opportunity, like I did, to participate in struggles, like Standing Rock, that have happened since then.

You also wrote some zines for people on the outside during this time, correct?

The zine for the public was different. I was never formally educated; I only went to community college after I got out of prison. The learning process of higher education was not something I experienced, so I kind of had to create it. I was being provided with so much information on so many subjects that I was interested about. I would read and read and read, but I had nowhere to process that information. If I was in a college class, I would have homework assignments and writing projects and prompts . . . interaction with other people. Not having that, I created it by putting time into writing about other issues, like the Irish Republican resistance. I would read three or four books and then write an article about it from my perspective. It was also a way to demonstrate that I was using this time to learn, that my struggle did not end in prison. For me, that meant learning about other struggles and resistance movements and how they could be applied to earth and animal liberation.

What was the general condition of books in the library?

I learned not to start reading a good book from the library unless you were certain it had all of the pages. Otherwise, you would get a couple hundred pages in and realize whole chapters were missing or something. During my second stint in 2011 there was so much material that I was not able to receive. I had so much mail confiscated because they said it was threatening to the peace of the institution.

What sort of resources there were for nonnative English speakers in terms of books?

The worst. So much worse than it was for English speakers. Nonexistent I would say. That was striking to me. I was in prison for very serious crimes, and I was there alongside people whose only crime was that they crossed the border too many times. They were in prison working in UNICOR,[1] sending their money home. It was actually working out for them, so far as it goes, because the lack of employment in their home countries was so dire. I couldn't believe that.

Any final thoughts?

I just want to say how great of a service it is to provide books to incarcerated people. These people are ignored, rejected, and thrown away by society. They are ripe for being educated, empowered, and liberated. . . . It is a great social responsibility to provide resources to incarcerated people to help them think about who they are going be when they get of prison. Our society is doing nothing to rehabilitate people. Any hope for people in custody is going to come from programs like PBPs and not from the state itself. I am convinced of that.

NOTE

1. Federal Prison Industries, Inc., doing business as UNICOR since 1977, is a wholly owned U.S. government corporation created in 1934 as a prison labor program for inmates within the Federal Bureau of Prisons and as a component of the Department of Justice. Incarcerated people manufacture a wide variety of products including office furniture, bedding, eyewear, clothing, and electronics. There are approximately 25,000 incarcerated people waiting to work in UNICOR. Only 8 percent of work-eligible inmates are employed, earning between 23¢ and $1.15 per hour. "Shop the UNICOR Online Store," UNICOR, https://www.unicor.gov/Category.aspx.

FUN(DRAISING): THE HALLOWEEN COVER BAND SHOW Patrick Kukucka

Prison book projects are generally volunteer run and organized through traditional grassroots methods. This means we're mostly broke. While large, monetary donations are always welcome, they're also rare. So, PBPs must do a lot of fundraising. The program I've been involved with for twenty years, Asheville Prison Books (APB), has done a lot of creative things to fundraise.... But the most long-standing and lucrative has been the Halloween Cover Band Show.

Every Halloween (or the weekend closest to it) we would set up a PA system, get a bunch of PBR (Pabst Blue Ribbon) beer, and charge people a cover to come and listen to their friends play Halloween-ish takes or spoofs of their favorite bands. Asheville has a plethora of talented musicians, and this event allowed them to contribute to prison books. There are also lots of folks, like myself, who have music equipment and the ability to run a soundboard. This community knowledge created a fantastic event. I've personally played in zombie Bikini Kill, a Queen cover band where the crowd was chanting "I want to ride my bicycle" so loud it could likely have been heard in space, The Smiths, Joy Division, Born Against, Gang of Four, PJ Harvey, Loretta Lynn, The Cars, Violent Femmes, Bruce Springsteen, and Unwoundead. Bands get really creative sometimes, like "Taylor Spliff"—Taylor Swift songs done Reggae style.

It's not clear if Asheville, North Carolina, is the only town with annual Halloween cover-band shows. There must have been someone with the original idea, perhaps from another town, but that origin has been lost in the many years of the event, and it is thoroughly an Asheville institution now.

OCTOBER 31st

Asheville Prison Books

PRESENTS

the 2008

HALLOWEEN COVER BAND SHOW

at APPLE ALLEY
428 Haywood Rd.

9-1 A.M. $5

8:30 - 9:30 Haunted House ($1)

DJ Abu Disarray!   Costume Contest!

kidlet press

Flyer for the Halloween
Cover Band Show

Each year before Halloween, friends new and old would get together a month or so before the holiday and brainstorm different bands to cover. The event is a direct benefit to the Asheville Prison Books and Tranzmission Prison Project (a fellow group in the area that nationally services LGBTQIA folks in prison). This annual show has been dramatically changed by COVID, but also by the change in Asheville and its gentrification and expansion

When I first moved to Asheville, downtown was largely boarded-up store-fronts. Rent was incredibly cheap, and landlords would rent to people they

We used to have this small portable tape player that moved around with us to our various volunteer spaces. One day, as I was shelving, a tape was playing some hot jamz, but it sounded slightly muffled and had some extra sounds. I looked closer at the tape that was playing and saw the mixtape was hand-labeled "hot sexy jamz." It was in fact very much that. It was a mixtape of music that had been dubbed to another tape player's microphone (old-school fashion). While recording the music, there was also extraneous spanking and moaning sounds . . . the whole time. I'd never contemplated that concept before, and I did not announce my discovery to the group with whom I was working. I wonder where the tape is now?

ONE TIME at PRISON BOOKS...

wouldn't even dream of renting to now. This meant that projects such as APB could find space to host events like the Halloween show. The first cover band show I recall was at a show space and living area in downtown called the Big Idea. This was an apartment off what is lovingly called "Chicken Alley" in downtown—a small alleyway where someone had spray-painted "Punk's Not Dead." Once this area began to be rented by more professional types, there were too many noise complaints, and we had to find a new venue. We moved the Halloween show to a short-lived community space called El Diablo. After that, the community was able to rent a small, basement space off Haywood Road in West Asheville, which had yet to become desirable real estate. Called El Nuevo, this space hosted lots of shows in its time, including the Halloween show. This space was also eventually lost because of noise complaints. People who started a hand-cranked print-making shop in West Asheville then offered up their shop for the show. During that Halloween show, adventurous partygoers climbed on the roof, and there was a gas-leak scare. . . . At this point, a friend who owned a custom motorcycle shop in the warehouse district offered up his shop for the Halloween show. Word was spreading about the show and attracting people outside the radical community. Some of these folks really let loose. It was like the choir boys in *Lord of the Flies*. . . . They parked their cars in the middle of street, which invited unwelcome calls from the cops. They sat on the sink in our friend's workshop and pulled it from the wall, and one (obviously very fucked-up person)

Flyer for Halloween Prison Bake Event

decided to take a shit on the front step of the only Black-owned business in this warehouse district. Needless to say—that put an end to that. We decided to hold the show at a "legitimate" spot: the bar and arcade downtown. It was a fiasco, albeit a well-intentioned one. We were told there would be plenty of space, but on the night of the show, many people were stuck waiting outside for hours trying to get in as other people shuffled out to give their friends a turn because the venue greatly limited the number of people who could be inside. Inside (apart from directly in front of the stage) it felt empty. Most of the bands got to play, but the last band (Minor Threat) was shut down, and the singer (dressed as a parrot) was choked by a bouncer. Fortunately, some

Flyer for Halloween
Cover Band Show

friends opened up a community theater space called The Toy Boat. This space was further out from downtown, but it was a big space that featured local theater and served as a practice space for an all-person circus in which I also participated. This space hosted the Halloween show for two years. The owners were badasses and didn't let shenanigans slide. But, unfortunately, the space closed. The final place—as of now—was the Mothlight, a sizable establishment in town. They graciously hosted us until the outset of COVID and their ensuing closure.

Halloween shows usually last until dawn. People have a great time. In the past, it brought community together in a way few other events do. It was joyful, and it benefits our friends and fellows who live locked away from community, unable to experience the joy of having fun together. The cover band show was the primary way APBS was funded each year. I remember one band that donated $100 each year because they loved to come together and cover their favorite bands while benefiting a local program that they cared about. The Halloween show demonstrates that activism doesn't have to be punishing, serious work. Creating the society we want can—and should— be fun. Joy is the bond that holds people in community.

While there is a definite future for such shows, the tide might be turning against the Asheville Halloween Show. After some of the more damaging incidents, rules had to be implemented that hindered the autonomous freedom of the event. Many people from outside the small, activist community that spawned it joined in, and this, alongside the burgeoning Asheville real estate market and the ever-growing tourism in town, meant that there is no longer a common ethos for the event. When people don't know, for example, not to park in the middle of the street or think they can vandalize the hosting venue because it's a "punk show," things get too difficult to maintain.

The Prison Book Halloween shows were more than just a bacchanalian fundraiser. Incarcerated people are made invisible. Their loss directly impacts people and communities. Shining a light on this is important, and I hope these benefits continue until the end of mass incarceration. Support and recognition of this practice is important, and although the shows did not solve any of these issues, they did help get some books to folks in prison and brought recognition that no one is truly free unless we all are.

INTERVIEW: DANIEL McGOWAN AND POLITICAL PRISONERS
Interview by Dave "Mac" Marquis

Did any of the prisons you were in have a library? If so, did you have access to it?

Ostensibly, every one of the institutions I was at had at least a book cart or a library. Your access to them is a whole other thing. When you are in federal transit and you are going across the country, as I was, you are held in segregation. . . . When you are in segregation there is cart, a two-sided cart, largely populated by mass market paperbacks. Mystery, thriller, spy, action, romance, that kind of stuff. . . .

To clarify, you have no control over what is in the cart.

No. The book cart is predetermined, it is rolled around, and usually you can take one, or two books if you are lucky. . . . When you are in the SHU (special housing unit),[1] like I was when I was in Oklahoma, they open up what is called a bean hole. It is just a little slot, and they put the book cart there. So, you are looking through that slot, and you have to reach out, and if you are lucky you can ask [to be handed a book], but you don't ask people for shit in prison. You are really just wrangling your arm through [the bean hole]. You can't get to the bottom [of the cart]. You might be able to get to the second shelf . . . you can't turn it. You can ask them to turn it, but more than likely they'll tell you to hurry up. Everything is "hurry up."

The jail in Brooklyn had a great library, it was quite large . . . whoever was their librarian got a lot of good donations. The problem was access—you could only go there once a week. A person that doesn't have a lot to do can read one or two (fiction) books a day. Nonfiction is a little slower.

Daniel McGowan

When I was at the federal prison in Sandstone, I was there for nine months. Sandstone had a really good library. Libraries in [federal] prisons are kind of like social centers. . . . The library at Sandstone was big, but again, it was mostly [mass-market] fiction. There was like one shelf of nonfiction with maybe six books. What I ended up doing over the course of time that I was there was that I donated all of my books to the library. I read a ton when I was there. It was at the start of my bit, and I was trying to figure shit out. People knew that I had good books, and so when I would go to the library with a stack [of books I had been sent], people would walk with me to the section. They weren't going to hassle me on the way, but they were like, "I'm going to check that out." I remember putting a book in there about Sam Melville, who was at the Attica uprising, called *Mad Bomber Melville*. Maybe it [the nonfiction section] had fifty books when I left.

Then I got moved to the communication management units (CMU) at Marion and Terre Haute.² The CMUs have shitty libraries. They were libraries for just the CMUs. When I first got to Marion there was nothing but a magazine rack. A few months later, they brought in some romance and mass-market books. That library was literally in a cell. They would swap the books out every so often, and since I would regularly talk to the librarian, I was asked to choose which ones to swap out.

Drawing by Nic Cassette

I was also using the interlibrary loan system. Essentially, we were using the public library, but the problem was that we didn't have a catalog. We would just write book titles down, and they would come back two weeks later with what they thought we wanted. I remember one time I ordered a book titled *Killing Rage*, which was about the Irish Republican Army, and they sent me *Killing Rage* by bell hooks, which was not bad (as far as errors go).

I didn't have the strongest need to utilize the prison library. . . . The reason why the CMU library was not that important to me personally was that I had the capacity to ask [people on the outside] for any book I wanted, short of something very expensive, and I could get that sent in. I received a lot of books and magazines when I was at Marion, and those would just go through the unit. I pretty much shared everything.

What was the sharing experience like?

You are not allowed to share your property, but everyone does it. It was kind of like how you weren't allowed in another person's cell, but we were always in each other's cells because there were only like twenty-five of us in the CMU. The cops look the other way. People share stuff. It was mostly a positive experience, but occasionally you get burnt.

After a while the unit got subscriptions to a bunch of mainstream magazines. My sister sent me *People* because she thought it was funny, but I got into it. I didn't watch a ton of TV inside comparatively, but I watched way more than I used to. I was trying not to become a fossil. When I went in, *Borat* had just come out, and I joked to my friends, "If I make a *Borat* joke when I come out, tell me to stop." That's what happens inside. Time just stops for you. But a lot of magazines stopped printing paper editions while I was inside. I was really disappointed. I just wouldn't get it, and I would ask my friends what happened, and I would find out they were now web only.

That brings up a point about why access to print media is important for incarcerated people because access to things online . . .

There is none. There is no provision by which you access the web in a meaningful way. You have access to a wired connection for the very limited email system, and then there is a limited bullshit legal research database. You pay for it. It is like using email in the early nineties. . . . There are word limits.

The two CMUs I was in had a lot of educated people, very different from being in general population. There were multiple authors, medical doctors, PhDs. It was a very different experience. The conversations were very different . . . but, yeah, access to print media is very important.

Drawing by Nic Cassette

You have mentioned that you had access to books from the outside through familial and political networks and so forth, but I was wondering specifically about prison books programs and if you ever received books from one and/or solicited them. And did you know of other people on the inside who did?

I volunteered briefly at NYC Books Through Bars before I went inside. I knew all of the people that did it, but I knew that I wasn't going to have to utilize their service, and I knew the they were stretched pretty thin. Back then, they were often hurting for money, and there were packages that just wouldn't go out because they had no money. [Before I went inside] I was working on pretrial release, I was putting money away, I was fundraising—most of that went to my lawyers—but my work money was being banked for books and commissary for when I was inside. I decided that I was not going to go in there and be like a monk, but I also wasn't going to just be buying ice cream and chips to drown my sorrow. I was going to allow myself to buy as many books as I wanted. I would get into topics, and I would read thirty on the topic. I probably read eight hundred books when I was inside, that's my guess.

I got two packages from PBPs. The first one I got was from NYC Books Through Bars. I think they reached out to my support network [and coordinated it]. I had just gotten sent to the CMU at Terre Haute after only four months in general population at Marion. I was pretty bummed. I got it [the package], and it had the NYC greeting reading letter, and it said my name with a little smiley face, and I knew it was people that I knew. They heard I was back in CMU, and they wanted to send me a lifeline. That was really nice. It is really hard to overstate [what it means] when people go out of their way like that. It kind of informs what I do now. I send a lot of packages to people inside. A lot of times in the beginning of people's sentence when they are facing the ennui and the crushing dread of starting their bit, I will send them a fat package.

The other PBP I got books from I think is now defunct. It was run out of Boxcar Books in Indiana. I had written them for a package. It was mostly because I had this idea that I could bulk up the Terre Haute CMU library. Like the Marion library it was almost all mass market. They sent me a package, but I realized that they probably had a lot of folks they needed to send stuff to. I was also told that I could not donate my books to the library because those books would eventually make their way out to the compound. So, I stubbornly lent them out and let people keep them or sent them home because I could then donate the ones I didn't want to Books Through Bars, which is what I ultimately did. In general population I could just put them on the shelf, but not in the CMUs. When I was in general population, I would make copies of the National Prisoners Resource List and leave them where I could. I know that people found them and used them because I was told [by a PBP] that they just started getting requests from Sandstone.

Can you tell me a little about that? What was the response when other people got books?

What I found was a very sad thing, and it fuels what I am doing right now. What I found . . . is that you have this embarrassing situation where your name gets called a lot, and the cops get mad at you and seem weirdly jealous, and they kind of stoke shit with other incarcerated people. When you go to mail call with 120 people, and only 6 people get mail, it's just like [grimace]. People get books, but not as much as you think. You think, like, my PBP is so busy it must be ubiquitous, but it isn't. To be honest, I never feel like these programs are utilized as much as they could be. Getting a book is kind of like Christmas. . . . You get a thrill. It's amazing. One of the coolest packages I got was when I got another person inside to get me a book about Rod Coronado by trading them some commissary items. I had tried to get it, but they [prison guards] wouldn't let it through.

So, did you experience issues of censorship other than that one book?

Oh yeah. I have a whole file of stuff they rejected. I would say I experienced pretty significant censorship of my political reading. When I was in general population, my mail went through [monitoring], but it was not being read by the Counterterrorism Unit (CTU), which is in Martinsburg, West Virginia.[3] Once I was sent to the CMU, the CTU was in charge of [reading my mail]. In the CMU your mail gets scanned and sent to the CTU, and they determine whether it is approved or not. Sometimes some of the books I got did not have a sneak peek available online, so they would send them to CTU, but CTU hid their role, so all rejections were signed by the prison warden. It made it nearly impossible to challenge. It turned into a litigation nightmare. I felt like I couldn't get a lot of the stuff I wanted, but then there would be days when I could not believe certain books made it through. . . . I got a book called *Let Freedom Ring: A Collection of Documents from the Movements to Free U.S. Political Prisoners.*

Your position as someone who had volunteered with a PBP, then was incarcerated, and is now out and volunteering with a PBP again is . . . we'll call it special. You have seen all of the sides of it, that is what makes it interesting. What advice or suggestions for PBPs?

I was a hardcore nonfiction reader before I went inside. If you tried to give me fiction, I would be like, "I don't have time for that." Almost as soon as I was inside I wanted fiction. Your life is goddamned serious inside. You want some light fiction. You want some escapist reading. Fiction is really great for inspiring people to think beyond. People need something that is different from their life inside, which is really challenging at times. I wasn't really interested in sending packages of mass market before I went inside. My perspective shifted within weeks. I have fought with people over the years at PBPs because I understand that there is a general consensus that most book carts and libraries [inside] are chock full of mass market paperbacks. That said, your life in prison is nonfiction. It's a pretty hard nonfiction . . . it's a fucking horror sometimes. So, I don't believe in legislating what people should be reading in prison. We [at NYC's Books Through Bars] are not going to put all of our energy to mass market, but if somebody is asking for James Patterson—I might send them Truman Capote—but if we have James Patterson, I am also going to send them James Patterson. I like to send packages to people that are diverse. I like to send people gussied-up versions of the shit they are asking for, but I'll (also) send six mass markets.

I think PBPs need to be political. We got into the political realm because the governor was stopping books from going to like twelve different prisons. They had this thing called TV prisons. If they had cable, they weren't going to be able to get books. We pushed back on that, and we became core members of a coalition that sent like ten thousand postcards to the governor. We have to push back, or it is going to get to a point where people locked up in federal prisons are not going to be able to get books, and that is a real fucking problem. I also don't think we can exceptionalize PBPs. I want any group or family to be able to send in books.

In 1846, Henry David Thoreau, while walking in town, encountered the tax collector, who asked Thoreau to pay his poll tax. Thoreau refused and was jailed for the night, during which time he wrote the beginnings of the essay now published as "Civil Disobedience." An abolitionist, Thoreau refused to pay taxes to a government that sanctioned enslavement.

NOTES

1. "Special housing units are cells within a correctional facility (prison or jail), whereby inmates who break prison rules are confined to severe isolation. These units, also known as 'solitary,' the 'box,' 'bing,' or 'special housing units,' are often 6 × 9 × 12 feet cells where the majority of the inmates will spend their days confined for 23 hours, only being given, at most, 1 hour of recreation. Individuals placed in special housing [units] are denied access

to rehabilitative programming, including educational opportunities and communication with families and friends." Pamela Valera and Cheryl L. Kates-Benman, "Exploring the Use of Special Housing Units by Men Released from New York Correctional Facilities: A Small Mixed-Methods Study," *American Journal of Men's Health* 10, no. 6 (2016): 466–73.

2. "In 2006 and 2008, the Federal Bureau of Prisons (BOP) created Communications Management Units (CMUs), prison units designed to isolate and segregate certain prisoners in the federal prison system from the rest of the BOP population. Currently, there are two CMUs, one located in Terre Haute, Indiana and the other in Marion, Illinois. These isolation units have been shrouded in secrecy since their inception as part of the post-9/11 'counterterrorism' framework implemented by the Bush administration." From "CMUs: The Federal Prison System's Experiment in Group Segregation," Center for Constitutional Rights, October 13, 2021, https://ccrjustice.org/home/get-involved/tools-resources/fact-sheets-and-faqs /cmus-federal-prison-system-s-experiment-group.

3. For information on CMUs see Will Potter, "The Secret US Prisons You've Never Heard of Before," TED Talk, TED Fellows Retreat 2015, https://www.ted.com/talks/will_potter_the _secret_us_prisons_you_ve_never_heard_of_before. For more on Daniel McGowan's mail being reviewed by the Counter Terrorism Unit see Daniel McGowan, "Court Documents Prove I Was Sent to Communication Management Units (CMU) for My Political Speech," *Huffington Post*, April 1, 2013, https://www.huffpost.com/entry/communication -management-units_b_2944580.

HOW TO START A PRISON BOOKS PROGRAM

CREATING A PBP Drawn by Nic Cassette and Written by Moira Marquis

Good will has lots of dictionaries.

Dictionary

They are the most Requested book!

Donation bins can be setup in schools

local businesses

Churches

Libraries can be a great Source of books

or hold a book drive

BOOK DRIVE!

Colleges are a great place to solicit books

be sure to get a wide variety of reading levels

6 Get a space

If you have a Room in your house that can hold bookshelves This is a great place To start!

Your partner bookstore May also have a space.

It's important that whatever you have is as close to Rent-free as possible

Nope

contract X

Although it is alluring to have a great space, having to pay rent can sink the ship

7 Get materials together! you will need: paper to wrap packages | paper Tape

sharpies | scissors

Printed invoices | wish you wer... ...he

Post cards!

Return labels are handy but Not required

Stamps can be used in lieu of return labels and you can stamp the inside covers of the books...

Postcard Stamps are cheap!

...That way wherever the book ends up, folks will know they can write and re-quest more!

You should also print copies of National Prisoners Resource List/ State specific Resource List/PARC Resource list. They are highly requested. You can also ask for free copies of Prison Legal News!

8 Make sure you know your states' Restrictions.

B. Book MAIL

see the Berkeley's Prisoner Lit project Restrictions list which is updated every few months by PLP librarian Jessica

9 know how to look up incarcerated folks in state and Fed prisons

check the address every time because people get moved A LOT. Lost 3 returned packages Cost $$$

Once you get your first letters...

You can start holding packing parties. Most P.B. programs do these once a week

BUT if you're just getting started and don't have many letters, you can do it less often

Do keep in mind that some prior approvals are only good for 3-4 weeks after being issued. Though. Prior approvals need to be filled first! Packaging can be fun social times

Play some music bake some cookies and hang out with friends while you work!

Book should be wrapped in paper with the return address of the bookstore you're affiliated with and the person's prisoner number underneath their name...

Write the address for the prison just as they wrote it in the letter to you. Also include an invoice that indicates there is NO money due. (see example)

11) develop a system to organize the letters you get that need more attention!

Special Requests and Prior approval

Special Requests are letters that ask for specific skills training, a specific book in a series the person hasn't been able to get their hands on!!!

AUTO

or foreign language materials

HOW TO DO IT

basically anything you don't regularly get donated

these can be put aside untill you have money to buy them or find a doner!

Prior approvals are restrictions where prisons make people get approval for books signed by the warden or other staff before they can receive them

ally
You
warden

Sometimes they make you switch titles

Sometimes they only last for a certain period of times

They are a pain

"Prior approvals"

You need a system to keep track of them. Here are some ideas: a bulletin board where pending prior approvals are displayed...

"...a shelf for prior approvals where the books are rubber-banded together with the original letter.

a spread sheet on a computer or paper where the names, DOI# address and book titles are written down

Once you're up and running

getting letters and sending out books, you can focus on two important things: Getting money and letting foks know you exist

IF you're already partnered with a local bookstore then the people in your community likely know about you.

It's possible you're getting donations from the change jar there.

That's great, but you will need more money.... You know how it goes...

SO. Here are some ideas that accomplish both goals

PBK

Create a website. If you're not a tech savvy person use a website builder. Put your contact info and a mission statement.

1

174

You should include a donate button linked to your bank account. If you're into writing, you can also have a blog that talks about current issues and events related to incarceration.

2) Get on social media. Even if you're not a social media person, there are A LOT of people who are. Whatever platform you feel most comfortable with, you can cultivate a wider audience for your work through social media. It's amazing how many people will follow accounts working for good things in their area.

3) Have a public Packing Party

You will likely have a small group of core volunteers, but when the letters start pouring in it can feel overwhelming.

One great way to make a huge dent in an accumulating letter pile is to hold a packing party that invites people to participate just for a day. You can target:

A) college and high school students that need community service hours.

B) Church groups that want to give back

We've played chess games (if you're a wiz), played instruments (a classic)...

...posed as human statues

...juggled or...

...performed magic tricks

Staged mini puppet theaters...

...drawn sidewalk art...

...or staged sidewalk dance performances.

ART AUCTIONS

...You can hold a silent auction

If you are lucky enough to know talented artists who are willing to donate a peice or two of work...

Shhh

Bid

While art galleries are great places, you can also hold these at coffee shops, bars and resturants.

These are fantastic fundraisers because people are willing to pay alot of money for good art.

D food benifits IF Someone in your Program Works for a restaurant you can hold a food benifit at the restaurant.

See if you can get the owner to donate the space durring a time when the restaurant might normally be closed

PRIVATE PARTY

Plan a simple menu of one plate (Prefered due to low food cost and less prep time

or you can offer the choice of one of two appetizers one of two entress and two or three sides. Get other service industry and Program folks to volunteer. Keep food costs LOW.

If the restaurant serves alcohol you can offer the owner that all alcohol Sales go to the restaurant? Don't forget to make sure the clean-up is done well so that you can do it again.

Sometimes bars with Karaoke set-ups will let you have the Space and the door covers

e Karaoke Benifits all youneed is a space and a Karaoke machine! These are superfun events.

You can charge a cover and if possible Sell beer.

This is great because people can buy drinks and theres NO cleaning up!

KEEPIN' THE DREAM ALIVE: MAINTAINING YOUR PRISON BOOKS PROGRAM Julie Schneyer

"Guys, I think Prison Books might be dead."

When I made this declaration, it was 2017, and I was tired. For over a year I'd been dragging a deflated project along behind me, stubbornly hoping that one day it would spring back to life as long as I didn't officially give up on it.

I had good reason to hold out hope. Having been around for nearly two decades, Asheville Prison Books (APB) was an institution in our small radical community in our small southern town. Its longevity was no small feat for an all-volunteer project with a shoestring budget, no formal legal structure, and hardly more infrastructure than a pretty nice tape dispenser and a printer that occasionally worked.

But as the months went by and the stack of letters grew, I had to face the truth. We were a year behind on requests, we didn't hold regular meetings or public events, and volunteers rarely communicated with or even saw each other. I felt ashamed that this twenty-year-old project could die on my watch; nothing about it felt right, but it felt *true*—and it was long past time to stop pretending.

So, as I sat with comrades from another prisoner support project in town, some of whom had been involved with APB in the past, and made this pronouncement, my friends reacted with sadness and some surprise. After all, APB had been a mainstay for as long as anyone could remember.

"Yea, I think the project is ending. We don't have enough volunteers, we're like a year behind on letters, nothing is getting done." Instead of just shrugging and saying, "Bummer," some folks who were present that day decided to

ASHEVILLE PRISON BOOKS
DOWNTOWN BOOKS & NEWS · 67 N LEXINGTON AVE · ASHEVILLE, NC 28801

Logo for Asheville Prison Books

mobilize to get the project back on its feet. And just like that, this crucial act of solidarity opened a new phase in the project. The change didn't happen overnight, but bit by bit we got things on track. It took a year to arrive at a place of stability, and another to feel like we were thriving. By the time COVID-19 hit, APB was strong enough to withstand the challenges of the pandemic: the early shutdowns that prevented access to our office space, the small chaos of daily life turning upside down, the bewildering isolation that made it hard to get tasks done and harder still to contemplate the despair of our correspondents inside, who knew very well they had been left to live or die.[1]

The goal of this chapter is not to define monolithically what it means to do prison books work well—in part because our projects are simply too diverse for that to make sense. Rather, it is to encourage groups to consider what

Austin Reed was a free Black man, born in the 1820s in New York. Despite this, he spent most of his early life as a forced laborer, in prisons, and as an indentured servant. His memoir, *The Life and Adventure of a Haunted Convict*, is the earliest prison memoir by an African American. Lost for 150 years, it was published by Yale University Press after researchers discovered the manuscript in the archives.

doing the work well means *for them*, and to try to do that the best they can. For APB, it meant becoming a resource people inside could count on while continuing to function as horizontally as possible. What follows is a discussion of some of the ways we made that happen and how others might apply the lessons we learned to their own work.

Make Hard Choices for Accountability

Who is your project accountable to? Has your group ever explicitly discussed this?

It's an important question, particularly because many PBPs aren't formally accountable to anyone. The truth is that when APB's backlog of letters was a yearlong, no one ever called us out on it. It's important to take an honest look at who or what your group is accountable to and, if you find yourself falling short in this regard, to take steps to address it. Importantly, accountability doesn't always mean doing more. In fact, for us, reaching a meaningful relationship with accountability meant doing less, and this required us to make two painful decisions:

> We contracted our coverage area, dropping down from serving four states to just two. This was a tough choice, but it meant we would have half as much work to do in the future, so that if we ever managed to get caught up, we might actually be able to *stay* caught up, and that was important to us.

Of course, that left the question: How could we possibly catch up?

> The hardest choice we made was to clear out our backlog of letters. Eight months' worth of letters—yes, *we threw them away*. It felt awful. But it also occasioned the closest thing we ever had to an explicit conversation about accountability, which went something like this:

"We can't just *not* fill these requests!"
"We're not filling them now. They're just sitting in the box. It's been a year."
"But . . . it feels bad."
"It should feel bad. We are failing."

Once we acknowledged how deeply we were failing, we couldn't go back to pretending the current state of affairs was acceptable. Beyond its absurdity, our yearlong backlog reflected a dehumanizing belief, so common in spaces that provide resources to people without social and economic capital, that anything is better than nothing. While I understood the significant capacity

Flyer for Valentine's Day Fundraiser, Asheville, North Carolina, 2011

challenges we faced, I wanted to see us hold ourselves to a higher standard of community care.

So, in addition to contracting our coverage area and clearing out our backlog, we also adopted an ongoing accountability model. To avoid reaching this abysmal milestone again, we agreed that we would never carry a backlog of more than three months, and that the result of getting more than three months behind would be the destruction of letters. These changes gave us a concrete benchmark at which to aim, and the motivation to avoid destroying letters lent urgency to long-overdue tasks such as volunteer recruitment and training.

Consider Multiplying Your Connections

Many smaller PBPs function as extensions of a subculture or even just a friend group. For years, APB was composed of mostly young, mostly white anarchists or other left-radical folks, many of whom ran in the same social circles or collaborated on multiple activist projects. Affinity-based organizing of this sort can have a powerful impact while holding meaningful space for those involved, so if your group is achieving its goals by working in this way, kudos! Keep at it. But for APB, it was clear that subcultural outreach alone had become a losing strategy. To maintain accountability, we had to reach out to the wider community.

We started holding monthly volunteer orientations and packaging parties, which we advertised widely, not just via activist word of mouth.[2] The results of getting out into public were immediate and dramatic. It was as if our town had just been waiting for an invitation to the party, and now it was enthusiastically RSVP-ing "Yes!"

Of course, the prospect of bringing in new folks carried challenges and worries. First and foremost, it raised the question of whether it made sense to spend scarce time onboarding new people who might not stick around when experienced volunteers could use that time to get stuff done *now*. Holding regular public events was labor intensive, and the social and mental effort involved in recruitment can be draining, especially for introverts. And for groups that operate nonhierarchically, there is an additional challenge of modeling what engaged membership looks like without reinforcing the image that experienced volunteers are "in charge."

In the end, a small handful of people took on an immense amount of work for about a year to grow our core group. And despite making good progress, we still struggle with this because building relationships takes genuine effort. But our experience yielded a few insights that may reframe ways of thinking about recruitment to reveal its transformative potential: *connections multiply exponentially*. Because of the challenges discussed above, it may be tempting to throw in the towel on recruitment before ever really beginning. After all, if you add up the time and effort it would take to train the number of additional people you think your project needs, you could easily conclude that a handful of seasoned if badly burnt-out volunteers is more effective than a shifting cast of characters with little prior experience. Fair enough. But the thing is, *that's not actually how it works*. What we discovered was that over time, having twice the number of people didn't double our effectiveness; it *tripled* it.

This makes sense if you view people not as isolated individuals but as members of existing communities and networks. When new volunteers arrive and see people working cohesively together and getting stuff done, it increases the chance they will stick around and get their own friends and family involved. Some percentage will deepen their engagement, possibly becoming new core members or bringing a valuable perspective or skill set the group previously lacked. Even those who stay on the periphery or eventually cycle through expand the density and diversity of your project's connections, causing them to radiate outward. Over time, these connections organically call in more people and resources until the project takes on a kind of self-sustaining momentum that requires *less* from the core to function stably, not more.

Outreach is a two-way street. Facilitating these connections requires putting some basic communication infrastructure and process in place. Throughout our quasi-dormant years, APB had email and Facebook accounts that were functionally useless because no one knew the passwords. When we started doing public events again, we made new accounts and created a listserv to stay in touch with volunteers. Initially we saw these channels mainly as ways to message outward, but the directionality quickly flipped. These days, we receive far more messages than we send, with offers for everything from volunteer support to book and monetary donations, to opportunities for community engagement and collaboration. So instead of thinking solely in terms of "getting the word out," consider whether you are creating reliable and welcoming ways for people to get the word *in*.

It bears mentioning that responding to a stream of external inquiries is more labor intensive than one-way outreach, since you don't control the volume or content of the communication. Because of this, low-capacity groups are more likely to make flyers and post about events than they are to respond to incoming messages quickly or consistently. But when people reach out and don't get a response, they tend to move on and put their energy and resources elsewhere. Responding to email and social media on a regular basis takes work, but it's a powerful way to access potentially deep wells of support.

Plug in computers, not people. A lot of recruitment-related language feels dehumanizing to me: talking about "investing" in training volunteers or finding ways to "plug people in" represents people as interchangeable units of productivity. But recruitment does not have to be about simply reproducing worker bees; it can be about giving people a door to walk through and getting curious about what they are bringing with them. Centering values of autonomy and creativity in recruitment helps avoid instrumentalizing people. And encouraging volunteers to bring their own special ingredient to the mix may also make your project more dynamic, perhaps allowing it to expand in new directions such as a pen pal project, book club, policy research, or advocacy. If you simply insert people into existing tasks and structures, you may miss out on the unexpected benefits of multiplying connections.

Choose Structures That Work for You

Many people doing PBP work have criticisms of the role the nonprofit sector plays in co-opting and demobilizing radical grassroots movements, and I share many of these; however, I don't believe that being incorporated as a 501(c)(3) will either doom or save your project, and our decision to remain unincorporated has been a primarily practical one. APB doesn't need much money, so it just never made sense to do the paperwork. Fundraising should support your goals and culture, not be an end in and of itself. But if after weighing the pros and cons you believe incorporation offers the greatest benefit, that's fine. The one thing you should *not* do is let people who don't understand or participate in your work convince you to adopt a particular structure just because it seems like what you "should" do.

Making financial and legal decisions can be tough, but thanks to the recent explosion in mutual aid projects, there is a lot of *great information* out there breaking down the complexities of these considerations.[3] For those who decide to remain unincorporated, here are a few tips and things to consider:

- Communicate openly about the legal structure of the group so that participants understand what your structure is (or isn't) and why those decisions have been made.
- If the account holding the project's money is just a personal account under one or more members' names, make sure it is used solely for organizational funds so that all transactions are easy to track and account for without being mixed up in someone's personal finances.
- Be transparent about money. For instance, you could regularly update a cloud-based document with your bank balance or make quick financial reports at meetings.

Don't Overlook Group Process

When people ask me about the innerworkings of APB, they always want to know where we get our books from or how we raise money. But group process—how volunteers communicate and share responsibility—is by far the most important, if least sexy, aspect of running a PBP or any other group. While there is no silver bullet, a few things have made a big difference for us:

Have recurring meetings. Ongoing meeting space is crucial for building relationships, reinforcing internal accountability, and giving the project a feeling of cohesion. This is particularly important for PBP work, which is deceptively well suited to solitary and decentralized activity. Meetings are also a good volunteer development tool; that is, not all participants have to come to meetings, but when you notice a volunteer's interest and energy level is high, inviting them to participate in meetings can help solidify and expand their engagement by giving them an avenue to greater ownership in the project. Relatedly, an internal communication channel such as a listserv for core volunteers is a great support and supplement for recurring meetings, offering a place to build meeting agendas, send out reminders, and post notes afterward. It also helps build your core by providing space for discussion *between* meetings so that you don't miss out on time-sensitive opportunities or lose momentum on exciting new ideas.

Make (or discuss) your budget together. Budgets are, above all, planning documents. Looking at the money your group has spent in the past and talking about the money you're going to spend in the future help participants zoom out from the day-to-day of filling orders and printing return address labels to consider the project's larger goals and vision. At the end of 2019, APB did a simple financial analysis and budgeting exercise. We looked at a printout of our bank account transactions and did some simple arithmetic to arrive at an expense and income breakdown. We then looked at each category of previous expense and said whether we thought we'd need more, less, or the same amount next year. Then we asked if there were things we should stop spending money on entirely, or if we weren't dedicating resources to something we should be. As a result, we decided to budget funds for buying dictionaries to avoid running out. We also discovered that the collective member who created our website was paying for hosting it, and we decided to reimburse them for it.

Share information, share responsibility. In nonhierarchical spaces where people participate in self-determining and unstructured ways, roles are emergent and organic. This is broadly a good thing, but documenting and evenly disseminating information can sometimes go by the wayside. Uneven workloads can develop, and some individuals may assume disproportionate influence in decision-making or determining group direction.

The best safeguards against these tendencies have already been mentioned: regular meetings and internal communication channels. With these structures in place, people know where and when they can raise concerns about access to information or allocation of responsibilities. But this isn't always sufficient. Discussing the operation of daily activities tends to dominate

Recent fundraising event promotion

meetings, so checking in about de facto hierarchies or ingrained group culture may not always make it on to the agenda. For this reason, it is helpful to create space for reflection on group roles and dynamics. An end-of-year debrief or "look-back" offers an opportunity to get everything that is being done out on the table so the group can collectively evaluate whether to redistribute tasks and what would be necessary to achieve this (skill sharing, changes to meeting times or other logistical factors, etc.).

You Are Awesome

Most people who do PBP work feel some amount of tension inherent in the activity: namely, in trying to do something "well" while wishing it didn't need to be done at all. The reason PBPs exist is that our society engages in the mass caging of human beings, and that the captors have little interest in dedicating resources to anything that acknowledges or nourishes the humanity of their captives. In other words, whatever your group's metrics are for success, the

THANK YOU FOR THE TWO BOOKS YOU RECENTLY SENT ME. BOTH . . . ARE GOING TO BE MUCH OF A HELP FOR MY WRITINGS. JUST IN CASE I DIDN'T TELL YOU ON MY LAST REQUEST, I WRITE ESSAYS AND POETRY ABOUT MY LIFE IN EL SALVADOR AND HERE AS WELL. LIKE SO MANY SALVADORANS I WAS IN EL SALVADOR WHEN THE REBELS AND THE ARENA PARTY LIT THE COUNTRY ON FIRE. AND I WAS THERE WHEN THE EARTHQUAKE OF OCTOBER 10, 1985 DESTROYED EL SALVADOR. . . . IT IS GOING TO TAKE A WHOLE LOT FOR THE PEOPLE OF EL SALVADOR TO RECUPERATE FROM THESE WOUNDS. SO THESE BOOKS ARE SURELY GOING TO HELP ME UNDERSTAND NOT ONLY WHAT OCCURRED IN THE 80S, BUT ALSO COME UP WITH FRESH IDEAS TO HELP MY SALVADORAN PEOPLE.

context of mass incarceration ensures that keeping that dream alive means simultaneously confronting a nightmare. So, if you are doing this work, or are considering jumping into it, you are awesome. And if you are actively thinking about how to do it better, you're even more awesome. Please keep doing it the best you can—whatever that means to you—until every cage is empty.

NOTES

1. As of mid-2021, 2,700 people (that we know of) have died from COVID-19 behind bars, making the COVID death rate for incarcerated people *five times* that of the general population. See "COVID-19 in Prisons and Jails," Prison Policy Initiative, https://www .prisonpolicy.org/virus/.

2. Packaging parties are events where people gather to wrap and address books for mailing. Packaging is easy to learn, hands-on, and social, making it a perfect entry point for new volunteers!

3. Michael Haber, "Legal Issues in Mutual Aid Operations: A Preliminary Guide," Hofstra University Legal Studies Research Paper 2020–06, SSRN Scholarly Paper, ID 3622736, Social Science Research Network, June 2020, https://dx.doi.org/10.2139/ssrn.3622736.

STARTING A UNIVERSITY-BASED PRISON BOOKS PROGRAM: PAGES FOR INDIVIDUALS IN PRISON Julia Chin

In the fall of 2019, shortly after joining the Associated Students Human Rights Board, a student government group, our campus support adviser brought to our attention several boxes of unanswered letters from incarcerated people requesting books. The letters were from 2018, and the person who might have known more about their origin had already graduated. We took it on ourselves to go through these letters and respond. After finding additional letters stashed in a storage closet, we counted over nine hundred letters sent from late 2016 to early 2018. I assembled a group of six dedicated volunteers to help go through the letters. We spent every Saturday systematically reading, cataloging, and scanning letters.

We were hoping to reply to them but were held back by our lack of knowledge about books-to-prison projects and the sheer number of letters. We read each letter, entered pertinent information (such as name, location, requests) in Google Forms, and scanned and uploaded a digital copy. We wanted to make sure no letter was left behind, and through this process we became more familiar with what was being requested (a lot of legal advice, dictionaries, science fiction, and mysteries) and when the requests were made (ranging from nine months to two years prior). Throughout this year, our costs were relatively low, and we spent solely on office supplies and food for our workdays. We tried to connect with the previous person on the Human Rights Board who solicited the letters and the partner organization from which he sought the letters, to no avail.

One of the turning points was when we reached out to the Prisoners Literature Project (PLP) in Berkeley, and they helped answer some initial questions about what might be entailed in the response process. We had so many questions. We asked what kind of restrictions prisons had (they kindly sent their internal restrictions list for all fifty states). What was the "National Prisoners Resource List" that so many people were requesting? We learned it was a short, free, resource directory of prison books programs, legal advice, and nonprofits that could help after release for all fifty states. Should we attempt to contact the letters writers first, or just blindly mail book packages back? We were advised to make contact before mailing packages out since people are moved very frequently when incarcerated, and we learned how to look up the location of individuals in the system (https://inmatelocator.cdcr .ca.gov/ for California state prisons and https://www.bop.gov/inmateloc// for federal prisons).

By our second year we finally had a name other than "Prison Book Program," which was the Pages for Individuals in Prison (PIP) project. We also had a logo, twice the number of volunteers (increasing from six to twelve), and the greatest support resource: the PLP. At the beginning of the year, we had a tough, but honest, conversation among our members about the direction in which PIP should go. We had spent all school year, including a summer, reading, cataloging, and scanning letters, yet we still had many steps before we could fulfill these requests. For instance, we had not even made contact with the original senders of letters to see where they were located and if they still wanted their dated request. During our first year, we randomly selected letters from the more than nine hundred letters we originally cataloged and fulfilled their requests as best as possible. Out of the ten packages

THANK YOU SO MUCH FOR THE BOOKS. I AM SO GLAD THAT THERE ARE PEOPLE LIKE YOU WHO ARE SO WILLING TO TAKE TIME TO SEND BOOKS TO US. IT MAKES IT SO MUCH EASIER IN HERE TO HAVE SOMETHING TO READ. I ESPECIALLY LIKED THE BOOK ON SUICIDE PREVENTION THAT YOU SENT. IT COULDN'T HAVE COME AT A BETTER TIME. I HAVE DEALT WITH THOUGHTS OF SUICIDE FOR MANY YEARS AND SO HAS MY CURRENT CELLMATE. I HAVE ALSO DECIDED THAT WHEN I GET OUT OF PRISON, I AM PLANNING ON STARTING MY OWN PRISON LITERATURE PROJECT IN PHOENIX, ARIZONA TO SERVICE ALL THE PRISONS AND JAILS IN ARIZONA. THANK YOU FOR ALL YOU DO.

of books or letters, half of what we sent was returned to us, two of those had "inmate paroled" stamped on them, and we received two thank-you letters weeks later from two that were successfully delivered. One of the thank-you notes was so heartfelt, it made everyone in the group weep when we read it. Despite garnering the emotional response from volunteers, a return rate of 50 percent was grim and expensive. Additionally, we still did not understand how to properly pack books, we did not know how we would source the books, and we did not know once we got started on the project how we would take any future requests once our return address was out there. With some advice from PLP and other groups we were connected with, such as the Appalachian Prison Book Project and Ithaca College Books Thru Bars, we decided to scrap the existing project of nine hundred letters due to the gap in time between when the letters were sent and when we would be able to realistically respond. Instead, we moved forward with a trial training system with the Prisoners Literature Project. They agreed to forward batches of more recent letters to us that we could fill. So, for that year, PIP used PLP letters and protocols with a mix of books given from PLP's overstock and our own book drive. This change in direction was an important lesson that despite the best of intentions when starting a new program, sometimes your original goals are not attainable, and you must change course. Without the information gained about the short turnaround time needed from letters being received to being able to respond, as well as how to circumvent the bureaucracy of prison restrictions, we would not have been able to execute this new phase of PIP.

Framing PIP: Explaining Our Name, Mission Statement, and Logo

Our name, mission statement, and logo encapsulate how we saw ourselves connecting to a larger system and network. When it came to creating and designing these, we wanted to be purposeful in how we used language and defined ourselves. PIP had numerous discussions about not defining the group as strictly reformist, abolitionist, and so forth as to not alienate potential allies. Yet, we also wanted to make clear that PIP is not just about books or surface-level intervention. We had to strike the right balance between what our members believed and what is more broadly palatable to the university and community. In crafting our mission statement and logo, we wanted to focus on this balance while also being sure not to take a "savior" lens either. Instead, we viewed our purpose as an organization as a partnership

AS Pages for Individuals in Prison   Logo for Pages for Individuals in Prison

with people who were incarcerated. Shirin Assadian, a member of PIP from 2020–21, summed it up by saying:

> By prioritizing the agency and voices of incarcerated individuals, PIP empowers others by fulfilling their own literary requests and sharing resources that combat the unjust reality of the carceral system. PIP's emphasis on humanity and dignity is essential to its mission of defying a prison system that does not prioritize the well-being and rehabilitation of individuals.

Hence in our name, UCSB (University of California, Santa Barbara) Pages for Individuals in Prison, we used "people first" language, instead of using their situation as their only identifier. Our mission statement also reflects this: "Sharing books as a source of knowledge, inspiration, and refuge with people who are incarcerated to combat the inhumane and alienating reality of the carceral system." Furthermore, our logo focuses on the growth, renewal, and new horizons that come from the knowledge derived from reading. We wanted to use earth tones such as greens and yellows to stay grounded and connected.

PIP knew that we could not change an entire system overnight, or even within a year. But we hoped that being thoughtful and intentional with our actions toward the work we do and how we treat each other does make a difference in countering the inhumanity of the incarceration system. Take it from one of PIP's current members, Montse Granados, who put it best:

> As a collective, PIP's integrity and intentionality is essentially what is at the foundation of our work. It really allows us to slow the process down and ensure we uphold our values. I feel as that translates to gratitude we are reminded of the fact that we are all humans maneuvering around and through the carceral state. With that, it really makes the work we do even more special!

How to Start a University Prison Book Project

The four essential parts needed to begin any prison book program are as follows: volunteers, funding, space, and books. Running a university-affiliated prison book program provides unique opportunities and challenges in securing these four things. Recruitment was simple enough the first year and even easier the second year when we became more well known. Since PIP is a subcommittee of the Human Rights Board, I was able to get approval to send out volunteer recruitment emails to academic major email lists. I could also get flyers reposted on the Human Rights Board social media platforms (which already had a substantial following and even led to reposts by other organizations). Most crucial to our volunteer recruitment was being able to send an email to the people in the honors program, who were required to complete volunteer hours. In our first year, all six volunteers were recruited from the honors program. Side note: due to the nature of the academic year, with breaks and examination weeks, students are only available to work a fraction of the year. At UCSB, we only worked approximately twenty-four weeks out of the year due to our schedule, which is something to take into consideration as you create expectations of your volunteer capacity. Lastly, due to the relatively short time students spend at a university, volunteer turnover can be high, and some projects fall to the wayside year to year. PIP is lucky to have a campus support adviser that can help assist with the transition periods and serve as a resource to help keep the longevity of a project going. This is crucial as the initial lack of consistency is how the original 944 letters became unanswered.

Another pro that comes with being affiliated with an already established student government group is funding. At UC Santa Barbara, every student pays a flat "Associated Students" fee, and our parent board gets a cut of this, from which they allocated a certain amount for PIP's use. For PIP, the funding comes from students, not the state or federal

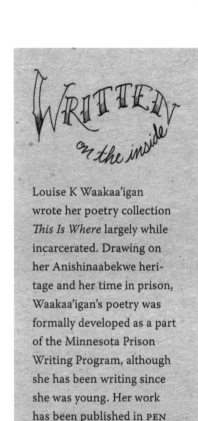

Louise K Waakaa'igan wrote her poetry collection *This Is Where* largely while incarcerated. Drawing on her Anishinaabekwe heritage and her time in prison, Waakaa'igan's poetry was formally developed as a part of the Minnesota Prison Writing Program, although she has been writing since she was young. Her work has been published in PEN America's *21: Mythologies*, *The Moon Magazine*, *Doors Adjacent*, *27th Letter*, *Words in Gray Scale*, and *The Asian American Writers' Workshop: A World without Cages*.

A glimpse into our packing days!

government, unlike other universities. Due to our unique student-funded status, we have an obligation to be transparent in how we spend the money. PIP has had the privilege of getting fully funded, which means we do not have to devote precious time and resources to fundraising.

Despite many attempts to change it, PIP did not have an office space for the first two years. This obviously poses some logistical problems when it comes to storing hundreds of books. As suggested by Ithaca College Books Thru Bars early in the year when we first connected, we adapted an "Adopt-A-Box" scenario where volunteers stored a box (or in reality, 3–7 boxes) in their homes. Given the state of COVID-19 and campus being shut down, we were not even able to meet in person until a third of the way through our second year. We met in a centrally located outdoor space undergoing every safety precaution possible to pack books. A substantial amount of time spent during our packing days was spent unloading, sorting, and cleaning up boxes of books at the end of the day. For this reason, I strongly suggest securing a dedicated campus space to pack books or, at the very least, storage space for books before you begin a prison books program. If you are unable to, you can still pack up books, but it causes some logistical problems that can be difficult to overcome. At the start of PIP's third year, we were finally able to secure permanent campus storage space, only after almost losing our whole library of books when we were unable to find storage over the summer months until the last possible minute. We secured this space through years of repeated networking with other university groups and the Associated Students president and director showing how vital these university connections were. Now with this space, the team can move forward and continue to expand.

As a university-affiliated program, we serve as a great resource connecting the student body to a much larger movement of which they may not have been previously aware. We can bring knowledge about prison books programs, at the very least, through our name. Additionally, we were able to source most of our books through a community book drive that resulted in over three hundred books. We utilized a campus-wide email distribution list that we were able to access, with the approval of the executive director of Associated Students, to publicize drop-off locations. We included the list of standard restrictions and were pleased that over 95 percent of the books donated were in usable shape. Part of the success of our book drive was having a centrally located contact-less drop-off bin at our University Center (a central building on campus) and boosting awareness by having other influential student groups repost and help support it. This proved to us how students who weren't necessarily volunteers could contribute greatly to this movement. Even while navigating the challenges of a pandemic in our first year sending out packages, we were able to find allies and campus partners who believed in our mission.

Leadership, Board Organization, and Self-Care

I was lucky enough to be the director of PIP for two years before graduating. With more time came the opportunity to be more reflective and thoughtful in my actions with help from the group and our campus support adviser. In the second year when we transitioned projects to respond to the letters that PLP forwarded, we were mindful about creating a process that was healthy and sustainable enough to maintain. We focused on the personal connections from answering the letters with books. If someone had a powerful letter, we all would stop what we were doing and listen as they read it aloud to the group. We were generous in managing our own expectations as we navigated the book-packing process for the first time during a pandemic. We created connections with each other before we even started working on PIP tasks by starting each meeting with a check-in question or icebreaker. It was intentional to be honest with ourselves when we struggled and when we needed help. All these lessons contributed to avoiding burnout. Our adviser, Tim, put it best:

> Me personally, I don't want to, you know, squeeze students for all they got for their time that they're with me. That's not at all the model that I would want folks to have. I don't want folks to be burnt out and unhealthy because of the work. . . . *I think that they still can accomplish a bunch of really good things if done in ways that center care* for the participants.

After a morning or several hours of packing, we would all eat lunch together and reflect. In the administration meetings afterward, we would share what went well in packing and what could be amended to make things simpler. There was no penalty for skipping any meetings or not showing up for a packing day, unlike other college clubs or activities.

While I may have been the director of PIP in name, we operated under the assumption that leaders are facilitators. As a result, it didn't matter if someone had a leadership role or was a general member—everyone had an equal opportunity to contribute. People could start whatever tasks they wanted if they had the initiative. When I was director, taking a step back and not micromanaging volunteers fostered more of a lateral, rather than a hierarchical, approach to meetings. We had two kinds of meetings. One was administrative meetings online over Zoom, where we worked out the details of running the program, and the second meetings were book-packing days. For the administration meetings, I created agendas that had talking points, but the group was the one to make decisions, and they could bring their own items to the agenda. Our board structure was unique because people supported where they wanted to and were needed, but certain people had specific roles that were delineated depending on what needed to get done. We had an "internal affairs coordinator," who facilitated our book drive and campus partnerships, and an "administrative coordinator," who helped me keep track of ongoing projects, just to name two examples. I'm including one

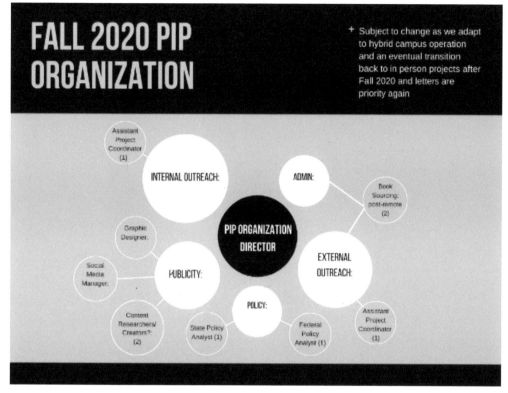

Infographic of PIP membership organization

early graphic of our membership organization, but we ended up scrapping most of it and creating roles as we went.

In the third year of PIP, roles adapted and changed again and will continue to do so as time goes on.

Final Thoughts

Founding PIP was not the easiest activity or job in which I participated in college, but it was the most worthwhile one. If you are considering starting a prison book project at a university, I highly encourage you to find a dedicated crew to work with. PIP would not have been able to find the success it has so far without the connections made between volunteers, within the university, with other prison books programs, and, most importantly, with the people behind the letters we are responding to.

Special thanks to Shirin Assadian, Montse Granados, and Timothy Grigsby for providing quotes for this chapter as well as Shirin Assadian, Mina Nur Basmaci, Montse Granados, Timothy Grigsby, and Sydnee Hoang for their help in creating the initial chapter outline. PIP would not have been possible without the support from the UC Santa Barbara Associated Students Human Rights Board, Peter Esmonde and the Prisoners Literature Project, and every single student volunteer who gave so much energy to this project. Finally, to the people who wrote the original 944 letters that started this project and every single one we've received since, we see you and will continue the fight to share literature and knowledge as a form of resistance.

THE FUTURE OF PRISON BOOKS

DRAWING BY WILLIAM ROSENCRANS

FORBIDDEN KNOWLEDGE
Kwaneta Harris

The Lonestar State wants to control women's bodies, but the abortion ban is not the only way.

It's 6:07 a.m. Out my window, I see the lady from the mailroom walking with a full cart of items. I skip the five steps to the door of this cell and announce, "Mailroom!" Everyone is excited. When I get books, I'm like a six-year-old on Christmas morning. In solitary confinement, the only pleasure I have is reading. Living in a cell the size of a parking space without a television, tablet, phone, or air-conditioning and an only temperamental radio signal, a book is more than entertainment and a much-needed distraction. It is a rare moment when I'm not reminded where I am. The average stay in solitary is seven years. I'm at five and a half.

People in solitary aren't allowed to go to the prison library. For some reason, we still receive the (rendered useless) library catalog. If we have been discipline-free for ninety days, we qualify for one book a week, delivered from the library. It's easy to receive an infraction. Examples include sharing reading materials or food with neighbors, covering your windows to block the blazing sun during triple digit temperatures, or questioning guards. Whether we request a specific book and author or a generic mystery, romance, or humor book, the librarian always sends a Christian-themed book. In 2018, I asked her, "Why don't you give me what I request?" She said, "I'm called to save your heathen soul." I'm locked in this cell twenty-three to twenty-four hours a day. Solitary confinement is where we need the books the

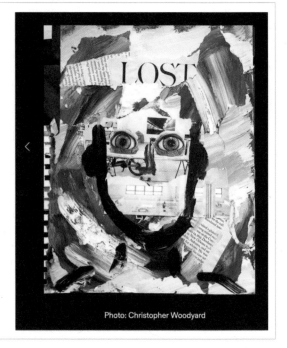

man looking into a mirror, in
despair after 15 years in solitary
confinement
—
For Rafael (NY)

REQUEST #91

An inmate standing and looking into a mirror and see a frail, eyes
sunken with pain and tears rolling down his face, while holding a
past photo of himself smiling, hair combed, primped, healthy
looking. The cell in disarray, 2 food trays not eaten. A calendar
depicting 15 years in S/C. a CO voice coming through the cell door
saying "no mail again". In the trash can showing a discarded Bible.

SPECIFIC INSTRUCTIONS

The photograph should depict a scene of despaired, depression,
given up on life, physically, mentally and spiritually. The cell door
should be made out of cinder blocks.

LOST

Photo: Christopher Woodyard

Art for Photo Requests from Solitary, an ongoing project that invites men and women held in long-term solitary confinement in U.S. prisons to request a photograph of anything at all, real or imagined, and then the organization finds an artist to make the image.

most. Yet, prisons put up innumerable barriers for people in solitary to receive books.

A recent example: we all heard the rumors, via CNN (Convict News Network) also called the grapevine, that the mailroom posed a "No Sexually Explicit Material" notice in General Population. Nobody paid attention to it. We thought, "That's for male prisoners." There isn't a market for partially nude celebrity photos in women's prisons. Little did I know how extreme this notice was to be enforced. In fact, its enforcement redefined "sexual."

A week prior, I was denied my *Good Housekeeping* magazine because of a supposedly sexually explicit image. In instances like this, they don't rip out the offending page. Instead, the entire magazine is denied. The thing is: the image was an advertisement for Depends—the adult diaper. It displayed an older woman wearing a Depends undergarment—which was deemed sexual.

My *usa Today* was also rejected due to a supposedly sexual image—Simone Biles, the Olympic gymnast, wearing her gymnastic leotard. The *New York Post* was also denied because it contained content regarding former governor Cuomo. *Allure Magazine* was denied because of a pregnant woman whose belly was exposed and painted with body paint. A bikini-clad model advertising a protein drink led to various magazines—*Vanity Fair, cg, Esquire, Cosmopolitan*—being denied. The decision is final, and I can't appeal. These bans are a result of all men at the table. It's hard to believe a woman of any race, age, political ideology, or religion would think a mature woman wearing incontinence underwear would be a sexual image for another woman to view.

But I'm not thinking about any of that as the mail lady approaches my door. I'm bouncing off the walls with anticipation. I'm hopping from one foot to the other. I notice my four books in a neat stack. She pushes a yellow carbon form through the gap in the door as she says, "I'm sorry. You're denied all four books." The art book is apparently sexually explicit. The book on menopause includes "sexual images." The book I wanted on healing from

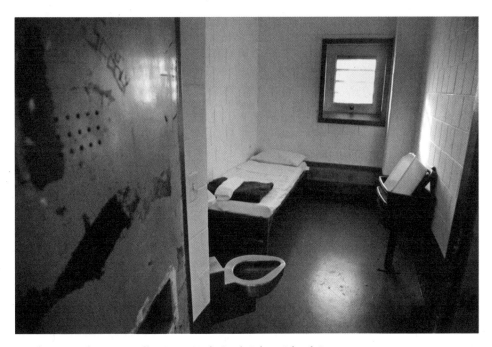

A solitary confinement cell in New York City's Rikers Island, January 28, 2016. Bebeto Matthews, the Associated Press.

childhood sexual trauma contains terms the prison has prohibited: "rape," "sexual assault," "sexual harassment," "sexual abuse," and . . . "sex." The book on prison abolition is denied because it would "incite violence." My mouth falls, and I realize my hand is wet with tears, already freely flowing. They can imprison our bodies but not our minds, or so I thought.

I don't read books. I completely immerse myself in them. As an only child, books were my companion. Inside my relationship with books has grown even stronger. I imagine alternate endings and visualize myself beside the characters. Books also build community with others who are locked up. We share books. We debate the plot and characters. Reading is how I remain sane in an environment designed to make people insane. Books matter just as much for people who don't or can't read as they do for those of us who do. Countless times I've stood at the adjoining vent until my feet were numb, reading aloud by streetlight to cell neighbors. Once the book has made the rounds, I donate it to the library. We call it "donating to the Bermuda Triangle" because you'll never see a donated book in your own prison library. We're told the books go to Huntsville, Texas, where they're redistributed to various other prisons.

Prior to solitary, my cellmates would hear me chuckling as I read and ask me to read aloud. It became a routine we called "story time." During that time, I lived in the "longtimer" dorm—a place reserved for people with a minimum of fifty-year sentences. The longtimers who wanted to learn or improve their reading were forbidden from attending the prison-offered schooling. The state doesn't see the value in teaching a person with a life sentence who's ineligible for parole, or who's serving three life sentences, to read. Many people inside struggle with reading, but shame and embarrassment forces some to choose even solitary over the embarrassment of being recognized as a struggling reader. I remember a lady named Tameka. She's been incarcerated since she was fourteen and was reading at a level where she only recognized sight words. One day, she was talking in her reading class, and the teacher reprimanded her saying, "If you shut up maybe you can learn to read." The class giggled. Tameka was twenty-five, and she immediately began doing anything to get placed in solitary. That was her last day in class. She would rather be in solitary than be embarrassed because she hadn't been taught how to read.

I couldn't do my time without reading. Usually, I hear about a book I'm interested in by listening to NPR or reading a review in a magazine. First, I write the prison mailroom to determine if the book and author are approved by the state. If so, I place it on a list I have for friends and family to purchase as gifts for holidays and special occasions. It's not a fail-safe. I've had books arrive, and the status has been changed from approved to denied. No appeal is permitted. Sometimes it's the mail lady who flips through pages at the door to your cell and reverses the decision. A neighbor could order the same book a week later and have a different mail lady who permits the book. It's within their discretion. If they won't let me have a book, I'm given a choice. They can destroy the book, or I can pay to send the book to someone on the outside. I'm lucky. I can usually afford to send them home. This involves purchasing a large envelope and eight to ten stamps per book. People inside can only purchase thirty stamps every two weeks. Spending ten stamps to mail one book is a big deal. Not everyone can do this. Times are hard. No one has money to waste.

The culture wars and political divisiveness have affected us in many ways in prison. Many of the books I read just a few years ago are now restricted under a new category termed "promotes racial division." I believe this is a by-product of the Black Lives Matter movement.

History warns us of the dangers of banning books, but the effects of information control on imprisoned women are intimate and profound. The majority of women living in solitary confinement were transferred from juvenile prison. At that age, talking back to prison staff or arguing about their treatment would be punished with time-out. However, once people turn seventeen, talking back or arguing earns a new charge and conviction of assault. This results in additional sentence time and transfer to solitary confinement in an adult prison. Being an adult in prison paradoxically means even less freedom. Many women in solitary were therefore in juvenile facilities when their menstruation began, which means that many incarcerated women don't have basic knowledge about our bodies and how they work. We don't have Google. Books that can answer these questions are banned—as they are deemed "sexual." This leaves not just younger women but my fellow menopausal friends and me to fall back on what was and often continues to be taught in public schools—the abstinence and fear-based lessons that boil down to three commandments: Don't touch your privates; don't touch other's privates; don't let others touch your privates. Following these rules makes people perfect victims for sexual predators and preventable illnesses. It's misinformation masquerading as education. The Lone Star State isn't satisfied by banning abortions to control women's bodies. It's also forbidding us knowledge needed to prevent one.

THE HIGH COSTS OF FREE PRISON TABLET PROGRAMS Valerie Surrett

In 2021, the Texas Department of Criminal Justice (TDCJ) announced a new tablet contract with Securus Technologies, a subsidiary of Aventiv Technologies (which also owns JPay). As in most free tablet contracts, Securus agrees to provide tablets for all eligible people incarcerated in Texas jails and prisons at no cost to incarcerated people or the state. In exchange, Securus will charge users a fee to send or receive emails, phone calls, and video calls or download premium content, such as movies, games, and music. The tablets, which use a secure internal network and do not have internet access, will include some free content, such as religious, educational, and law resources, and a limited selection of ebooks.

Texas is the latest in a growing number of states to implement "free" tablet programs in recent years. From the TDCJs' perspective, the partnership with Securus is a win-win. In addition to providing tablets at no cost to the TDCJ, Securus shoulders the total cost of installation and maintenance as well as any infrastructure upgrades needed to accommodate the widespread use of secure-network tablets. Bryan Collier, executive director of the TDCJ, identifies several potential benefits of the tablet program to incarcerated users, including expanded access to resources and educational materials, more frequent contact with the outside world, and increased technological literacy. Each of these benefits correlates with lower recidivism rates and suggests the program is congruent with nationwide prison reform efforts. TDCJ representatives are also optimistic that increased access to email will relieve pressure on overstrained and understaffed prison mailrooms, reducing the occurrence of contraband items entering prisons and jails through the mail.

Tweet from APBP informing readers on the use of tablets inside prisons.

Users can also file grievances through tablets, and tablets open the possibility of telehealth programs and increased access to online higher education programs in the future.[1]

At first glance, free tablet programs seem like a step forward, finally pushing antiquated incarceration practices into the twenty-first century at the mutual benefit of the incarcerated, departments of corrections, and prison industries—all with the oh-so-appealing tagline: "at no cost to taxpayers." Advocates of free tablet programs have a point; the introduction of tablets could bring life-changing benefits to incarcerated people. Unfortunately, current free tablet programs rely on predatory contracts between departments of corrections (DOCs) and two juggernauts of prison industry, Aventiv

OCTOBER 11, 2002
THIS LETTER IS NOT A
REQUEST FOR BOOKS, BUT
RATHER A DECLARATION
OF GRATITUDE FOR ALL
OF THE ASSISTANCE THAT
YOU HAVE GRACIOUSLY
PROVIDED THROUGH THE
YEARS. THANKS TO YOU, NOT
ONLY HAVE I MASTERED THE
ENGLISH LANGUAGE, BUT
CREATIVE WRITING AS WELL.
AND NOW—WHILE I MAY
NOT BE ANOTHER STEPHEN
KING OR LOUIS L'AMOUR—
BOTH MY KNOWLEDGE
AND SKILL HAS SOARED;
AND, MORE IMPORTANTLY,
DELIGHT IN HELPING OTHERS
EXTEND THEIR MINDS
BEYOND THE LOCKED DOORS
AND RUSTED IRON BARS. FOR
THIS, I SIMPLY WANTED TO
SAY, " THANK YOU! " FROM
THE HEART.

(Securus and JPay) and Global Tel Link (GTL). These companies have long histories in prison communications, histories checkered by charges of exploitative practices. Tablets do offer the incarcerated unprecedented access to their loved ones as well as new ways to fill time inside, but these benefits come with steep prices to the incarcerated and their families. The tablets may be free, but using them isn't. Users are charged exorbitant rates for technologies and services that are usually free for citizens who aren't locked up, and prices for games, movies, and music are often much higher than fair market value. Seeing as the average wage range for non-industry prison labor is $0.14–0.63 per hour in states that pay incarcerated people for the work they do (Texas, Georgia, Alabama, Florida, and Arkansas do not pay wages), free tablet programs divert the costs to the families of the incarcerated.[2]

The Price of Free

Tablet contracts between DOCs and prison communications companies vary by state, making it difficult to assess overall costs to the incarcerated; however, most contracts share a set of common features. The Prison Policy Initiative studied twelve free tablet contracts since 2017 and concluded that most "guarantee the Department of Corrections a portion of tablet revenue," "allow tablet providers to alter the prices of services—such as email, music and money transfer—without state approval," "allow providers to terminate tablet services if the tablets aren't profitable enough," and "exempt providers from replacing a broken tablet if they think it was 'willfully' damaged—a loophole ripe for exploitation, as prison tablets are cheaply made and break easily."[3]

Commissions paid to DOCs vary widely by state. For example, Colorado DOC (GTL contract) receives an annual flat payment of $800,000; Connecticut DOC (JPay contract) receives a 10–35 percent commission on replacement technology, accessory sales, email fees, media downloads, and subscriptions; Missouri DOC (JPay contract) earns a 20 percent commission on entertainment media purchases; and West Virginia Division of Corrections and Rehabilitation (DCR) and Indiana DOC (GTL contracts) receive a commission on all gross revenue, 5 percent and 10 percent, respectively. Contracts that

APBP
@AppalachianPBP

···

"Free" tablets in prisons come at a significant cost to users and their families, making it more difficult to access books. Here's how you can help:

appalachianprisonbookproject.org
The Cost of "Free" Prison Tablets - Appalachian Prison Book Project
Prisons across the country have started offering "free" electronic tablets to people behind bars. But these devices contain hidden costs. Learn more here.

3:04 PM · Nov 20, 2019 · Twitter Web App

Tweet from APBP informing readers on how they can help incarcerated people maintain access to books.

include revenue sharing funnel money paid by the incarcerated and their families back into the systems that incarcerate them. Such contracts also discourage DOCs from advocating for fair pricing on behalf of incarcerated people. The higher the rates for emails, video calls, and movies, the more commission the DOC receives. Revenue-sharing contracts that also allow the contractor to terminate the contract if expected profits aren't met place DOCs in a bit of a double bind in which low revenues threaten their ability to make any commission.

Prices for email and video chat services also vary by contract. According to JPay's website, sending and receiving emails cost one "stamp" per page of text. The average cost of a stamp is $0.35. Adding a picture to an email costs one additional stamp. Adding a "videogram" costs an additional three stamps. A thirty-minute video call costs $3.95. GTL contracts include prices for emails ranging from $0.25 to $0.47. Unsurprisingly, media download prices vary as well. Song download prices can range from $0.99 to $9.99 and audiobooks from $0.99–19.99. Some GTL contracts offer media subscription services, such as a music-streaming service for $24.99 per month,[4] but as noted by *Prison Legal News*: "GTL's music service costs twice as much as Spotify or iTunes for less than one-tenth the number of available songs. And with video games usually available outside prison for no more than $8 each, two months' worth of GTL's gaming fees could pay for all eight of the most popular games available from the Google app store."[5] JPay has recently introduced a $5.00 monthly subscription for its SecureView tablet, and the free tablet contract between Securus and Dallas County lists a $5.00/month rental fee for tablet use.[6]

Most contracts mention the availability of e-books, and both Securus/JPay and GTL reference generous e-book offerings on their websites. Both companies have also expanded access to a limited number of free e-books in the face of public pressure to curb the steep cost of book downloads and price-per-minute reading charges on prison tablets. However, neither company is forthcoming about what books are available and how many. While some GTL press releases boast availability of thousands of free e-books, stories have emerged, such as a story from Allegheny County (Pennsylvania) Jail, of jails banning physical books completely and limiting incarcerated people's access to reading materials to the 241 free e-books and 49 free religious texts available on GTL tablets.[7]

Same Old Story with a New Name

In important ways, "free" tablet contracts represent the next generation of predatory contracts between DOCs and prison communications conglomerates Aventiv and GTL. The prison phone business currently generates $1.4 billion in profits each year,[8] and the history of exploitative prices for phone calls within prisons is long and well documented. In 2015, the FCC moved to cap price-per-minute rates after reporting exposed phone rates reaching upwards of $1.00 per minute. Prior to the FCC capping, a 15-minute phone call in many states came with a $5.00 price tag. In addition to per-minute rates, incarcerated people and their families are often charged connection fees, voicemail fees, and fees for loading money onto prepaid debit and phone cards used for calling. In a 2015 letter to the Federal Communications Commission (FCC) signed by fifteen U.S. senators, the authors claim "in extreme cases, when all associated fees are incorporated in the aggregate cost, a phone call can cost as much as fourteen or fifteen dollars for a single minute."[9] Though the letter prompted the FCC to act, capping rates in state and federal prisons to $0.11 per minute and rates in jails to $0.14–0.22 per minute, the FCC reversed its position two years later under the leadership of Trump appointee Ajit Pai.[10] The Prison Policy Initiative, writing in 2019, shows that exorbitant phone prices in jails are still the norm, resulting in staggering costs to pretrial callers and their families. In Illinois, for example, the average cost of a fifteen-minute in-state call from jail in 2018 was $7.11, 52.7 percent higher than the average cost of a call from an Illinois state prison.[11]

Predatory prison phone contracts share a common feature with free tablet contracts: DOC commissions on revenues. In June 2021, Connecticut passed legislation making all phone calls from state prisons free, the first state to do so.[12] The legislation, which will undoubtedly benefit the incarcerated and their families, comes at a high cost to the DOC's budget. According to reporting by *The Atlantic*, Connecticut "had one of the highest prison-phone-call rates in the country" as part of its contract with Securus: "the state raked in a 68 percent commission on in-state calls from state prisons, which in 2019 translated to about $7 million."[13] A 2011 report by *Prison Legal News* claimed that, on average, prison communications companies paid a 42 percent commission on gross revenues to DOCs.[14] The Louisiana Department of Public Safety and Corrections (DPSC), under contract with GTL, received a 55 percent commission on the gross revenue of prison phone calls that year, a deal that generated $3.3 million dollars for the DPSC.[15]

Under JPay, Aventiv's reach extends beyond prison communications. JPay also offers banking services, including sending money to incarcerated loved ones—*for a fee*—and issuing "release cards," prepaid debit cards loaded with a person's remaining "inmate account" balance upon release from prison. Prisons with JPay release card contracts do not give

Civil rights icon Martin Luther King's "Letter from Birmingham Jail" (1963) is perhaps the most well-known letter or essay ever written from inside prison walls in the United States. "While confined here in the Birmingham city jail," the letter opens as M.L.K. addresses recent criticisms from white moderates of the civil rights movement. In this letter M.L.K. reminds us, "Injustice anywhere is a threat to justice everywhere." By the end of his several-page letter M.L.K. jests his letter "would have been much shorter if I had been writing from a comfortable desk, but what else is there to do when you are alone for days in the dull monotony of a narrow jail cell other than write long letters, think strange thoughts, and pray long prayers?"

Amanda Klonsky
@amandaklonsky1

Katy Ryan from the Appalachian Book Project, explaining the trend toward charging people in prison by the minute to read books on "free" tablets that are increasingly replacing access to books. "Can you imagine reading Don Quixote at 3-5 cents per minute?" #NCHEP2019

4:26 PM · Nov 15, 2019 · Twitter for iPhone

813 Retweets   **339** Quote Tweets   **1,244** Likes

Katy Ryan giving a talk on the cost of so-called free tablets.

incarcerated people a choice of whether to participate. Upon a person's release, they are given a JPay debit card with their remaining balance. JPay then charges high fees for checking the balance and making purchases, as well as monthly fees for inactive accounts and a fee to close the account. In October 2021, the Consumer Financial Protection Bureau (CFPB) found that JPay violated the Consumer Financial Protection Act as well as the Electronic Fund Transfer Act by charging people exorbitant fees "to access their own money on prepaid debit cards that consumers were forced to use" as well as "requir[ing] consumers to sign up for a JPay debit card as a condition of receiving government benefits,"[16] including "gate money," or funds provided by the state upon release from prison to help returning citizens purchase food, transportation, and other essentials. JPay was fined $6 million dollars for these violations.

The costs associated with free tablets add to the staggering costs of incarceration for people who are locked up. Free tablet programs are consistent with burgeoning trends to contract out prison services to private companies, invariably resulting in new costs to the incarcerated and their families. Most items a person needs to survive in prison must be purchased at prison commissaries or ordered through approved vendors at prices much higher than market value.[17] According to the Prison Policy Initiative, private companies reap a combined annual revenue of $2.9 billion for supplying commissaries and providing phone services.[18] These costs are often crippling to the families of the incarcerated. DOCs routinely justify privatizing prison services by quipping that the move will save taxpayers money. Unacknowledged in this sentiment is the fact that the families of the incarcerated, who by and large foot the bill for privatized products and services, are also taxpayers.

How APBP Got Involved — *Reading with a Meter Running*

In the fall of 2019, Katy Ryan, the founder of the Appalachian Prison Books Project (APBP), began researching prison tablet programs and their impacts after learning that the West Virginia Division of Corrections and Rehabilitation (DCR) had recently signed a free tablet contract with GTL. She quickly noticed a disturbing detail in the contract—a $0.05 per-minute standard fee for accessing reading materials, with an introductory discount bringing the cost to $0.03 per minute. We investigated further. The books offered on the tablets were exclusively from Project Gutenberg, an online archive of older texts that have entered the public domain and are now freely available to anyone with internet access. We did the math. For a person who can read thirty pages in an hour, reading George Orwell's *1984* would cost about $20. New paperback copies sell for $7.54 on Amazon. For strong readers, the price is exploitative. For new readers and readers with disabilities, such as dyslexia, the price is prohibitive.

Katy gave a presentation about prison tablets at the 2019 National Conference on Higher Education in Prison in St. Louis. During her presentation, she mentioned the per-minute charge for reading detailed in the WV DCR-GTL contract. Amanda Klonsky, who was in the audience, tweeted the stat, and the tweet spread. The next day, sitting in the airport, we began working on our first blog post, "How Much Does It Cost to Read a Free Book on a Free Tablet?," and a campaign was born.

Part of the reason our campaign caught fire, particularly among other prison books projects and groups that advocate for education in prisons, was because our exposure of the per-minute rate coincided with another trend prison books projects around the country were noticing; prisons were beginning to implement new book restrictions and occasionally banning donated books altogether. We already knew prisons were tightening approved book vendor lists, often limiting people's options for ordering books to one private vendor with limited selections and marked-up prices. A few states—Maryland, New York, Washington, and Pennsylvania—attempted to quietly implement complete bans on donated books after introducing tablet programs. Thankfully, all four states reversed course following successful campaigns to spread the word to the public, campaigns often led by prison books projects. Nonetheless, we all saw the writing on the wall. DOCs can easily offer free tablet programs as justification for crackdowns on physical books and reading materials in prisons and jails. Prior to free tablet programs, several prisons already had avenues for incarcerated people to purchase JPay and GTL tablets on their own, avenues that continue in states that have not yet signed free tablet contracts. The costs range from $70–140 per tablet with additional use fees. However, free tablet programs, which provide tablet access to the entire eligible prison population, can easily be invoked as justification for limiting donated books, as DOCs can point to free tablets as providing access to reading materials on demand.

K2 Spice, Liquid Meth, and Greeting Cards

The crackdown on donated books is part of a larger effort to eliminate paper entering prisons and jails through the mail. The reason? Primarily, K2 Spice (synthetic cannabinoids) and liquid meth, liquid drugs that can be sprayed onto paper and dried. The drugs have gained popularity in prisons and jails in recent years, and in response, DOCs and the federal Bureau of Prisons (BOP) have launched an all-out crusade to get them out of prisons. The front lines of attack: mailrooms and in-person visitations. The official line is that the majority of contraband drugs and cell phones must be coming in through in-person visitations and—especially liquid drugs—the mail, sprayed on cards, letters, books, and children's drawings.

As part of the effort to curb contraband entering through the mail, several state departments of corrections and the federal Bureau of Prisons now scan original mail and then print copies of the scans.[19] Incarcerated people are given the copies only. This includes greeting cards, handwritten letters from loved ones, photographs, and children's colorful drawings. Incarcerated people report that copies are poor quality, making it difficult to read handwriting or see faces in photographs. There is an added racial component in this regard, as people have reported that facial features of Black and brown people are especially difficult to see. Considering the disproportionate representation of Black and brown people behind bars, this is particularly troubling. Photocopies also remove the personal touch of letters, cards, and pictures. People can't run their fingers over the grooves left by pens held in loved ones' hands, or smell the wax of the crayons their children used to color purple oceans and pink suns. Scanning all mail also raises important legal questions about DOCS' and the BOP's practices of data collection and surveillance, especially in states such as Pennsylvania, where scanning and copying services have been outsourced to private, out-of-state companies.[20]

The DOCS' second strategy to curb contraband has been to limit or eliminate in-person visitations. Even before COVID-19, many jails and some prisons were limiting in-person visitations in favor of video visitations.[21] In 2016, NPR reported on Cheshire County (New Hampshire) Jail's switch to all video visitations, eliminating in-person visits. The superintendent of the jail, Richard Van Wickler, cited two reasons for the switch: less potential for contraband coming in through visitors and reduced staff time dedicated to strip searches before and after visits. Significantly, the elimination of all in-person visits was also a condition of the contract Van Wickler signed with Securus, a contract that stipulates the jail will receive a 20 percent commission on all revenues generated through video visitation fees, fees paid by the incarcerated and their families.[22]

Prison and jail staff deserve to work in a safe environment. However, the ends, in this case, may not justify the means. DOCS and the BOP have been less than forthcoming when pressed to provide data for the frequency of drugs and other contraband items entering prisons and jails through the mail or in-person visitations. Incarcerated people and prison staff have long reported that the majority of drugs and contraband that enter prisons and jails are brought in by staff. Texas may have unintentionally corroborated such allegations during the COVID-19 pandemic. Prior to the pandemic, Texas prisons had already implemented new mail restrictions, including bringing in more drug dogs and banning postcards, greeting cards, colored paper, and artwork and limiting photographs to ten per envelope.[23] During COVID-19, Texas prisons also eliminated in-person visits. The result? Despite limiting mail and eliminating in-person visits, the suspected culprits for drugs and contraband in prisons, the drug problem got worse: "The main source of the drugs, according to more than a dozen people who lived or worked in Texas prisons over the past year: low-paid employees and understaffed facilities."[24]

Like video visitations and scanning mail, tablets are also being touted by prison representatives as an offensive strategy in the war against drugs and contraband. If incarcerated people have easy (albeit expensive) access to email, perhaps their friends and family will send less mail, and perhaps they will be less tempted to purchase contraband cell phones. If they have easy access to reading materials, perhaps they'll need fewer physical books. To date, we do not know of a single incident of drugs or other contraband entering a prison or jail from a donated book mailed by a prison books project. That hasn't stopped prisons from including donated books in the growing list of dangers to staff and prison safety.

The Call for Fair Tablet Practices

APBP is not anti-tablet. We are pro-tablet, but anti-predatory contracts. Tablets in prisons could bring life-changing benefits to people locked up. Tablets could easily be used to give people free access to quality resources and services in addition to offering ways for them to speak to those they love more frequently. Tablets could be of particular benefit to people with vision problems and other disabilities. APBP frequently receives requests for large-print books. We hardly ever receive large-print book donations. Tablets, which allow users to change font sizes, could make reading possible for people who currently cannot read standard font sizes. This is particularly helpful in states with "one good eye" policies for imprisoned people that deny eye treatments and surgeries if the person still has one good eye.[25] And, of course, tablets could be instrumental in expanding access to higher education in prisons.

Those of us who are now able to email and video message our friends inside understand the power and potential of tablet access. What we are seeing, however, is that the introduction of free tablets is coinciding with moves to eliminate other things, such as original mail, in-person visitations, and, yes, books. Tablets should be affordable and should supplement existing services. Provide tablets *and* original mail, tablets *and* in-person visits, tablets

Current tablets by the prison communication company JPay

and donated books, tablets *and* in-person higher education opportunities, tablets *and* law libraries.

The reduction of original mail, in-person visits, and books, while ostensibly used as a strategy to reduce drugs and contraband, fits historical patterns of GTL and Aventiv contracts, from the companies' demands for exclusivity to the commissions DOCs receive from revenues generated. To date, we see no evidence that the free tablet programs will depart from Aventiv and GTL's exploitative modi operandi.

Prison Books Projects and Tablets

Prison books projects have a role to play in the coming days as more states will inevitably sign on to free tablet programs. Prison books projects have been instrumental in pressuring states to walk back bans on book donations, and APBP's tablet campaign pushed GTL to offer a limited number of free books on tablets in West Virginia prisons. More recently, several prison books projects joined a coalition including PEN America, the American Library Association, and forty-five additional "groups and individuals concerned with the rights and dignity of incarcerated people" to request that GTL and Aventiv Technologies drop tablet access fees during COVID-19 while most incarcerated people were locked in their cells for twenty-three hours a day.[26] Each of these campaigns garnered public support by using social media to inform the public of hidden prison practices.

Most policy changes that happen within prisons go largely unnoticed by the public. Details about prison contracts and prison practices are difficult to find, and press releases written by DOC and BOP representatives, such as announcements regarding free tablet contracts, generally don't divulge troubling minutiae. Prison books projects can, and should, make clear what is often hidden through social media campaigns and coalitions with other prison books projects, groups, and organizations dedicated to advancing the rights of the incarcerated and improving access to educational and reading materials.

We believe that education is a basic human right. We know that books are lifelines to people in prisons. We've seen that change can happen—albeit slowly and incrementally—when we engage the community in educational justice efforts. And, after seventeen years and over fifty thousand books mailed, we are still stunned by how difficult it can be to send a free book to a person who needs it. Free tablet programs are here, and more are coming. But we can keep telling people about the costs, we can keep exposing the connections to disappearing prison services, and we can keep demanding "tablets *and* books." It must be both.

NOTES

1. Jason Whitely, "110,000 Texas Prison Inmates to Get Computer Tablets with Apps, Radio, and Email," WFAA-TV, September 16, 2021, https://www.wfaa.com/article/news/local/texas /texas-prison-inmates-to-get-computer-tablets-with-apps-radio-and-email/287-cf570e10- 8b24-436c-a858-72a20882f94b; Earl Stoudemire, "Texas Inmates Soon Receiving Computer Tablets to Help with Rehabilitation and Reintegration," KFDA-TV September 27, 2021, https:// www.newschannel10.com/2021/09/27/texas-inmates-soon-receiving-computer-tablets-help -with-rehabilitation-reintegration/; "Tablet Program Coming Soon to the Inmate Population," Texas Department of Criminal Justice, https://www.tdcj.texas.gov/news/tablet_program.html.

2. Wendy Sawyer, "How Much Do Incarcerated People Earn in Each State?," Prison Policy Initiative, April 10, 2017, https://www.prisonpolicy.org/blog/2017/04/10/wages/.

3. Mack Finkel and Wanda Bertram, "More States Are Signing Harmful 'Free Prison Tablet' Contracts," Prison Policy Initiative, March 7, 2019, https://www.prisonpolicy.org/ blog/2019/03/07/free-tablets/.

4. Tonya Riley, "'Free' Tablets Are Costing Prison Inmates a Fortune," *Mother Jones*, October 5, 2018, https://www.motherjones.com/politics/2018/10/ tablets-prisons-inmates-jpay-securus-global-tel-link/.

5. Matt Clarke and Ed Lyon, "Tablets and E-messaging Services Expand in Prisons and Jails, as Do Fees," *Prison Legal News*, April 2, 2018, https://www.prisonlegalnews.org/news/2018 /apr/2/tablets-and-e-messaging-services-expand-prisons-and-jails-do-fees/.

6. "RFP Number 2019-064-6828 between Dallas County, Texas, and Securus Technologies LLC," *Prison Phone Justice*, https://www.prisonphonejustice.org/media/phonejustice /TX_-_Dallas_County_-_Securus_contract_-_2020-2025.pdf.

7. Charlie Deitch, "Fahrenheit 412: New Rule Bans Allegheny County Jail Inmates from Receiving Books; Reading Limited to 214 Select E-books," *Pittsburgh Current*, November 18, 2020, https://www.pittsburghcurrent.com/fahrenheit-412-new-rule-bans-allegheny -county-jail-inmates-from-receiving-books-reading-limited-to-214-select-e-books/ (site discontinued).

8. Rosalie Chan and Belle Lin, "The High Cost of Phone Calls in Prisons Generates $1.4 Billion a Year, Disproportionately Driving Women and People of Color into Debt," *Business Insider*, June 30, 2021, https://www.businessinsider.com/high-cost-prison-communications -driving-debt-racial-wealth-gap-2021-6.

9. KTVZ News Team, "Wyden to FCC: Cut Exorbitant Inmate, Family Phone Rates," *News Channel 21*, October 15, 2015, https://ktvz.com/news/2015/10/15/wyden-to-fcc-cut-exorbitant -inmate-family-phone-rates/.

10. Cooper Brinson, "FCC Caps Prison Phone Rates," Civil Liberties Defense Center, October 26, 2015, https://cldc.org/fcc-caps-prison-phone-rates/; Ann E. Marimow, "FCC Made a Case for Limiting Cost of Prison Phone Calls. Not Anymore," *Washington Post*, February 5, 2017, https://www.washingtonpost.com/local/public-safety/fcc-made-a -case-for-limiting-cost-of-prison-phone-calls-not-anymore/2017/02/04/9306fbf8 -e97c-11e6-b82f-687d6e6a3e7c_story.html?hpid=hp_local-news_prison-calls-330pm %3Ahomepage%2Fstory&utm_term=.17eb58fa9aad.

11. Peter Wagner and Alexi Jones, "State of Phone Justice: Local Jails, State Prisons, and Private Phone Providers," Prison Policy Initiative, February 2019, https://www.prisonpolicy .org/phones/state_of_phone_justice.html.

12. Lauren M. Johnson, "Connecticut Become First State to Make Calls Free for Inmates and Their Families," CNN, June 22, 2021, https://www.cnn.com/2021/06/22/us/connecticut -free-prison-phone-calls-trnd/index.html.

13. Clint Smith, "The Lines of Connection," *The Atlantic*, July 29, 2021, https://www .theatlantic.com/ideas/archive/2021/07/phoning-home-connecticut-state-prison/619586/.

14. John E. Danneberg, "Nationwide PLN Survey Examines Prison Phone Contracts, Kickbacks," *Prison Legal News* 22, no. 4 (April 2011),

https://www.prisonlegalnews.org/media/publications/pln%20april%202011%20cover %20story%20on%20prison%20phone%20industry.pdf#:~:text=An%20exhaustive%20analysis %20of%20prison%20phone%20contracts%20nationwide,obtain%20exclusive%2C %20monopolistic%20contracts%20for%20prison%20phone%20services.

15. Brian Byrne, "Addressing the High Cost of Prison Phone Calls," meshDETECT (blog), February 7, 2012, https://prisoncellphones.com/blog/2012/02/07/addressing-the -high-cost-of-prison-phone-calls/.

16. "CFPB Penalizes JPay for Siphoning Taxpayer-Funded Benefits Intended to Help People Re-enter Society after Incarceration," Consumer Financial Protection Bureau, U.S. Office of Inspector General, October 19, 2021, https://www.consumerfinance.gov/about-us/newsroom

/cfpb-penalizes-jpay-for-siphoning-taxpayer-funded-benefits-intended-to-help-people
-re-enter-society-after-incarceration/.

17. Beatrix Lockwood and Nicole Lewis, "The Hidden Cost of Incarceration," The Marshall Project, December 17, 2019, https://www.themarshallproject.org/2019/12/17/the-hidden -cost-of-incarceration.

18. Peter Wagner and Bernadette Rabuy, "Following the Money of Mass Incarceration," Prison Policy Initiative, January 25, 2017, https://www.prisonpolicy.org/reports/money.html.

19. Lauren Gill, "Federal Prisons' Switch to Scanning Mail Is a Surveillance Nightmare," *The Intercept*, September 26, 2021, https://theintercept.com/2021/09/26/surveillance -privacy-prisons-mail-scan/.

20. Mia Armstrong, "Is This What Prison Mail Looks Like Now?" *Slate*, December 5, 2018, https://slate.com/technology/2018/12/pennsylvania-prison-scanned-mail-smart -communications.html.

21. Sarah Watson, "When Jails Replace In-Person Visits with Video, What Happens When the Technology Fails?" Prison Policy Initiative, June 18, 2019, https://www.prisonpolicy.org /blog/2019/06/18/video-failure/.

22. Natasha Haverty, "Video Calls Replace In-Person Visits in Some Jails," *All Things Considered*, National Public Radio, December 5, 2016, https://www.npr.org/2016/12/05 /504458311/video-calls-replace-in-person-visits-in-some-jails.

23. Keri Blakinger, "No Glitter, No Glue, No Meth?," The Marshall Project, March 2, 2020, https://www.themarshallproject.org/2020/03/02/no-glitter-no-glue-no-meth.

24. Jolie McCullough, "Texas Prisons Stopped In-Person Visits and Limited Mail. Drugs Got in Anyway," *Texas Tribune*, March 29, 2021, https://www.texastribune.org/2021/03/29 /texas-prisons-drugs/.

25. Shannon Heffernan, "For Some Illinois Prisoners, One Good Eye Is Enough," National Public Radio, November 19, 2019, https://www.npr.org/local/309/2019/11/19/780757859 /for-some-illinois-prisoners-one-good-eye-is-enough; "Inmate Sues over Pa. DOC's 'One Good Eye' Policy," Corrections 1 by Lexipol, January 14, 2015, https://www.corrections1.com /correctional-healthcare/articles/inmate-sues-over-pa-docs-one-good-eye-policy -HCtJAIPnykfc5EsM/#:~:text="This%20policy%20is%20referred%20to%20as%20the %20'One,legal%20or%20total%20blindness%20in%20the%20diseased%20eye.

26. "Letter: Organizations Demand Prison E-Book Readers Drop Access Fees during COVID-19," PEN America, https://pen.org/letter-ereader-ceos/.

INTERVIEW: ZOE LAWRENCE ON LGBTQ PEOPLES INSIDE
BY DAVE "MAC" MARQUIS

Tell me about the first time you went to the prison library.

My first time going in the library was a little intimidating. The Dewey Decimal System was in place, but ignored. The inmate clerks responsible for organizing the books were too busy with their own hustles so the books weren't in any particular order. The library also housed a section for educational television use, further restricting space. If you had a problem with enclosed spaces or crowds, you would have an issue. As time went on, though, the TVs were removed, and we lost several shelves of older books. Now there is a system for organizing as well, so I would say it is improved.

There is a decent library here. Romance, science fiction, drama, reference, true crime, urban, westerns, nonfiction, war, and just odds and ins like medical, psychology, travel. The most common book is romance—in numbers that are shocking. At one time I could have sworn that half the library was Nora Roberts (not that I am complaining). LGBTQ was the one topic that seemed taboo. Maybe because this prison is in the South, maybe because the concern that reading a gay book makes you look weak. I am not sure of the thought process there. All I knew then was that I had little to read (at least in terms of being able to relate to the characters). I had an underground library running out of my locker. In a weird way it felt like I was starting a movement. "If you wanted an LGBTQ book, go talk to Zoe. She'll be on the rec yard tonight after 5 pm." I donated my own books, along with a few other inmates, to establish the section in the library. I wanted to donate my books simply to reclaim the other half of my locker! I am in a large room with sixty-four sets of bunk beds only eight feet apart. Those beds are separated by six-foot walls creating a cubicle-style living space of nearly eighty square feet. Each cubicle has two standing foot lockers and one table. So, not a lot of space.

I donated biographies and erotica to everything in between. My personal contributions included books like *Trans Bodies, Trans Selves, If I Was Your Girl*, and *She's Not There* . . . all trans books. After a while we took the books to the head of the library and asked that the books be added. After some meetings the books made it to the shelves. Even then it was a struggle to maintain because of people's dislike or religious feelings. Many times I would find books missing for weeks, only to be returned damaged.

During the COVID-19 pandemic, there is no library. We are restricted to our housing units. Our "library" is a simple metal book cart with a variety of this and that. Before the lockdown the library was clean and organized. It took several years of dedicated work to get it to the standards that we had. I hope when this is over we can return to that state of organization.

If you were in charge of the library, what would you do to continue to improve it?

I would make calls every day to bookstores and ask for donations of newer books. We have newspapers and magazines, but newer books are sometimes harder to obtain. I would also work with the local college to perhaps volunteer their time to have an instructor come teach any kind of creative writing.

How important are books to you during incarceration?

Very. In the beginning of the incarceration, I would read books to my child over the phone. Being a parent in prison is very difficult. I have been incarcerated for thirteen years so far. My little baby went from being eight to twenty-one before I had a chance to say anything. My son loved *Where the Wild Things Are*. Each and every night that was the only book. [I think] mostly because I would make silly voices. After a while, though, I had a great idea. What if there were more monsters? So, I started making my own version up. This became a new thing with us. I can say books helped, but there is such a gap between us that no Band-Aid can fix. Only time. I know that my reading to him helped, but it can only help so much. If I could suggest anything, it would be to offer inmates that have children books on how to parent from inside. I came on here with no knowledge or hints. I was scared that I would completely lose him. I didn't have anyone to tell me it would be OK. Even a simple, one-page pamphlet called "It Gets Better" would have helped.

Drawn by Nic Cassette

When he grew up some he would read to me. Now I read more nonfiction work on PTSD and DID (dissociative identity disorder). I suffer from both, and information on trauma recovery helps. Books I have received that I recommend are *The Body Keeps the Score* (PTSD), *Coping with Trauma-Related Dissociation* (DID), *Seeking Safety* (both). Plus, I am an artist, and the art books I have received were handy. Finally, I was able to spend some time learning how to write screenplays, furthering my education while incarcerated. My greatest joy was writing a beautiful script with my best friend and sending it to different companies. While it has not yet been made into a movie, many of the producers said the story was great and needed only a few fine touches. I have a copy if you'd like to read it. But seriously, I am thrilled that I was able to read everything from the books sent to me and do something with it. So, I would say books play a very important role.

Did you ever solicit or receive books from a prison books program? If so, tell me about the process.

Yes, many times. In my first year someone gave me the address for LGBTQ Books 2 Prisoners. That began a long and wonderful relationship with the bookstore. The process was easy. Simply write and request a type of book (nonfiction, fantasy, sci-fi . . .) and in a few months I would receive two or three books. Most were very helpful. Since then, I have received many books from as many as ten different programs. I donate all books when I am done, expanding our library further.

I have spent a decade here at my prison writing to them and spreading the word to other inmates. Word of mouth is still the best way to learn about PBPS. The first time that John [not his real name] received his books he actually cried. He didn't think he was going to get anything. John was a great man. Never judged, always gave. But because he'd had a hard time reading, he tended to stay to himself a lot. He lived in the cubicle next to me. He would actually tease me about my reading so many books. "Ain't nothing in them books you can't learn on the street," he'd say. I told him about several companies that sent books to me. He scoffed. Told me he'd never get any books because no one writes him anyhow. After a good heart-to-heart, he told me that the letters moved when he tried to read. So, I wrote to a company on his behalf explaining the situation. Instead of sending me the books, they sent *A Workbook for Dyslexics* by Cheryl Orlassino directly to him. We worked on that book for a while until he was comfortable on his own. The day before he left, I said, "There ain't nothing in them books he can't learn from the streets." His response was a long, wordless hug. Good enough for me.

I love getting books because it means my name gets called during mail call. I don't receive much mail from the outside world. To get something always feels like you are cared for in some way. I particularly enjoy the little notes from the volunteers who work so hard to fill those orders. In one particular case I became good friends with a volunteer. We try to read some of the same books so that we can talk to each other about them. It is like I am in a small book club. Being trans in a male facility, I find that I miss that feminine element a lot, so this helps fill the void. I have enjoyed each and every delivery of books.

Were there any restrictions on the types of books you and/or other imprisoned people are allowed?

Yes. Any book containing nudity, martial arts, anti-government rhetoric are typically banned. That doesn't mean they don't slip through. But as staff changes, so do the opinions of what we are allowed. For instance, years ago Japanese manga were perfectly fine. There was an inmate here that filled his locker with manga. When he left prison, he attempted to bring all the books home with him. The person who picked him up said that he couldn't bring them with him. So he left them here. They were donated to the library

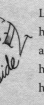

Leonard Peltier is of Anishinaabe, Dakota, and Lakota heritage and grew up on the Turtle Mountain Chippewa and Spirit Lake Reservations in North Dakota. Peltier has been incarcerated for forty years, during which time he has written extensively. His work *Prison Writings: My Life Is My Sundance* (1999) uses the Sundance religious ceremony to explain how Peltier endures despite the torture of imprisonment. Peltier's Native perspective sheds light on the plight of all Native peoples who are incarcerated at higher rates than any other group in the United States.

because they were books. When the library received them and reviewed them, red flags went up. The library staff destroyed the books and brought the issue up with the executive branch. After that manga was difficult to obtain for a while. Not impossible, but certainly under more scrutiny than before. This was years ago, nearly six I believe. Now the mailroom considers them to be pornographic works. In a few years, who knows?

While it is policy to inform inmates when a book has been rejected, that rarely happens. And the fear of a book being rejected has influenced my decisions when ordering books. I attempted to get *Our Bodies, Our Selves*, a women's health guidebook. It was rejected on the grounds that I was not a woman. I didn't get a chance to fight that decision because the book was sent back before I ever had the chance. Such is life in a system designed for minimum results with maximum effort.

In the SHU (solitary housing unit) you are limited in many cases to only one book. To get that one book you have to wait for some guard to bring the book cart around. It is filled with romance novels for some reason. The area is loud during day and night. Food is brought to you in little trays, and while you get enough calories, I can honestly say the food is terrible. That is with most prison fare though. In the end, segregation is not a good place to be. People are placed there now for quarantine because of COVID-19.

Update: On the first week of April 2021, Ms. Zoe Lawrence was transferred to a female medical facility within the Federal Prison System. She leans on books more than ever.

GOING POSTAL: CENSORSHIP, POLICY, AND CORRESPONDENCE REJECTION WITH TEXAS PRISONS Paul Tardie

Returned mail is one of our least favorite things at Inside Books Project (IBP). Returns mean that someone didn't get what they needed, possibly when they needed it most. It also means that we have more mail in addition to our standard influx of requests for literature, and in this case, it means there will be troubleshooting involved. Returned packages cost us money, we pay for the original package, and then we pay once again if we can navigate the problem that caused the return and then successfully get the books inside. There are several stickers or rubber stamp marks that might be found on returned packages that outline the reasons for a return: the person was moved or released, the person has received too much mail, the person could not be found, or the contents are presumed to conflict with mail policy. An issue that creates front- *and* back-end problems is banned material, which is discussed later.

Understanding prison policy is key to ensuring that mail is not rejected. The Bureau of Prisons (BOP) is under federal jurisdiction, so it has policies that apply to most facilities under their authority, such as not allowing hardback books. The Texas Department of Criminal Justice also has policies that can be generally applied and observed but may differ greatly on certain content being deemed as contraband. Arbitrary definitions and enforcement procedures leave us in the position of a de facto censor. Will anatomical drawings in medical textbooks or bare bodies in classical art be considered nudity? Is there a point at which art history becomes pornography? Even if a page is excised from a book in order to remove banned content, this may put

DEAR FAMILY,

I WANT TO LET YOU KNOW THAT YOUR PRISONERS LITERATURE PROJECT IS ONE OF THE BEST BOUND TOGETHER BOOKS IN THIS WORLD. IT HELPED ME TO SET MY LIFE TOGETHER. THIS WISDOM HAS TAUGHT ME SO SO MUCH, THANK YOU SO MUCH FROM MY HEAR AND SOUL. I'M DOING NINE YEARS. I HAVE DONE FIVE YEARS ALREADY. I LOST EVERYTHING. I LOVE MY KIDS, MU LADY, MY FAMILY. I'VE ALSO WANTED TO DIE OR KILL MYSELF, BUT YOUR ADVISED HELP AND SUPPORT SHOWED ME THE RIGHT WAY OF LIFE AND HOW TO LIVE IT. WORDS WOULD NOT SAY THE LOVE I HAVE FOR YOU. I'M NO LONGER ALONE.

the book at risk of rejection in the mailroom for being altered. To mitigate the risks involved in these gray areas, many books do not get sent in.

Our database allows us to keep track of whose mail has been processed, providing the postage date an individual sent their request for books and notable details of the contents, if pertinent. IBP policy is to allow requests every three months. If their request is too early within the allotted time frame, it cannot be fulfilled and is cataloged. Another way it cannot be fulfilled is if the person has been released, which is a pleasant surprise. The only drawback to this good news would be if they asked us for material necessary for their reentry in the current request and could now no longer receive it due to their release. This type of request is common and can include reentry guides, job search material, or printouts of requested material key to their well-being upon reentry. Many of these materials are compiled and stocked by IBP volunteers or published by local governments working in coordination with regional groups such as the Travis County (Texas) Justice and Public Safety Division. We have also kept in stock books such as *Beyond Bars* to act as a general guide and supplemental material that goes into social and psychological aspects of reentry, for which a book such as *What Color Is Your Parachute?* isn't designed.[1]

Another reason we may receive a mail return or are unable to fulfill a request is due to transfers. People are often moved to another facility, and this is especially problematic if they have gone to another state. IBP only serves Texas due to the large volume of imprisoned people in the state (about

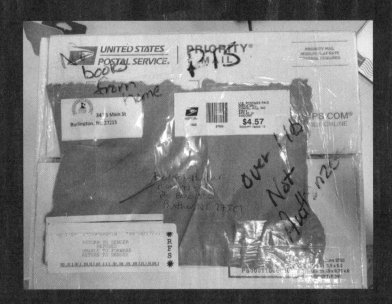

Recently returned books, repackaged due to the original packaging being destroyed.

The volume of mail Inside Books Project received.

120,000 in the Texas Department of Criminal Justice [TDCJ] alone, not to mention federal prisons, jails, state-run halfway houses, juvenile facilities, migrant detention, etc.). We are a volunteer-run nonprofit, and our limited resources mean that we can only effectively serve people in Texas. Federal prisons under the authority of the Bureau of Prisons may transfer people to another state within the time it takes to get a package out of our doors and to the destination. We are unable to know exactly when a someone will get transferred, the BOP keeps this information secret, even down to the county level of incarceration. State prisons in Texas are included in a database that we can reference online for information to ensure that packages are going to their correct destination and will reach the requester before they are released if their sentence is about to end.

A major obstacle that we and other PBPs face is that it is not always easy to find and understand any particular institution's guidelines for sending packages inside. Even if you can find the guidelines on the prison website (if they have one), they might be outdated. Of course, even if you find the guidelines, many decisions about what constitutes a violation of them is left to the discretion of individual guards working in the mailroom. For example, we recently had an issue with returns coming from Carswell Federal Medical Facility, a federal medical prison primarily for women. It began by having many packages returned with no clear reasoning, despite BOP guidelines that state: "When correspondence is rejected, the Warden shall notify the sender in writing of the rejection and the reasons for the rejection. The Warden shall also give notice that the sender may appeal the rejection."[2] When we reached out to Carswell for a reason why our packages were being denied, we were met with hostility, dismissiveness, and no responses to our messages. When Carswell finally responded, they stated that they had done a search engine map view of IBP's address, and it was not the bookstore we have partnered with over the years as a physical address to receive mail. We updated our address, but Carswell continued to deny us access. After reaching out to other books-to-prisoners projects, we found that Carswell had been denying mail from them as well. One cited reason was that envelopes were the wrong color, yellow instead of white. We then sent postcards to Carswell, informing our correspondents that we were unable to send them books for the foreseeable future and were seeking remediation. We contacted Carswell beforehand to ensure that postcards were allowed. The officer handling the call said that they were unsure if cardstock was permitted and to check the policy on their website. The website did not have any clear specifications about cardstock so it was assumed that postcards would be allowed in. Weeks later, all our postcards were returned. We then called the prison to see if they could provide us with their current policies since the policy on their website was from 2011 and was the only available reference to the public. Taking a chance, we sent enveloped letters to the same people who didn't receive their books, these envelopes containing printed articles on how to file a grievance under BOP requirements as well as the original postcard content informing them of our discontinuation of services. This experience demonstrates that no matter what the policy may be on a website or from the mouth of a corrections officer (CO), there is no guarantee of consistency. Arbitrary enforcement of policy is the norm in prisons and jails and is solely dependent on who is in charge at any level on any given day. This Kafkaesque experience with the Carswell mailroom is not unique.

Within the time spent writing this article, we have received contact from Carswell stating the mail ban on IBP has been lifted. This reversal was the result of COs reading the letters stating that we could not mail packages anymore as well as an incarcerated person at Carswell filing a complaint. Overzealous interpretation of policy had led to months of denials, extra work from IBP core staff, and stress to all parties involved. Fortunately, our determination and tactics led to resolution of this problem. We were anticipating having to acquire legal representation, inmates filing grievances, potential retaliation against inmates, and in the worst-case-imaginable scenario—possible chain reactions with other federal prisons clamping

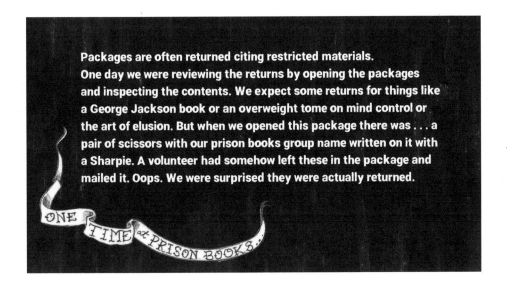

Packages are often returned citing restricted materials.
One day we were reviewing the returns by opening the packages and inspecting the contents. We expect some returns for things like a George Jackson book or an overweight tome on mind control or the art of elusion. But when we opened this package there was . . . a pair of scissors with our prison books group name written on it with a Sharpie. A volunteer had somehow left these in the package and mailed it. Oops. We were surprised they were actually returned.

ONE TIME at PRISON BOOKS

down on mail policy. While we were all relieved not to have this problem anymore, it was demoralizing to have to put up with it in the first place.

Sometimes a package of literature may be rejected in the mailroom and simply discarded. If any content is deemed contraband (including perfume in a magazine, photographed or illustrated nudity, maps of Texas, pornography, photos of drug use, banned books, etc.), then the entire package may be discarded or confiscated. We often receive letters from people who did not receive a package we sent, or they only received part of it. Other reasons packages don't make it to people include retaliation from guards or a person being put on restricted mail access as a form of punishment or purported security measure. Unfortunately, it is difficult for us to confirm any reason for a return other than the rationale provided by the prison.

Currently, there is a list of over 6,200 banned books in Texas (although this is 4,000 fewer titles from the 10,000 it once had). What is most noticeable at IBP is that many of the titles that had *once been banned* are still on our radar and tend to create hesitancy and uncertainty when we put a package together. Adjusting to policy change is a bit of a shock to protocol. There is a lingering sense of expecting mail to be rejected when we send Paolo Freire's *Pedagogy of the Oppressed* (Penguin, 2017) or similar titles, even though we haven't seen these on the updated list but have seen them returned by prison officials in the past. Going back to the Carswell policy/fiasco, it can be up to the discretion of the warden or lower-ranked staff to make these decisions. Naturally, we are always testing the waters to see what titles will make it through, and we get a thrill every time we send in a copy of Angela Y. Davis's *Are Prisons Obsolete?* (Seven Stories Press, 2003) or Alex S. Vitale's *The End of Policing* (Verso, 2018). So far, such titles have not been returned as contraband, but this is only in our experience and may not be the case in other states. Alternatively, as Kwaneta Harris's chapter explains, these books could simply be thrown out by people in the mailrooms, or imprisoned people could be asked to pay to mail them home.

Prior approval is not an issue that IBP has had to deal with, but it can be a major restriction, according to the zine *How to Start a Prison Books Collective*:

One of the tougher policies is requiring a prisoner to get a form signed by a prison administrator which is then sent to you and must be attached to the outside of the package. The forms often have a specified time period during which

A recent thank-you note from someone inside.

the books can be received by the prisoner. If your backlog of requests prevents you from answering this request within the allowed time period, the prisoner will have to get a new form and start over again.[3]

According to Saxapahaw Prison Books, it is not uncommon to receive a letter with the approval form after the deadline has passed. In Texas, there may be a need for prior approval in cases of bulk donations. A corporal from a county jail contacted us to receive books, we agreed, and then they informed us that approval from a judge was required to move forward with the process. According to them, even a dozen books required judicial authorization.

Mail returns may gum up the works at PBPs. They happen all of the time and are to be expected. We hope that one day we will never receive another letter from an imprisoned person, for that will mean that prisons have been abolished, but until then we will keep honing our troubleshooting skills and sharing what works to get books to people inside.

NOTES

1. Jeffrey Ian Ross and Stephen C. Richards, *Beyond Bars: Rejoining Society after Prison* (New York: Alpha Books, 2009); and Richard N. Bolles and Katherine Brooks, *What Color Is Your Parachute* (Berkeley: Ten Speed, 2022).

2. "Notification of Rejections," in "Correspondence," Program Statement, U.S. Department of Justice, Federal Bureau of Prisons, April 5, 2011, p 7, https://www.bop.gov/policy/progstat/5265_014.pdf.

3. "Checking Restrictions," in *How to Start a Prison Books Collective*, https://prisonbooks.info/img/resource-starting-a-group.pdf.

AFTERWORD Megan Sweeney

"Pessimism of the intellect, optimism of the will." This maxim is often attributed to Antonio Gramsci, an Italian philosopher, journalist, and Marxist organizer who spent eleven years in prison for resisting Benito Mussolini's fascist regime. Gramsci actually borrowed the maxim from French writer Romain Rolland, but he repeatedly draws on the idea in his *Prison Notebooks*, written during his incarceration from 1926 to 1937.[1] "I'm a pessimist because of intelligence, but an optimist because of will," Gramsci explained in 1929. "Whatever the situation, I imagine the worst that could happen in order to summon up all my reserves and will power to overcome every obstacle."[2] Gramsci's sensibility captures what I find so moving about *Books through Bars: Stories from the Prison Books Movement*. Despite myriad, ever-shifting reasons to feel pessimistic about possibilities for reading and education in jails and prisons, the contributors featured in the volume—incarcerated people, teachers, advocates, and activists—model in concrete, embodied ways what it means to know the worst, to be fully aware of all the grim facts, and to keep doing the work anyway. Enacting optimism in penal contexts is not a simple matter of maintaining a positive attitude; it requires grit, determination, and often grueling forms of individual and collective labor. But as *Books through Bars* reminds us, such labor not only fosters crucial opportunities for reading, understanding, and meaning making; enacting optimism enables powerful—even joyful—forms of human connection and community in contexts of profound isolation and constraint.

In many ways, reading *Books through Bars* felt eerily familiar to me, as if time had stood still since I completed my own research about reading in women's prisons in 2009. I found myself nodding in recognition when I read contributors' descriptions of both the contents of prison libraries (romance novels, Christian-themed books, urban fiction, mysteries, westerns) and the mercurial, irrational censorship policies that regulate such content, often with no options for appeal, let alone notification that the material has been censored. It's the same story, too, with prisons banning books that, as James King notes in his chapter, "either help contextualize the Black experience in America or are merely authored by notable Black authors" (83), from Harriet Jacobs's *Incidents in the Life of a Slave Girl* to Toni Morrison's *The Bluest Eye*, from Patricia Hill Collins's *Black Feminist Thought: Knowledge, Consciousness, and the Politics of Empowerment* to Bryan Stevenson's *Just Mercy*. With their insistent denial of books about educational inequities, race and public housing, historical events such as the 1921 Tulsa race riot, and any topic that "promotes racial division"—a category established in the wake of the Black Lives Matter movement—prison administrators continue to act as if refusing to address historical and ongoing manifestations of racism will make them magically disappear.

Efforts to censor sexually explicit material lead to similarly absurd outcomes, such as the denial of magazines that feature an older woman wearing a Depends undergarment, or Olympic gymnast Simone Biles wearing a leotard. Particularly wrenching is the deliberate denial of much-needed resources: books about menopause and women's health, books about surviving schizophrenia or healing from childhood sexual trauma, books about prisoner reentry and victim offender conferencing, and books that center children with incarcerated parents and strategies for parenting from prison. *Books through Bars* also draws important attention to the ways in which prison regulations position books-to-prison advocates and teachers as de facto censors forced to predict whether the anatomical drawings in a medical textbook or a book with an excised page will be rejected in the prison mailroom.

Even as it highlights the seemingly timeless ways in which penal authorities limit incarcerated people's access to books, *Books through Bars* illuminates ever more insidious forms of control and deprivation. I'm thinking of the corrections officer who presumes that LGBTQ people only want books that focus on sex transitions, or the librarian who presumes that all readers in solitary confinement need Christian books regardless of the genres they request. I'm thinking of the host of obstacles to incarcerated people receiving books, including time-limited authorizations required from prison

GOOD BOOKS AND BAKED GOODS BENEFIT SALE FOR ASHEVILLE PRISON BOOKS

SUNDAY JUNE 25th – 9AM–2PM

201 BROADWAY

ALL BOOKS 25¢–$1

Fundraiser from the early days of Asheville Prison Books.

administrators and even judges. And I'm thinking of how state and federal prisons—in an effort to reduce contraband—hire private companies to scan the handwritten letters, greeting cards, photographs, and children's drawings that many incarcerated people receive, a process that blurs loved ones' handwriting, obscures faces and erases traces of caring hands, and drains the exuberance, scents, and textures of colorful crayon creations.

Reading about current practices for introducing digital tablets into jails and prisons particularly piqued my pessimism of the intellect. As contributors note, free tablets potentially offer incarcerated people increased access to loved ones, telehealth programs, higher education programs, varied reading materials, and materials in fonts and formats that meet the needs of variously abled readers. Yet, as I learned about the predatory partnerships between prisons and private corporations such as JPay, Securus Technologies, and Global Tel Link, I was reminded of the endlessly inventive ways in which profit trumps people. *I shouldn't be surprised*, I thought over and over as I read about these companies charging $.03–$.05 per minute to read books available for free in the public domain, charging incarcerated people twice as much as Spotify or iTunes to download a limited range of songs, or charging $3.50 to deposit $5 into an incarcerated person's account. *I shouldn't be surprised*, I thought as I read about the fees incarcerated people must pay every time they send or receive an email, make a phone call, or download a movie or game, fees that get funneled right back into the penal system as departments of correction receive a portion of the profits. *I shouldn't be surprised*, I said to myself as I learned about states' efforts to ban all physical books and give incarcerated people access only to the free e-books and religious texts available on tablets. *Shouldn't be surprised, shouldn't be surprised*, I thought, but I couldn't help wincing when I read the words of Kwaneta Harris, currently incarcerated in Texas: "They can imprison our bodies but not our minds, or so I thought."

At the same time, however, *Books through Bars* offers a vivid picture of what it looks like when incarcerated and non-incarcerated people collaboratively counter efforts to imprison bodies and minds, reminding us—in the words of Lorenzo Kom'boa Ervin—that "no army can stop an idea whose time has come." Optimism of the will assumes many forms in penal contexts. It's embodied by a prisoner scratching the address of a prison book program onto their cell wall, or giving a friend the address for LGBTQ Books to Prisoners, or feeling like a valued member of a book club in corresponding with a books-to-prison volunteer. It's embodied by reading a tattered paper-back or "light fiction" in an effort to "think beyond," to experience "peace-ful absorption" rather than the depression and anxiety stoked by pandemic lockdowns and lengthy sentences. Optimism takes the form of standing at the vent that adjoins prison cells and reading aloud by streetlight for neigh-bors who do not or cannot read. It takes the form of running an underground LGBTQ library out of a prison locker and then helping establish an LGBTQ section in the prison library. Optimism of the will is embodied by an im-prisoned mother reading *Where the Wild Things Are* night after night to her eight-year-old son, embellishing the story with silly voices and extra mon-sters, until the day comes when the son reads to his mother. And it's em-bodied by a heartbreaking attempt to seek understanding in the midst of unspeakable loss and state-sanctioned violence: "I would like to know if you have anything on Death by Execution. I had two brothers who was Executed. One was Executed in 1977 by a firing squad at the Utah State Prison. My other brother got the death sentence in 1990. I would very much like to get a book on Execution."

In prisons and jails, optimism of the will frequently takes the form of rad-ical self-education designed to counter the profound racial and class ineq-uities perpetuated by American schools. Enacting optimism entails form-ing Black radical study groups, creating a widely disseminated legal guide, organizing prisoner-led lawsuits to defeat bans on revolutionary literature, and working across racial lines to disempower the Klan. Enacting optimism involves circulating books about Native American history and politics, and gathering each week with other Native incarcerated people to share cookies, coffee, and a photocopied zine.

Enacting optimism looks like letters written on a commissary request form folded and taped together to form an envelope. It looks like envelopes adorned with elaborate pictures as thanks for books received. It looks like a volunteer reading her first letter from an imprisoned reader and feeling a human connection through the handwriting and drawings on the page. It looks like volunteers drawing family members and friends into the work by sharing moving passages from incarcerated people's letters. Enacting opti-mism looks like trusting each person to know what reading materials they would like: a Tagalog-English dictionary, a crossword book, a calendar with pictures of dogs. It looks like meeting in outdoor spaces to pack up requested books during COVID-19, or learning the hard way that envelopes must be yellow, not white. Enacting optimism looks like insisting—as many times as necessary—that prisons at the very least adopt rational, clear, ethical practices relating to incarcerated people's access to books.

As contributors to *Books through Bars* emphasize, practicing optimism of the will is most often a collaborative endeavor. Before email, it meant tracking down possible volunteers through phone calls, word of mouth, and snail mail sent to P.O. boxes checked every other week. Now, it means forming partnerships between books-to-prison programs and independent used bookstores, far more affordable "authorized distributors" than Amazon. It means organizing multiday symposia about educational justice and prisons. It means sending ten thousand postcards to the governor of New York to stop "TV prisons," which treat access to cable as a substitute for access to books. It means suing the state of Mississippi for attempting to make religious books the only reading materials available in prisons. It means pressuring departments of correction from all sides when they try to prevent prison books programs from operating in their states. Practicing optimism means launching a "Freedom to Learn Campaign"—a network of incarcerated students, library associations, authors, unions, civil liberties organizations, campus organizations, and books-to-prison programs—dedicated to making learning more accessible to people in prison. It means forming a broad-based coalition to demand that digital tablet providers drop access fees when COVID keeps incarcerated people locked in their cells twenty-three hours per day. It means doggedly insisting, as Valerie Surrett does, that protecting imprisoned people's right to read requires providing access to "tablets *and* original mail, tablets *and* in-person visits, tablets *and* donated books, tablets *and* in-person higher education opportunities, tablets *and* law libraries." And in the midst of all this exhausting labor, practicing optimism means inventing joyful, creative, collective ways to keep doing the work: a Halloween Cover Band Show, a twenty-four-hour book-packing party, a party dedicated to burning donated books about gay conversion therapy or Confederate soldiers winning the Civil War. As Patrick Kukucka reminds us, "Joy is the bond that holds people in community."

"To ask questions of the universe, and then learn to live with those questions," James Baldwin writes, is the necessary groundwork for creating social change.[3] In *Books through Bars*, the contributors push us to ask questions, to absorb the distressing facts, to be fully cognizant of the many reasons why pessimism is a warranted response to current conditions for reading in prisons. At the same time, *Books through Bars* offers ample, embodied demonstrations of what it means to live with those questions. Enacting optimism, the contributors suggest, means doing the work, relentlessly, in both solitary and collective forms. It means making a way out of no way, one letter and one free book at a time.

NOTES

1. In an article published in the periodical *L'Ordine Nuovo* on March 4, 1921, Gramsci quoted the motto of French writer Romain Rolland when he asserted: "Our motto is still alive and to the point: Pessimism of the intellect, optimism of the will." See Susan Ratcliffe, ed., *Oxford Essential Quotations*, 5th ed. (Oxford: Oxford University Press, 2017), https://www.oxfordreference.com/view/10.1093/acref/9780191843730.001.0001/q-oro-ed5-00018416.

2. Antonio Gramsci, *Letters from Prison* (New York: Harper & Row, 1973), 158–59.

3. James Baldwin, "A Talk to Teachers," in *The Price of the Ticket: Collected Nonfiction, 1948–1985* (New York: St. Martin's Press, 1985), 326.

APPENDIX: PRISON BOOKS PROGRAMS BY STATE

Alabama	Books to Prisons Alabama
	4413 5th Avenue South
	Birmingham, Al. 35222
	burdockbookcollective@gmail.com
	https://www.burdockbookcollective.com/books-to-prisons
	SERVES: Texas and Alabama via D.C. Books to Prisoners
Arizona	Read Between the Bars
	c/o Daily Planet Publishing
	P.O. Box 44014
	Tucson, Ari. 85733
	readbetweenthebars@gmail.com
	https://readbetweenthebars.com/
	SERVES: Arizona
California	Pages and Time
	P.O. Box 66583
	Los Angeles, Ca. 90066
	(310) 487-7538
	4pagesandtime@gmail.com
	http://pagesandtime.com/
	SERVES: Libraries at Wasco and Delano State Prisons and Chino Women's Prison

Prison Library Project
586 West First Street
Claremont, Ca. 91711
(909) 626-3066
claremontforum@gmail.com
http://www.claremontforum.org/prison-library-project/
SERVES: All U.S. states except Massachusetts

Prisoners Literature Project
c/o Bound Together Books
1369 Haight Street
San Francisco, Ca. 94117
prisonlit@gmail.com
https://www.prisonlit.org/
SERVES: All U.S. states except Texas
Address for volunteering:
Grassroots House
2022 Blake Street
Berkeley, Ca. 94704

UC Davis Books to Prisoners
DavisBookstoPrisons@protonmail.com
https://twitter.com/Books2Prisons

. . . .

Colorado

Pages for Prisons
Boulder, Co.
https://www.facebook.com/pg/pagesforprisons/posts/?ref=page
  _internal
SERVES: Colorado

. . . .

Connecticut

Connecticut Prison Book Connection
P.O. Box 946
Rocky Hill, Conn. 06067
https://www.facebook.com/ctprisonbook
SERVES: All U.S. states

District of Columbia   D.C. Books to Prisons Project
P.O. Box 34290
Washington, D.C. 20043
btopdc@gmail.com
http://dcbookstoprisoners.org/
SERVES: Federal prisoners in Arizona, DC residents in federal
prisons. All other states *except* Connecticut, Florida, Illinois,
Massachusetts, Maine, Michigan, New Hampshire, New
Jersey, New York, Oregon, Pennsylvania, Rhode Island, Vermont,
Washington, and Wisconsin.

Florida   Open Books Prison Book Project
1040 N. Guillemard Street
Pensacola, Fla. 32501
(850) 453-6774
openbookspcola@riseup.net
https://www.openbookspcola.org/
SERVES: Florida

Illinois   Chicago Books to Women in Prison
4511 N. Hermitage Avenue
Chicago, Ill. 60640
chicagobwp@gmail.com
https://chicagobwp.org/
SERVES: Women and trans people in Arizona, California,
Connecticut, Florida, Illinois, Indiana, Kentucky, Mississippi,
Missouri, and Ohio

Liberation Library
c/o In These Times
2040 N. Milwaukee Avenue
Chicago, Ill. 60647
https://www.liberationlib.com/
SERVES: Youth in all Illinois youth prisons and select Illinois youth jails

Midwest Books to Prisoners
1321 N. Milwaukee Avenue
PMB #460
Chicago, Ill. 60622
midwestb2p@gmail.com
http://midwestb2p.com/
SERVES: Iowa, Illinois, Indiana, Kansas, Michigan (libraries only),
   Minnesota, Missouri, North Dakota, Nevada, Ohio, South Dakota,
   and Wisconsin

Reading Reduces Recidivism
http://www.3rsproject.org/
SERVES: Librarians of prison libraries in Illinois

Urbana-Champaign Books to Prisoners Project
P.O. Box 515
Urbana, Ill. 61803
(708) 782-4608
http://www.books2prisoners.org/

Indiana

Midwest Pages to Prisoners Project
P.O. Box 1324
Bloomington, Ind. 47402
(812) 727-0155
mwpp@pagestoprisoners.org
SERVES: Arkansas, Iowa, Indiana, Kansas, Minnesota, Missouri,
   North Dakota, Nevada, Oklahoma, and South Dakota

Kentucky

Louisville Books to Prisoners
c/o McQuixote Books & Coffee
1512 Portland Avenue #1
Louisville, Ky. 40203
(502) 625-LB2P (5227)
louisvillebtp@gmail.com
louisvillebookstoprisoners.org
SERVES: Kentucky and Virginia

Louisiana	Louisiana Books 2 Prisoners
	3157 Gentilly Boulevard #141
	New Orleans, La. 70122
	books2prisoners@gmail.com
	https://lab2p.org/
	SERVES: Alabama, Arkansas, and Louisiana; women and Louisiana prisoners are prioritized
Massachusetts	Great Falls Books Through Bars
	P.O. Box 391
	Greenfield, Mass. 01302
	gfbooksthroughbars@riseup.net
	www.greatfallsbooksthroughbars.org
	SERVES: All U.S. states *except* Massachusetts
	Prison Book Program
	c/o Lucy Parsons Bookstore
	1306 Hancock Street Suite 100
	Quincy, Mass. 02169
	(617) 423-3298
	info@prisonbookprogram.org
	https://prisonbookprogram.org/
	SERVES: All U.S. states *except* California, Illinois, Michigan, Maryland, Nevada, and Texas
Michigan	Unitarian Universalist Ann Arbor Prison Books
	First Unitarian Universalist Congregation of Ann Arbor
	4001 Ann Arbor-Saline Road
	Ann Arbor, Mich. 48103-8739
	(734) 665-6158
	https://uuaa.org/index.php/social-justice/faith-in-action /prison-books
	SERVES: Select Michigan institutions

Minnesota	Women's Prison Book Project 3751 17th Avenue S Minneapolis, Minn. 55407 womensprisonbookproject@gmail.com https://wpbp.org/ SERVES: All U.S. states *except* Connecticut, Florida, Illinois, Indiana, Massachusetts, Michigan, Mississippi, Ohio, Oregon, and Pennsylvania
Mississippi	Big House Books P.O. Box 55586 Jackson, Miss. 39296 bighousebooksms@gmail.com https://bighousebooksms.org/ SERVES: Mississippi
Missouri	Missouri Prison Books Program 438 N. Skinker Boulevard St. Louis, Mo. 63130 moprisonbooks@gmail.com https://missouriprisonbooks.org/ SERVES: Missouri
New Jersey	Books Behind Bars P.O. Box 2611 Wildwood, N.J. 08260 info@booksbehindbarsnj.com https://www.booksbehindbarsnj.com/ SERVES: New Jersey
New York	NYC Books Through Bars c/o Bluestockings Bookstore 116 Suffolk Street New York, N.Y. 10002 info@booksthroughbarsnyc.org https://booksthroughbarsnyc.org/ SERVES: All U.S. states *except* Alabama, Florida, Louisiana, Massachusetts, Michigan, Mississippi, North Carolina, Ohio, and Pennsylvania, with a priority on New York

North Carolina	Asheville Prison Books Program
	c/o Downtown Books and News
	67 N. Lexington Avenue
	Asheville, N.C. 28801
	Ashevilleprisonbooks@gmail.com
	https://avlpb.org/
	SERVES: North Carolina and South Carolina
	N.C. Women's Prison Book Project
	ncwomensprisonbooks@gmail.com
	https://ncwomensprisonbookproject.wordpress.com/
	SERVES: Women in North Carolina
	Prison Books Collective
	P.O. Box 625
	Carrboro, N.C. 27510
	(919) 443-9238
	prisonbooks@gmail.com
	https://prisonbooks.info/
	SERVES: Men in North Carolina and Alabama
	Tranzmission Prison Project
	P.O. Box 1874
	Asheville, N.C. 28802
	tranzmissionprisonproject@gmail.com
	http://www.tranzmissionprisonproject.org/
	SERVES: LGBTQ prisoners nationwide
Ohio	Athens Books to Prisoners
	30 1st Street
	Athens, Ohio 45701
	athensbooks2prisoners@gmail.com
	http://athensbookstoprisoners.weebly.com/
	SERVES: Ohio
Oklahoma	Oklahoma Prison Books Collective
	P.O. Box 52255
	Tulsa, Okla. 74152
	https://twitter.com/okpbc
	SERVES: All Oklahoma

Oregon

Portland Books to Prisoners

pdxbookstoprisoners@riseup.net

https://www.ewobglobal.net/portland-books-to-prisoners

Incarcerated persons book requests should be mailed to the address under the listing for Books to Prisoners, Seattle, Wa.

SERVES: All U.S. states

Rogue Liberation Library

P.O. Box 524

Ashland, Ore. 97520

https://peacehouse.net/RLL/

SERVES: Oregon, California, Indiana, Nevada, and Texas

Pennsylvania

Pittsburgh Prison Book Project (formerly Book 'Em)

P.O. Box 71357

Pittsburgh, Penn. 15213

pghprisonbookproject@gmail.com

https://pghprisonbookproject.org/

SERVES: Pennsylvania

Books Through Bars

4722 Baltimore Avenue

Philadelphia, Penn. 19143

(215) 727-8170

volunteer@booksthroughbars.org

https://www.booksthroughbars.org/

SERVES: Pennsylvania, New Jersey, New York, Delaware, Maryland, Virginia, and West Virginia

Rhode Island

Providence Books through Bars

Unitarian Universalist Bell Street Chapel

5 Bell Street

Providence, R.I. 02909

https://provbtb.org/

SERVES: All U.S. states *except* Alabama, Arkansas, Florida, Illinois, Kentucky, Louisiana, Massachusetts, Maine, Mississippi, New York, North Carolina, Ohio, Pennsylvania, South Carolina, Washington, and Wisconsin

Tennessee	Tennessee Prison Books Project
	P.O. Box 22846
	Nashville, Tenn. 37202
	https://tnprisonbooksproject.wordpress.com/
	SERVES: Tennessee
Texas	Inside Books
	3106 East 14 1/2 Street
	Austin, Texas 78702
	(512) 655-3121
	insidebooksproject@gmail.com
	https://insidebooksproject.org/
	SERVES: Texas
Vermont	Vermont Books to Prisoners
	P.O. Box 234
	Plainfield, Vt. 05667
	https://www.facebook.com/
	VT-Books-to-Prisoners-268181000703935/
	SERVES: Maine, New Hampshire, Vermont
Virginia	Books Behind Bars
	c/o Friends of the Jefferson-Madison Library
	1500 Gordon Avenue
	Charlottesville, Va. 22903
	info@jmrlfriends.org
	https://booksbehindbars.info/
	SERVES: Virginia
Washington	Books to Prisoners
	c/o Left Bank Books
	92 Pike Street Box A
	Seattle, Wash. 98101
	(206) 527-3339
	bookstoprisoners@live.com
	https://www.bookstoprisoners.net/
	SERVES: All U.S. states

Olympia Books to Prisoners
Center for Community Based Learning and Action
Evergreen State College
Olympia, Wash.
olybtp@gmail.com
https://olympiabtp.org/
Incarcerated persons book requests should be mailed to the address
 under the listing for Books to Prisoners, Seattle, WA
SERVES: All U.S. states

Books to Prisoners Spokane
https://www.facebook.com/B2Pspokane/
Incarcerated persons book requests should be mailed to the address
 under the listing for Books to Prisoners, Seattle, Wa.

Wisconsin

LGBTQ Books to Prisoners
c/o Social Justice Center Incubator
1202 Williamson Street Suite 1
Madison, Wis. 53703
lgbtbookstoprisoners@gmail.com
https://lgbtbookstoprisoners.org/
SERVES: LGBTQ prisoners in all states *except* Texas

Wisconsin Books to Prisoners
1202 Williamson Street Suite 1
Madison, Wis. 53703
wisconsinbookstoprisoners@gmail.com
https://www.wisconsinbookstoprisoners.org
SERVES: Wisconsin

CONTRIBUTORS

Lauren Braun-Strumfels, PhD, is an associate professor of history at Cedar Crest College in Allentown, Pennsylvania. She taught U.S. and women's history to people incarcerated in New Jersey from 2013 to 2019. In her professional advocacy she seeks to bring more humanity and authenticity to the teaching and writing of history, and she works actively to build community inside and outside the classroom. In 2020 she held the Fulbright Research Lectureship in U.S. History at the University of Rome III. She is the author of *Partners in Gatekeeping: How Italy Shaped U.S. Immigration Policy over Ten Pivotal Years, 1891-1901* (University of Georgia Press, 2023) and the editor and contributor to *Managing Migration in Italy and the United States* (DeGruyter, 2024). Her work has also appeared in *Labor: Studies in Working-Class History*, *Perspectives on History*, and *World History Connected*.

Nic Cassette is a Saxapahaw, North Carolina–based visual artist and musician who has been active in local organizing against voter suppression and racism. His art has also been integral in raising awareness of Wyatt Outlaw, a local Black community leader who was lynched in the public square in 1870.

Andy Chan is a volunteer and board member of Books to Prisoners in Seattle. Andy has been volunteering with Books to Prisoners since 1994 (but is only the second longest serving volunteer). Andy led the first efforts at communications between prison book programs at a national level in the late 1990s. He has a PhD in politics from the University of Bristol, England, is a board member of the Social Justice Film Festival Institute, and is a former editor and contributor to the academic journal *Anarchist Studies*.

Melissa Charenko is an assistant professor in Lyman Briggs College and the Department of History at Michigan State University. She has been involved with LGBT Books to Prisoners for nearly a decade and has served on the board of Chicago Books to Women in Prison.

Julia Chin is a proud feminist, abolitionist, and reader who believes in the radical power of empathy. As an undergraduate at UC Santa Barbara, Julia was founder and organizing director of the Associated Students Pages for Individuals in Prison as well as serving as special projects chair of the AS Human Rights Board, advocate for University of California tuition reductions through the Fund the UC campaign, and researcher of gender, sexuality, and critical mixed-race studies. After graduating with her BA in sociology and minor in feminist studies, Julia has been working at Over Zero, a nonprofit aimed at peacebuilding and identity-based violence prevention, since 2023.

Rod Coronado is a lifelong environmental activist of Yaqui heritage. He was a crew member for the Sea Shepherd Conservation Society and a member of Earth First!, and he has been imprisoned four times for his involvement with the Animal Liberation Front, Earth Liberation Front, and Earth First!. After completing his sentences and federal probation, Rod started the Wisconsin citizen's monitoring group, Wolf Patrol, which for eight years monitored wolf conflicts with bear hunters and opposed hound hunting practices and wildlife-killing contests. Currently, Rod lives in Vermont, where he started Vermont Wolf Patrol to support legislative efforts to ban controversial trapping and hound hunting practices. Rod's work was recently the subject of the documentary *Operation Wolf Patrol* (2021), https://wolfpatrol.org/home/.

Michelle Dillon is the former program coordinator for Books to Prisoners Seattle as well as the former public records manager for the Human Rights Defense Center. Michelle holds a master of library and information science and has been working to organize librarians into the fight against prison censorship since 2013, when she completed her master's capstone project on the chronic needs and barriers of prison book programs.

Lorenzo Kom'boa Ervin is an anarchist, civil rights activist, and author who was a member of the Student Nonviolent Coordinating Committee, the Black Panther Party, and Concerned Citizens for Justice. In response to credible threats on his life, Ervin fled to Cuba and then Czechoslovakia. He was later extradited to the United States and sentenced to prison. Ervin remained politically active while inside. Through public support and his own legal challenges he secured his own release after fifteen years. He remains politically active.

Rebecca Ginsburg is associate professor and director, Education Justice Project, which she cofounded in 2008, at the University of Illinois Urbana-Champaign. Her teaching and research spans apartheid and Atlantic slavery to prison education, the history of punishment, and prison abolition. She is the editor, most recently, of *Critical Perspectives on Teaching in Prison* (2019) and coedited two architectural history books with Clifton Ellis, *Slavery in the City* (2017) and *Cabin, Quarter, Plantation* (2010). Her monograph, *At Home with Apartheid* (2011), received the Abbott Lowell Cummings Prize. She is currently working on a reader on prison abolition.

Kwaneta Harris, is a former nurse, business owner, expat, and now incarcerated journalist in the largest state prison, Texas. Her powerful and shocking stories expose how the state-sanctioned, gender-based violence directly maps onto broader, misogynist U.S. culture. An abolitionist feminist, she advocates for non-carceral solutions for those who harm as well as showing how mainstream issues including abortion, gun debate, and climate change affect systems-impacted people.

James King is the campaign manager for the Ella Baker Center for Human Rights. James is also a writer and organizer, having written numerous op-eds and a weekly blog that gave a first-person perspective of the true impact of mass criminalization and living within the prison-industrial complex. As an organizer, he founded a think tank of incarcerated people passionate about criminal justice policy and built relationships with multiple California criminal justice reform organizations. In 2019, James co-wrote and presented a TEDx Talk, "From Proximity to Power," at California Polytechnic State University that advocated for recognizing the value and expertise of people who come from marginalized communities. His current policy interests include decarceration and improving the living conditions for incarcerated people, with the ultimate goal of creating alternatives to incarceration based upon investing in under-resourced communities.

Patrick Kukucka moved to Western North Carolina in 2001 and began volunteering with the Asheville Prison Books Program. He has worked with APBP off and on ever since. In 2005, Patrick and a few others revived APBP within the Asheville Community Resource Center after the program had been defunct for about a year. Patrick a has BS in music technology and records music in addition to his longtime work in bookstores, including Downtown Books and News. He opened his own bookstore, Bagatelle Books, in 2019.

Victoria Law is an author and freelance journalist focusing on the intersections of incarceration, gender, and resistance. Her writings about prisons and other forms of confinement have appeared in the *New York Times*, *The Nation*, *Wired*, *Bloomberg*

Businessweek, the *Village Voice*, *In These Times*, *Rewire News*, and *Truthout*. She is a cofounder of NYC Books Through Bars and for years, was the editor of the zine *Tenacious: Art and Writings by Women in Prison*. Her books include *Prison by Any Other Name: The Harmful Consequences of Popular Reform*, *Resistance behind Bars: The Struggles of Incarcerated Women*, and *Don't Leave Your Friends Behind: Concrete Ways to Support Families in Social Justice Movements and Communities*. Her newest book, *"Prisons Make Us Safer" and 20 Other Myths about Mass Incarceration*, was published in 2021. She is currently working on a book about the pandemic in prisons.

Zoe Lawrence is a trans woman currently incarcerated in Alabama. Zoe is a Louisiana-born, Mississippi-raised belle who traveled all over the world in search of tough answers to tough questions. She will be released from prison in March 2026, after serving eighteen years.

Jodi Lincoln has been involved with the prison books program Book 'Em (now Pittsburgh Prison Book Project), which serves people incarcerated in Pennsylvania, since 2015. As an ardent abolitionist based in Pittsburgh, she's also a part of the Coalition Against Death by Incarceration and efforts to improve conditions at Allegheny County Jail. To pay the bills Jodi is an affordable housing developer with ACTION-Housing, Inc.

Dave "Mac" Marquis is a lifelong activist. He has worked with Earth First!, the Concerned Family and Friends of Mumia Abu Jamal, the *Asheville Global Report*, and several PBPs as well as innumerable other organizations, small and large. He has a PhD in history from the College of William & Mary and is currently a postdoctoral fellow at the University of South Carolina. He is currently writing a graphic history of the Brotherhood of the Timber Workers, an interracial union in the Piney Woods during Jim Crow.

Moira Marquis manages the Freewrite Project based in PEN America's Prison and Justice Writing program. She has worked with Asheville Prison Books and the Prison Books Collective in Carrboro, North Carolina, and started Saxapahaw Prison Books. She has a PhD from UNC Chapel Hill. Her academic writing can be read in *Resilience: A Journal of the Environmental Humanities*, *Science Fiction Studies*, and *Green Letters: Studies in Ecocriticism*. She is the author of the PEN America published report "Reading Between the Bars: An In-Depth Look at Prison Censorship."

Annie Masaoka assisted the Asheville Prison Books Program for several years, packaging and sending books out to prisoners as well as organizing fundraising events, often with the help of their mom, Julia. Annie is now living in Detroit, practicing acupuncture and looking to start a local prison books program in Detroit.

Robert McDuff is an attorney practicing in Jackson, Mississippi. In addition to his private practice, Rob is the director of the impact litigation project of the Mississippi Center for Justice. He has handled trials and appeals in several states and has argued four cases before the U.S. Supreme Court involving civil and constitutional rights. Rob is the recipient of numerous awards, including the Pro Bono Service Award of the International Human Rights Law Group of Washington, D.C.; the William Robert Ming Advocacy Award of the national NAACP; and the Frederick Douglass Award of the Southern Center for Human Rights. He has been a member of the faculty of the Trial Advocacy Workshop at Harvard Law School. A native of Hattiesburg, Mississippi, Rob is a graduate of Millsaps College and Harvard Law School.

Daniel McGowan is a former political prisoner and former member of the Earth Liberation Front (ELF). He was incarcerated for seven years, most of which were in experimental "communication management units." Daniel has been involved with political prisoner support and prison struggles for most of his activist life. He is currently a member of the Certain Days collective, NYC Books Through Bars, and the Anarchist Black Cross Federation. Daniel is from Queens, New York, and works as a paralegal for the ACLU.

Beth Orlansky is a retired lawyer from Jackson, Mississippi, who was the advocacy director at the Mississippi Center for Justice from 2006 to 2022. In addition to private practice prior to joining MCJ, Beth was a charter member of Parents for Public Schools and served on many community boards, including Stewpot Community Services and the Religious Action Center. A native of Memphis, Tennessee, Beth is a graduate of Stanford University and the University of Tennessee School of Law.

Julie Schneyer is a prison abolitionist working with Asheville Prison Books since 2011. Julie also participates in numerous groups challenging state repression, including the Asheville Community Bail Fund and Blue Ridge ABC. She holds a master's degree in literacy, culture, and language education and teaches reading and math to adult learners.

Ellen Skirvin is a college instructor and fiction writer. She received her master of fine arts degree in fiction from West Virginia University, where she first became involved with the Appalachian Prison Book Project (APBP) and assisted a college

Literature course inside a Pennsylvania prison. Currently she serves on the board of APBP and teaches at Penn State University.

Valerie Surrett is currently serving as copresident of the Appalachian Prison Book Project (APBP). Valerie began volunteering with APBP in 2015. She has since worn many hats there, including graduate student intern, graduate research assistant, member of the women's book club, and co-facilitator of the men's book club at Federal Correctional Institution (FCI) Hazelton, service-learning coordinator, volunteer coordinator, and board member. Valerie is an assistant professor of English at the University of North Georgia, Gainesville, where she teaches courses on representations of incarceration in American literature and film.

Megan Sweeney is Arthur F. Thurnau Associate Professor of English, Afroamerican and African Studies, and Women's and Gender Studies at the University of Michigan, Ann Arbor. Sweeney's publications include an award-winning monograph, *Reading Is My Window: Books and the Art of Reading in Women's Prisons* (2010); an edited collection, *The Story within Us: Women Prisoners Reflect on Reading* (2012); a collection of lyric essays called *Mendings* (2023); and numerous articles about African American literature, reading, and incarceration. Sweeney has received fellowships from the Radcliffe Institute for Advanced Study at Harvard University, the Institute for the Humanities at the University of Michigan, the Ford Foundation, and the Woodrow Wilson Foundation. Deeply committed to teaching, she has been awarded the John D'Arms Award for Distinguished Graduate Mentoring in the Humanities (2021), a Class of 1923 Memorial Teaching Award (2010), and an Arthur F. Thurnau Professorship (2014), the university's highest award for undergraduate teaching.

Paul Tardie has been a collective member of Inside Books Project based in Austin, Texas, since 2018. After spending a year incarcerated in 2016, Tardie wrote *Inside: Dissecting a County Jail*, a book detailing life in a Tennessee jail. It can be found at Monkeywrench Books in Austin as well as online through lulu.com. Tardie is currently pursuing a biology BS at the University of Texas, Austin, with a focus in environmental justice. He enjoys propagating abolitionist street art and info sheets.

Sarah West is an artist living and working in Raleigh, North Carolina, who cofounded Asheville Prison Books. Sarah earned a BFA in metal design from East Carolina University and a bench jewelry certificate from North Bennet Street School. Sarah splits her time between teaching at Pullen Arts Center, exhibiting her jewelry at retail craft markets, and creating custom installations for public spaces. Sarah was a recipient of a North Carolina Arts Council Fellowship, and her distinctive linear works have been selected for exhibitions nationwide.